VFW
OUR FIRST CENTURY

By Herbert Molloy Mason, Jr.

ADDAX PUBLISHING GROUP
Lenexa, Kansas

Contents

 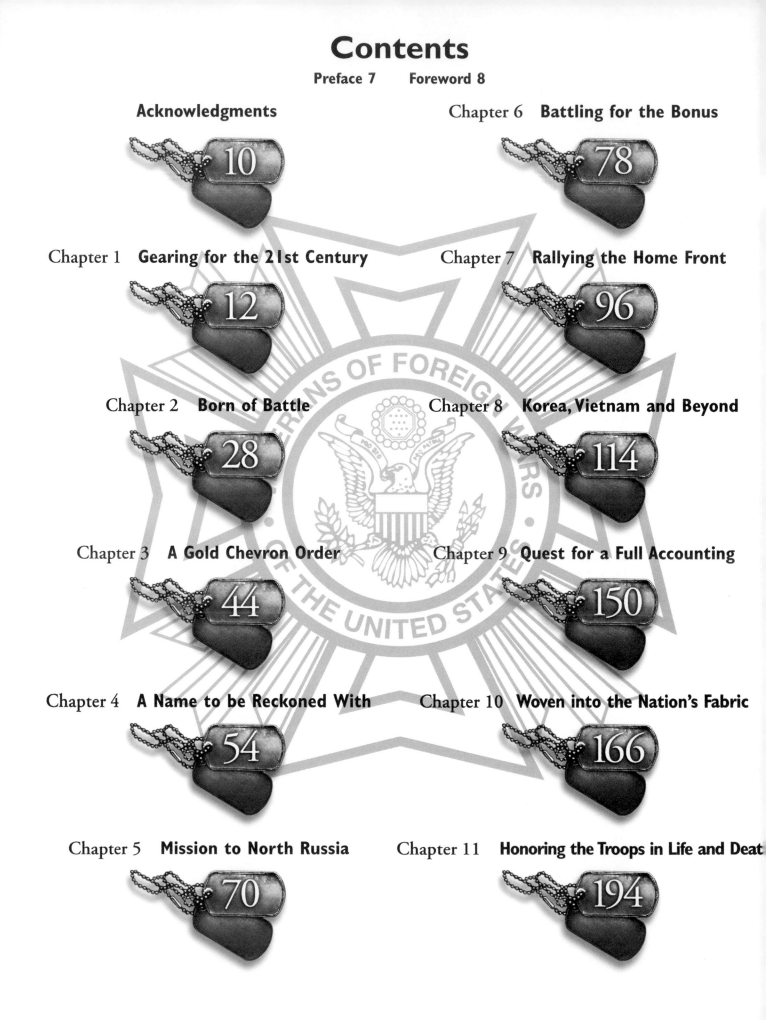

Special Features

PUBLISHER, *Bob Snodgrass*

EXECUTIVE EDITOR, *Richard K. Kolb*

BOOK DESIGNER, *Jerry Hirt*

COVER DESIGNER AND PRODUCTION MANAGER, *Robert Widener*

PRODUCTION ASSISTANCE: *Pat Brown, Tim Dyhouse, Dawn Christy, Janie Blankenship and Joe Moran*

Published by Addax Publishing Group

8643 Hauser Drive - Suite 235

Lenexa, Kansas 66215

Distributed to the trade by Andrews McMeel Publishing

4520 Main Street

Kansas City, Missouri 64111

Library of Congress Catalog Card Number: 99-24943

ISBN: 1-88611072-7

By the Same Author

The Lafayette Escadrille (1964)

High Flew the Falcons: French Aces of World War I (1965)

Bold Men, Far Horizons (1966)

The New Tigers: The Making of a Modern Fighter Pilot (1966)

The Great Pursuit (1970)

Duel for the Sky: Fighter Pilots of World War II (1970)

The Rise of the Luftwaffe (1971)

Missions of Texas (1974)

The U.S. Air Force: A Turbulent History (1976)

To Kill the Devil (1978)

The Luftwaffe (1981)

For younger readers

The Commandos (1966)

Famous Firsts in Exploration (1967)

The Texas Rangers (1967)

Ants (1974)

Secrets of the Supernatural (1975)

Preface

The Veterans of Foreign Wars of the United States was conceived a century ago by a small group of veterans who returned from campaigns on Cuba and in the Philippines in 1898 and 1899. They banded together to create a veterans organization that would outlast themselves, and in effect, last as long as Americans put on uniforms to defend their country.

This is the story of the genesis of the VFW, and its steady growth. It is the story of dedication to the welfare of those who served overseas and a chronicle of civic presence throughout the nation.

Not every contribution by VFW and its Ladies Auxiliary could be cited. But all members share the same spirit of patriotism and pride in what the VFW has accomplished through 10 decades of service.

—**H.M.M.**

San Antonio, Texas, February 1999

Foreword

By Nebraska Sen. Chuck Hagel

The story of the Veterans of Foreign Wars (VFW) is the story of America. Far from being an organization set apart from the mainstream of American history, it has been an integral part of the nation's growth and development. Entering the 20th century as an obscure association among many back when joining was a national mania, the VFW soon charted an independent course that earned it a distinctive niche in an ever-evolving society.

VFW's confidence in the future was evidenced in the very beginning. Upon the merger of the two veterans groups that constituted VFW in 1914, the October cover of the national publication proudly proclaimed: "We have entered a new epoch in the history of veterans organizations. Such societies have come and gone. Others are fast fading away. But ours is destined to live as long as our country exists — forever! Our house is built upon the rock of eternity, not upon the sands of time." VFW has surely withstood the test of time, leaving an indelible legacy.

Americans often ask me what makes the VFW unique. How is it different from a host of other veterans organizations? Besides being the oldest major group of ex-servicemen and women in America, the VFW has a special appeal. Membership has always been based on more than simply wearing the uniform — itself a noble gesture. VFW members all served overseas in an actual war zone or in a situation demanding arduous duty. The camaraderie that results from such sacrifice is legendary. Bonds formed in combat are not easily dissolved. VFW's founders, fresh from campaigning in the tropics of Cuba and the Philippines at the century's turn, readily recognized this reality of war. And VFW's prestige is undeniable: eight Presidents have been among its ranks, ranging from Teddy Roosevelt and Harry Truman to George Bush.

Yet the essence of the VFW is not merely this invisible and spiritual link. Members quickly realized that fulfilling one's obligation of citizenship extends beyond military service. America was fast becoming a world power; changes at home were radically altering the social landscape. If veterans were to influence these rapidly changing times, they would have to adapt. That meant not only tending to the needs of returning warriors, but also having a say in the course of the country. Instead of being a single-interest society, the VFW was determined to affect the nation's direction in several spheres — community service, defense and foreign policy among them.

While the VFW may be best known as an organization that has provided a center for social life in small town America, it is much more. As expected, it always played a pivotal role in passing legislation beneficial to disabled veterans and easing the transition to civilian life of millions of returnees from four major wars.

Beyond this realm and behind the scenes, VFW also has provided morale-boosting support to troops in the field, from France in 1918 to Bosnia in 1999. When natural disasters strike, its members are often among the first to offer assistance to victims. If youth need guidance in growing up, VFW Posts sponsor it in the form of sports and educational opportunities. The Voice of Democracy program, for example, is widely respected. Instilling patriotism is another VFW specialty.

Teaming up with other civic groups such as the March of Dimes and American Red Cross has demonstrated the organization's commitment to community betterment on countless occasions.

Perhaps President John F. Kennedy capsulized the VFW's mission most succinctly with these words: "By your magnificent wartime service you have defended America's freedom and security. Today, as veterans, you serve with equal tenacity, devoting brain and heart to the task of keeping our country strong."

Indeed, the VFW is a vibrant organization dedicated to a set of principles that all Americans can identify with. The four pillars of its foundation — care for veterans, national defense, patriotism and community service — are as relevant today as ever. As the VFW heads into its second century — the 21st — I, like my father before me, am proud to claim membership in the nation's premier veterans organization.

EDITOR'S NOTE: *Chuck Hagel was elected the Republican senator from Nebraska in 1996. A VA assistant administrator from 1981-82, he has been a member of VFW Post 3704 in Columbus, Neb., since 1968 and a life member since 1983. In Vietnam, he served with B Company, 2nd Battalion, 47th Infantry, 9th Infantry Division, in the Mekong Delta during 1967-68. He was wounded twice, earning the Purple Heart with oak leaf cluster.*

Acknowledgments

For help of every kind, the author is indebted to the following:

AT VFW NATIONAL HEADQUARTERS IN KANSAS CITY, MO.:

To *VFW* magazine Editor-in-Chief Rich Kolb — a sure and relentless navigator through 100 years of VFW history. Without his unstinting help and editing, this book would not exist in its present form. Also to his associates on the *VFW* magazine staff: Art Director Robert Widener, Production Assistant Pat Brown, Senior Editor Tim Dyhouse, Staff Writer Janie Blankenship and Graphic Artist Joe Moran. And Dawn Christy who took on the duties of an editorial assistant extraordinaire, tirelessly perfecting the manuscript in preparation for layout. For the cover design, full credit goes to Robert Widener.

National officers, past and present, as well as staff members, freely gave their time to discuss the VFW's past and future. I wish to thank: Howard Vander Clute, Mike Gormalley, Bob Greene, Cooper T. Holt, Curt Jewell, Bob Merrill (who died in January 1999), Larry Rivers and Gordon Thorson. Each provided insights not otherwise obtainable.

AT THE WASHINGTON OFFICE:

Sidney Daniels, Frederico Juarabe, Jr., William G. Smith, Ken Steadman and Robert E. Wallace. Each provided overviews and current information about services and issues at that end of the VFW spectrum.

Others who provided pertinent and invaluable research include:

Nick Natonson, Reference Section, National Archives in Washington, D.C.; Helen McDonald of the Nimitz Museum of the Pacific War in Fredricksburg, Texas; Daniel Smith, Sr., of the Medal of Honor Museum in Chattanooga, Tenn.; Richard B. and Peter Harrington, curators of the Anne S.K. Brown Military Collection at Brown University in Providence, R.I.; Danny Crawford, head of the reference section at the Marine Corps Historical Center, Washington, D.C.; and Stanley Bozich, director of Michigan's Own Military & Space Museum, Frankenmuth, Mich.

In San Antonio, Texas, the author is indebted to Margaret Zapatos, Bob Stevens, Richard Fields and Mary Green, knowledgeable staff members of the Great Northwest Library. Rodger Johnson of Computize, Inc., effortlessly sorted out software problems on the Macintosh. And to Maury Maverick, Jr., WWII Marine combat veteran, state representative, author and confidant of U.S. public officials since the days of Franklin D. Roosevelt. Maury's observations on the political process on Capitol Hill are worth chiseling on tablets.

This book could not have been completed without the patient endurance and steadfast support of my wife, Rigmor. To her, I owe the greatest debt of all.

To the millions of war veterans who have made

the Veterans of Foreign Wars the premier veterans

service organization of the 20th century

"It is impossible for the nation to compensate for the services of a fighting
man. There is no pay scale that is high enough to buy the services of a single
soldier, sailor, Marine or airman during even a few minutes of the agony of
combat, the physical miseries of the campaign, or the extreme personal
inconvenience of leaving his home to go out to the most unpleasant and
dangerous spots on earth to serve his nation."
—GEN. GEORGE C. MARSHALL
U.S. ARMY CHIEF OF STAFF, 1939-45

Chapter 1

Gearing for the 21st Century

**VFW's story is America's story.
It is full of exciting events
and dynamic personalities. Today,
it occupies a place of prestige in society.**

General Douglas MacArthur called the Veterans of Foreign Wars "the greatest organization in the world." Members, no doubt, would readily agree. VFW, after all, has had a profound impact on American society. Its crusades for social justice have touched many lives. World War II's GI Bill literally transformed postwar society. VFW had a direct hand in that transformation.

But the GI Bill is among the better-know chapters in the history of America's oldest major veterans organization. Its past is filled with adventure and drama. Founding members and early leaders displayed genuine heroism on the battlefields of Cuba, Philippines and France. VFW's odyssey to North Russia to recover remains of Americans killed there, the fight for the WWI Bonus and the Doughboys march of 1932 are episodes made for movies.

A national home built by proceeds from a World Series baseball game, movie stars who supported VFW programs, connections to Hollywood and making the *Star-Spangled Banner* the national anthem form some early-day VFW tales from the "Roaring '20s" and Great Depression.

During WWII, VFW not only helped create the landmark GI Bill, but raised $150,000 to buy 15 training planes, actually prepared 44,300 pilots for combat duty and was consulted on the creation of the United Nations. It raised millions in war bonds, too.

Human interest stories abound from all eras. VFW-sponsored ice hockey teams in Minnesota that produced Olympic champions, immensely popular national marble tournaments originating at Boy's Town, young men who sacrificed their lives in war from VFW's National Home, VFW leaders as diplomatic emissaries, the generosity of VFW members to war's casualties in Korea and Vietnam are all part of the story.

Dynamic personalities have peopled its ranks: Pennsylvanian Jimmy Van Zandt, Bob Woodside, the charismatic Marine Smedley Butler, literary giant Carl Sandburg, Sgt. Alvin York and world boxing champion Gene Tunney, to name a few. Some of these men are legendary figures in U.S. history, but they all had one thing in common — VFW membership.

Humanitarian impulses have guided VFW's principles. Concern for destitute vets during the Depression, severely disabled war wounded, servicemen exposed to atomic radiation, victims of the defoliant Agent

**Opposite page:
VFW's Washington Conference in 1997 focused on vital legislative and national security issues. Marine Commandant Gen. Charles C. Krulak told the audience: "VFW is the only organization to consistently understand the sacrifices of today's servicemen." Such conferences, conducted for 50 years, provide VFW leaders with the opportunity to directly lobby Congress.**

Orange, the homeless, families suffering from Gulf War Syndrome, wives and children enduring the mental anguish of having a loved one missing in action and health care for the elderly are among the issues that motivate VFW.

Volunteerism in the community is VFW's least-known activity: a clean environment, aid to victims of natural disasters, safety programs for the young and old, volunteering in hospitals, youth sports sponsorship, citizenship education and college scholarships for thousands of students every year are all priorities. Such contributions are seldom recognized by the public.

Yes, few Americans are aware of VFW's historic achievements. As the country's premier organized group of war veterans enters the 21st century, it is ready to carry on a tradition grounded in the unshakable values of the past.

VFW is rooted in a sense of boundless confidence. Sen. Chuck Hagel's quote in the *Foreword* bears repeating. VFW's founding fathers loudly proclaimed: "We have entered a new epoch in the history of veterans organizations. Such societies have come and gone. Others are fast fading away. But ours is destined to live as long as our country exists — forever! Our house is built upon the rock of eternity, not upon the sands of time." Indeed, the VFW will not fade away. The charter on its mission is perpetual.

Destiny and eternity are powerful words yet they apply to this unique organization of dedicated Americans. From the start, VFW members have proved their mettle on both foreign and domestic battlefields. Their legacy is felt in every aspect of our society. The time has come to tell their story. But before we begin that story — an exciting chapter in the entire nation's saga — let's briefly explore what the VFW is today and where it is headed.

More than 600 residents of Mooresville, Ind., braved bitter cold to show support for Americans serving in the Persian Gulf. This 1991 rally, sponsored by VFW Post 1111, was typical of rallies held across the country.

In 1999, Commander-in-Chief Thomas Pouliot, a Navy veteran of the Vietnam War, looked to the 21st century and reminded members: "The future is bright for the venerable VFW. The organization has an opportunity to shape the nation's destiny. Merely being part of the flow of events will not assure our place in history. VFW must assert itself by strengthening the bonds between its members and the communities in which they live."

VFW's future hinges on how closely tied it is to the community. Because it is a mass membership organization, individuals acting in concert will ultimately determine its fate.

Joe L. Ridgley, VFW's chief financial officer and chairman of the 100th Anniversary Committee, attributes VFW's success to the grassroots efforts of

14

Cross of Malta

The Cross of Malta is VFW's official insignia. Each design aspect symbolizes something special. The cross, radiating rays, and Great Seal of the U.S. together symbolize the character, vows and purposes distinguishing VFW as an order of warriors who have traveled far from home to defend sacred principles.

Its eight points represent the beatitudes prescribed in the Sermon on the Mount: Blessed are the poor in spirit, the meek, the pure, the merciful, the peacemakers; blessed are they who mourn, seek righteousness and are persecuted for righteousness' sake. VFW added the sun's rays between the eight points and the cross. These emphasize the vigor and warmth with which the present-day brotherhood is pledged to defend the nation and to extend its mercy. Superimposed over the cross is the American eagle — the sacred symbol of a proud nation and people.

While the Maltese Cross has religious origins and was used by the crusading Knights of St. John as a battle standard centuries ago, it is equally relevant today as a symbol of all those battling for noble ideals.

VFW's venerable symbol dates to 1899, when the organization was founded as the American Veterans of Foreign Service. The Cross of Malta harks back to the Crusades, launched during the 12th century.

VFW's 2 million members. "The strength, power and influence we have in Washington, D.C., is based on what we do in the field," he said. "In the VFW, power flows upward, not the other way around. The Posts — and there are 9,781 of them — and the 54 Departments form our base of strength. They send a message of commitment to Washington, allowing us to be successful in protecting and extending veterans entitlements — and in influencing national defense and foreign policy."

Prestige and stature are all-important in today's world and VFW has something to boast about in this area. *Fortune* magazine, in 1998, rated interest groups by clout. VFW ranked No. 16 in the nation among 120 groups and No.1 in veterans circles.

But making "The Power 25" is not enough. Esteem in one's home base is critical, too. VFW's sponsorship of a senior golf tournament for two years benefited ailing children, and earned the respect of the community. As the *Kansas City Star* noted: "The venture takes the 2-million member VFW to a new level of commitment. It stands to win a wider recognition of the VFW — recognition difficult to obtain through other resources."

Presidents and the VFW

VFW has counted eight Presidents among its ranks, ranging from Theodore Roosevelt who joined in 1917 to George Bush who left office in 1992. Here's what they had to say about the organization:

■ **Harry S Truman** saw VFW membership as a "source of pride and personal satisfaction because of the high ideals that have been exemplified throughout the lifetime of the VFW. The VFW will ever stand in the forefront of unselfish devotion to our nation."

■ **Dwight D. Eisenhower** appreciated VFW's ceaseless efforts to keep the armed forces ready for any contingency: "As strong defenders of peace, you exemplify the highest quality of American citizenship. The record of the VFW, working today on behalf of our national security, adds honor to your proud tradition of military service in all parts of the world."

■ **John F. Kennedy** paid this tribute: "By your magnificent wartime service, you have defended America's freedom and security. Today, as veterans, you serve with equal tenacity, devoting brain and heart to keeping our country strong."

■ **Lyndon B. Johnson** said: "The conviction of the Veterans of Foreign Wars that our heritage of freedom must be protected is a signal to all your fellow citizens that courage and commitment continue to be honored and celebrated."

■ **Richard M. Nixon:** "My membership in the Veterans of Foreign Wars has always been a source of pride to me. Its meaning has taken on a new substance during the period since my inauguration. America's veterans constitute the finest element of our population. I know their deep devotion to their country."

■ **Gerald R. Ford:** Members of the VFW and Ladies Auxiliary are "men and women whose patriotism has been tested and proven."

■ **George Bush:** "The VFW has become part of the fabric of our nation. For many years now, I've been inspired by the motto of the Veterans of Foreign Wars—'Honor the Dead by Helping the Living.' I congratulate all of you for the work you've done to enhance the lives and well-being of those veterans and families who are less fortunate than others."

PRESIDENT	TERM	WAR	POST
Theodore Roosevelt	1901-1909	Spanish-American War	At-Large, New York
Harry S Truman	1945-1953	World War I	35, Kansas City, Mo.
Dwight D. Eisenhower	1953-1961	World War II	3279, Abilene, Kan.
John F. Kennedy	1961-1963	World War II	5880, Brockton, Mass.
Lyndon B. Johnson	1963-1969	World War II	856, Austin, Texas
Richard M. Nixon	1969-1974	World War II	2081, Whittier, Calif.
Gerald R. Ford	1974-1977	World War II	830, Grand Rapids, Mich.
George Bush	1989-1993	World War II	4344, Houston, Texas

President John F. Kennedy, famous for his exploits aboard PT-109 in the South Pacific, commanded Post 5880 in Brockton, Mass., after WWII.

In 1965, President Lyndon B. Johnson traveled a rocky road with the VFW over VA hospital closings. Nevertheless, the Texan was a member of Post 856 in Austin.

As Vice President, Richard M. Nixon, WWII Navy vet, was greeted in Dallas in 1956 by Commander-in-Chief Timothy J. Murphy. As President, Nixon worked closely with VFW. He held a membership card from Post 2081 in Whittier, Calif.

In 1975, President Gerald R. Ford reaffirmed May 1 as Loyalty Day — made a national holiday by the VFW 17 years earlier. Another WWII Navy vet, he belongs to Post 830 in Grand Rapids, Mich.

As Republican presidential nominee, George Bush saluted delegates at the Joint Opening Session of the 1988 VFW National Convention in Chicago. Bush, then a member of Post 4344 in Houston, Texas, was endorsed by the VFW.

Editor's Note: Teddy Roosevelt is not pictured here because he joined the VFW after leaving the presidency.

ADVERTISING

VFW Fights for Respect With Ad Blitz

By Lisa Brownlee
Staff Reporter of The Wall Street Journal

The Veterans of Foreign Wars, one of the nation's oldest veterans' groups, is trying to boost its image – and that explains some unusual ads running lately on ESPN.

Many people still associate the VFW with old war stories, sparsely attended parades and World War II veterans like Bob Dole, who is a lifetime member. About half of the organization's 2.1 million members are over the age of 65.

"If you go back 30 or 40 years, almost every family had a veteran or knew a veteran," says Steve Van Buskirk, spokesman for the VFW, which is based in Kansas City, Mo. But today, veterans' concerns are no longer the "sacred cows" they were after World War II, when the GI Bill showered veterans with benefits

bers seeking more visibility, Mr. Van Buskirk says. "We wanted quality air time. We wanted to reach the largest audience that we could possibly reach." ESPN reaches 71 million households with cable TV.

The pitch isn't aimed just at veterans, although the VFW has a stagnant membership base and is hungry for new recruits. "Obviously, we're a shrinking organization," says Paul E. Connors, a Vietnam veteran and accountant in Blue Springs, Mo., who is a VFW member. With an annual budget of about $50 million, the VFW gets most of its money from membership dues ($20 a year, or as much as $200 for a lifetime membership.) Only about one in six eligible veterans now join.

The VFW also hopes to counter the notion that veterans are a fringe, special-interest, political group, rather than a core part of mainstream American society.

ADVERTISING

The VFW Fights for a New Image

& Witteborn Advertising in Kansas City, Mo. "Had this been an actual emergency, you'd have been scared pretty much out of your wits. Fortunately, we've never had a national emergency in this country because millions of veterans risked their lives so the rest of us could take it for granted." The tagline: "We'd do anything for this country."

government funds] showed it could afford to pay for a splashy ad campaign, the VFW might find it harder to get free air time for public-service announcements.

But the VFW, whose current leadership is made up largely by Vietnam vets, decided to take the risk. The group was frustrated that its public-service messages often were relegated to the wee hours of the morning. There was "an ongoing line and far from rank-and-file VFW mem-

Vietnam veteran and VFW member. Far from deeming the TV ads extravagant, he believes they are crucial to keeping veterans' concerns on people's minds.

Even Congress and state legislatures, traditionally bastions of veteran support, have declining numbers of vets among their ranks. This session, an estimated 35% of U.S. representatives and 40% of senators are veterans, down from...

Please Turn to Page B3, Column 5

When VFW began airing public service announcements through ESPN in 1995, the message came across loud and clear. They combatted what the *Wall Street Journal* observed: "Many people still associate the VFW with old war stories, sparsely attended parades and World War II veterans like Bob Dole, who is a lifetime member." Paul E. Connors, a Vietnam vet and VFW member from Blue Springs, Mo., spoke for many when he said: "It was about time. It was worth every dime."

VFW National Headquarters occupies a 12-story building in Kansas City, Mo., in the shadow of the nationally famous WWI Liberty Memorial. The building was leased by VFW in 1930 and has been owned outright since 1946. An outdoor wall contains soil from 200 battlefields on which Americans have fought and died. Decorated with three flagpoles, the sweeping wall is a symbolic part of VFW's patriotic legacy.

This special property serves as the organization's nerve center. "Services provided by the administrative side of national headquarters are vital to VFW's efficient functioning," said Adjutant General John Senk. Assistant Adjutant General Larry LeFebvre concurs: "Despite the fact that this aspect of the organization forms the nuts and bolts of the daily routine, few members understand and appreciate its value to the overall operation of the VFW."

From this hub, VFW reaches out to America by coordinating a variety of community programs with local Posts. These programs are administered by the staff of the office of the Adjutant General. Activities include Citizenship Education & Community Service, National Youth Development, Scholarship & Recognition and Voice of Democracy. To keep the organization a well-oiled machine and in touch with the public as well as members, the Membership, Post Services, Buddy Poppy, Marketing Services, Publications, Public Affairs and VFW Foundation departments are housed in Kansas City, too.

VFW also reaches out in other ways. Working traditionally with established groups such as the Red Cross, Salvation Army, American Association of Retired Persons, Boy Scouts of America, Muscular Dystrophy, March of Dimes and Keep America Beautiful, it has recently formed partnerships with other prominent volunteer groups. VFW is a major supporter of *Make a Difference Day* (sponsored by the Points of Light Foundation/*USA Weekend*) and America's Promise — Alliance for Youth and Freedoms Foundation. In fact, the commander-in-chief is now on the *Make A Difference Day* advisory board.

VFW's National Headquarters building is prominent on the Kansas City, Mo, skyline. Headquarters occupied this building on Jan. 1, 1930. It serves as the nerve center for the worldwide organization.

VFW charitable activities are notable. Voice of Democracy raises $2.6 million annually for college scholarships. Between national headquarters and various states, at least $2 million has gone to disaster relief. Some $1.1 million has been donated to memorial efforts. Minnesota's VFW alone has given some $1 million to a cancer center. The USO received $406,000. VFW has given $250,000 to VA's National Veterans Golden Age Games in the past four years. One Pennsylvania library has garnered $126,000. March of Dimes gets $100,000 per year. VFW's newest endeavor — free telephone calling cards for hospitalized vets and active-duty troops — contributed hundreds of thousands of dollars worth of calling time in only two years.

Sen. John Glenn (D-Ohio) addresses Voice of Democracy (VOD) winners on tour of the U.S. Capitol Building in 1997. VOD is the crown jewel of VFW's youth programs. Glenn became a VFW life member in 1962 after the astronaut hero returned to New Concord, Ohio, for a celebration. Representatives from Post 1058 in Zanesville were on hand when he joined.

The base of the flagpole that stands in front of VFW National Headquarters in Kansas City, Mo., boasts unique contents — dirt from bloody battlefields around the globe. Placed there in 1986, these special soil samples are a way of paying tribute to America's warriors. Indeed, because of them, VFW's flagpole merits mention on trolley car tours of the city.

In 1969, commander of Illinois' 6th District, Otto Osterburg, began collecting soil samples from various wars in which Americans served. By the time he graciously turned his collection over to the VFW, he had samples from over 200 battlefields worldwide. It's thought to be the only one of its kind in the country. Each sample contained a synopsis of the engagement from which the dirt was taken. Little-known details and irreplaceable photos help prove the soil's authenticity.

Samples date from the 1600s

to the Vietnam War. There is even a sample from the Great Swamp Fight that took place Dec. 19, 1675, just west of Wickford, R.I. Soils from major battles in each war are included. For example, soil from Attu, Austria, Buna and Burma are included with WWII samples.

Regrettably, Osterburg was unable to obtain samples of Russian soil from where Americans fought in the Archangel area of North Russia and Siberia. The Chinese Communist government and Fidel Castro's Cuba wouldn't cooperate, either. However, the Spanish-American War was not ignored — soil from Puerto Rico represents sites where Americans and Spaniards clashed in 1898.

"I wanted to do something to let the people — especially the youth — know what Americans have fought for," explained Osterburg when he donated his collection in 1983.

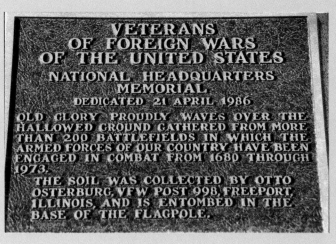

This plaque commemorates efforts of VFW member Otto Osterburg, who gathered soil from more than 200 battlefields where Americans shed their blood. Part of the flagpole's base, the sacred soils were dedicated in 1986.

All this is only possible by maintaining a healthy membership base. By the beginning of 1998, VFW had reached another milestone: The number of *life* members surpassed the 1 million mark for the first time in its history. That equates to about half the organization's total membership. And efforts are continually under way to keep VFW infused with young, new members. Bosnia and Gulf veterans now joining the ranks ensure VFW will remain "evergreen." It is the melding of generations that has kept the organization vital for a century.

On the financial side of the house, functions are quite diverse. The Quartermaster General Department includes Emblem & Supply, Insurance, Receipts Processing & Member Benefits, Life Membership & Member Dues

Processing, Information Technology, VFW Properties and Finance & Human Resources. All contribute significantly to the bottom line.

Combined with revenues generated by Marketing Services and *VFW* magazine, the Quartermaster General Department boasts an annual $60 million operating budget.

"In looking forward to the next century," Quartermaster General Joe Ridgley said, "we must focus on our accomplishments, but more important, our potential. Although the financial road ahead is filled with challenges and difficult changes may be forced upon us, we have the resources at our disposal to meet those challenges."

VFW's legislative control center is inside the Washington Memorial Building, a few blocks from Capitol Hill. The building was dedicated on Feb. 8, 1960, when President Dwight D. Eisenhower addressed a crowd of more than 2,000, including 19 past commanders-in-chief. Today, that shop is run by Executive Director Ken Steadman and his assistant director Bob Wallace, a past commander-in-chief.

The behind-the-scenes lobbying of the Washington office is carried out by VFW's National Legislative Service (NLS). Personnel spend their days meeting with congressional staffers, testifying before committees, answering queries from legislators and filing reams of paper with background data to defend, support and further the causes of America's veterans.

Meanwhile, VFW's National Veterans Service (NVS) monitors benefits developments on the federal level and provides training to a large cadre of VFW service officers. VFW's network of service officers is the most important aspect of the NVS. Service officers — professional and volunteer — are available to all veterans, not just VFW members. NVS in any given

The Washington Memorial Building is the center of VFW legislative activity. The battle for veterans rights begins there and carries over to Capitol Hill a few blocks away.

President Dwight D. Eisenhower addresses a crowd of more than 2,000 as the VFW Memorial Building is dedicated on Feb. 1, 1960. Eisenhower was a life-long member of Post 3279 in Abilene, Kan.

year handles 15 percent of the claims for the Department of Veterans Affairs. Veterans benefit greatly. In the VFW's 1997-98 fiscal year, tens of thousands of veterans claims worth hundreds of millions of dollars were recovered by VFW service officers. In some unique, individual cases, retroactive claims of $300,000 are not unheard of, according to NVS personnel.

The NVS network includes seven field representatives, all of whom operate out of Washington except for one at national headquarters in Kansas City. The primary mission of "field reps," as they are called, is evaluating VA operations and services — health-care facilities, regional offices, cemeteries and vet centers.

NVS Director Frederico Juarbe, Jr., says "the jewel on the crown" for NVS are two annual conferences to train Department service officers. They undergo intensive workshops and lectures that keep them current on VA policy changes and medical advances. Juarbe adds, "The expertise of our service officers separates VFW from all other veterans organizations."

VFW's National Veterans Employment section actively lobbies for laws to provide training for vets, offer tax incentives to companies that hire veterans, guarantee that veterans can get their old jobs back when they leave active service and protect veterans preference.

The National Veterans Service (NVS) keeps track of benefits and oversees training of VFW service officers. At the Washington Office, NVS employee Jimmy Lee Wallace (seated) and Jim Jewell, assistant director of Veterans Health Care Policy, monitor VFW's helpline for incoming calls from veterans seeking answers to health care questions.

Within a year of its establishment in 1997, VFW's Tactical Assessment Center had helped 6,000 veterans.

National Security and Foreign Affairs is an integral part of the Washington office, too. Regular communication with the Pentagon and State Department, where contacts provide background information enabling VFW to get a head start on influencing upcoming policy decisions, is essential to assuring a strong national defense and well-cared for armed forces.

Grass-roots political activism is coordinated by VFW Action Corps, now in its seventh year of fielding a special legislative strike force of volunteers. These 1,600 VFW members respond when congressional committee members of their same zip code areas are considering legislation of concern to veterans. A community team-leader program will soon put team leaders in each county of all 50 states to add more striking power.

Washington office staffers each day pass a reminder of why they dedicate their working lives to veterans — a 36-foot-high memorial called the *Torch of Freedom*. Each face of the shaft is adorned with heavy bronze high-relief depictions of America's wars from the Revolutionary War to Vietnam. The imposing structure was created by Felix de Weldon, best-known for his Iwo Jima Memorial bronze sculpture across the Potomac River in Arlington, Va.

The *Torch of Freedom* was dedicated by Commander-in-Chief Thomas C. Walker on March 8, 1976. Walker told the crowd: "Here in the capital of our nation, no one—not individual, state or federal government — has thought to raise a memorial to those who enabled this great country to evolve to what we see today — the man who fought for his country when called on to do so. So, very simply, the Veterans of Foreign Wars and the Ladies Auxiliary have undertaken to give such a memorial as their Bicentennial gift to the nation."

The three-sided memorial is based on a marble tribute near Athens to Greek warriors of 600 B.C. And like that ancient memorial, VFW's tribute is topped with bronze flames, symbolic of peace and the future.

Most of VFW's "allied" organizations have been with it from the start. VFW owes much of what it has achieved locally to the Ladies Auxiliary. Some 728,000 members strong, it became VFW's "Partner in Service" in 1914, and has expanded its contributions to American communities ever since.

A prime example: the Auxiliary has raised $3 million for its Cancer Aid and Research program for 10 consecutive years. Add to that $30 million another $42 million raised previously and the total is a staggering $72 million. A cancer hotline also helps members take an active role in their own treatment. Moreover, the Ladies donated some 2.6 million volunteer hours in VA medical centers and other hospitals in one year.

The Auxiliary also recently provided $100,000 worth of pre-paid long-distance telephone cards to hospitalized veterans and active-duty military personnel through VFW's *Operation Uplink*. It serves, too, as a Gold Medal Sponsor of the annual National Veterans Wheelchair Games. These are just a few of the wonderful contributions of this outstanding organization.

VFW's National Home, which opened in 1925

VFW's Torch of Freedom, standing 36-feet tall, honors Americans who fought during a dozen wars since 1776. It was dedicated during the Bicentennial. The work was executed by Felix De Weldon, known for his massive Iwo Jima Memorial in Virginia.

in Eaton Rapids, Mich., served 108 children and 26 single-parent families in 1998. It also graduated four residents from high school and one from graduate school. It is a privately funded child care facility that provides youth with guidance, stability and love in a safe, nurturing family environment. Situated on 629 acres, the National Home also has a single-parent family program to assist parents and their children.

The Military Order of the Cootie, whose community volunteer efforts date from 1921, now numbers 30,576 colorfully uniformed members. They help meet the needs of the children of the National Home, as well as hospitalized veterans through the *Keep 'Em Smiling in Beds of White* program. Also, Cooties have a hand in supporting VA's National Golden Age Games and National Wheelchair Games.

VFW's Political Action Committee (PAC) will celebrate its 20th year coincident with the organization's 100th anniversary. Its basis for endorsement is a candidate's roll-call vote record on issues concerning veterans legislation and national security. VFW is the only major veterans organization to maintain a PAC.

The Ladies Auxiliary contributed $12,000 to the National Veterans Wheelchair Games in San Diego in 1997. The Auxiliary is a visible presence in community activities across the nation.

VFW's affiliated groups, national headquarters and the Washington office work for the members: Power is invested in a genuinely grass-roots organization. Member resolutions passed by voting delegates at annual national conventions set policy. The resolution process is the most important mechanism VFW has for shaping domestic and foreign policy.

While delegates at national conventions form the supreme governing body, the National Council of

The Military Order of the Cootie was founded in 1921 as a VFW auxiliary. Cooties are active volunteers at the National Home and devote much time to raising funds for other worthwhile causes. Their unusual uniforms were chosen to reflect their trademark levity and high spirits.

Administration (NCA) bridges the gap between them and national leaders during an administrative year. Part of the system of checks and balances, NCA has been likened to a "third branch of VFW government." Providing "advice and consent," it has the power to approve or reject appointments by the commander-in-chief. NCA also grants and revokes Department charters. Pulling the purse strings and amending bylaws are other functions. Finally, it acts as a sort of board of directors, composed of regional representatives elected for two-year terms by delegates at state conventions.

Another major mechanism exists to formulate and advocate policy, too. VFW's annual Washington Conference, held every year since 1949, provides an opportunity for leaders from the states to be updated on current events and personally lobby their respective lawmakers. So besides the national convention, these three days of intensive meetings cover all the crucial issues. Guest speakers are invited to address members, with the keynote appearance on Monday.

Richard Wyatt, Sr., Post 7284 of the District of Columbia, looks on as national honor guard David Long debates the issues at the 1997 Salt Lake City convention.

The conference is best-known for visits to Capitol Hill and the Congressional Banquet. Hundreds of VFW members pack the Cannon Caucus Room to view the joint session of the House and Senate Veterans Affairs committees. That evening, members and dignitaries gather to hear the speech of the Voice of Democracy winner. All Department VOD contestants are present. For half a century, VFW has used this occasion to communicate directly to Congress and advance the best interests of the nation's veterans.

VFW's democratic foundations, above all else, ensure it will be a factor in American society for a long time to come. The future of VFW— what it hopes to achieve — remains an ever-present topic. As the VFW 100th Anniversary Committee Chairman Joe Ridgley pointed out: "A lot of our success depends on how well we adapt in the media age. We must project the image we want the American people to have of VFW. We must educate our non-veteran friends and gain their support." That is precisely what founding father James Putnam meant when he said veterans must be placed "in the front rank of American citizenship."

"Everything we do," said past Commander-in-Chief John Moon in 1998, "harks back to the organization's origins. VFW was founded by genuine war veterans who served under fire on Cuba and in the Philippines nearly 100 years ago. We owe it to them to perpetuate the legacy left us."

That legacy will be explored in the next 10 chapters.

Robert B. Handy: "Mr. VFW"

Robert B. Handy, Jr., served in WWI with the 318th Infantry, 80th Division. In 1920, just two weeks out of the Army, Handy became the director of VFW's fledgling National Service Bureau in Washington, D.C.

A mere three years later he became quartermaster general and later took on the additional role of adjutant general. He served in that dual capacity until 1950. Thereafter, he was solely quartermaster general. Business manager of *VFW* magazine was another of his roles. Often referred to as "Captain Bob," Handy organized the first Buddy Poppy sale in 1922 and saw sales reach 17 million poppies in 1947.

It was once said that he probably knew more veterans on a first-name basis than any other member of the organization. He was personally acquainted with many Spanish-American War veterans and was a

Robert B. Handy, known as "Mr. VFW," served the organization for 41 years in almost every executive capacity. In the 1920s, he borrowed $3,000 from a bank and loaned it to the VFW to meet pressing bills. Handy retired in February 1962 after a lifetime of dedicated service.

"buddy" to thousands who served in World Wars I and II. He was the last of the WWI vets to hold a major VFW administrative office.

"No man has made a greater contribution to a greater organization," 1962 Senior Vice Commander-in-Chief Byron Gentry said of the native of Northampton County, Virginia.

In essence, the history of the VFW is bound up in the chronicle of Captain Bob's service to the organization. After his retirement in 1962, Handy continued to serve the VFW as national historian and quartermaster general emeritus.

Handy died on April 13, 1971, in Kansas City at the age of 85. He justly earned the title bestowed upon him by his peers: "Mr. VFW."

Above, V.C. LeClerg of the First Federal Savings and Loan Association, VFW Commander-in-Chief Paul C. Wolman, Adjutant General R.B. Handy and H.F. Dunton, president of First Federal, at a veterans housing site in Altadena, Calif., in 1946. VFW made sure veterans moved into quality housing made possible by the GI Bill.
At left, Handy places a wreath at the Tomb of the Unknown Soldier in 1931.

James E. Van Zandt: VFW Statesman

James Van Zandt had an incredible impact on the VFW. So much so that at the 1987 National Convention, VFW passed *Res. 625*, which noted: "Van Zandt has dedicated over 65 years of his life to the betterment of our nation and its deserving veterans." He was the only person ever to serve three terms as commander-in-chief.

Born in Altoona, Pa., on Dec. 18, 1898, Van Zandt served in the Navy during both world wars, as well as Korea. He was a member of Post 3 in Altoona for 67 years. He was first elected commander-in-chief in 1933. Five years later, in 1938, Van Zandt was elected to his first of 11 terms in the House of Representatives.

When he announced to Congress that he was enlisting for WWII, President Franklin Roosevelt told him he envied him. Tapping his paralyzed legs, Roosevelt said, "If I didn't have these, I'd do the same thing."

During his years as commander-in-chief, he willingly accepted any and all tasks assigned. One was his chairmanship

James E. "Jimmy" Van Zandt was a three-war naval officer, congressman, three-term VFW commander-in chief and tireless crusader for veterans rights. He was easily the most popular man ever to lead the organization.

of the VFW National Memorial Building project. In 1958, as Van Zandt turned a spade of dirt at groundbreaking ceremonies, he recalled a building the VFW wanted to buy some 20 years earlier. "I am confident that the VFW would have made much better use of that building than the Soviet Embassy has," he said.

He also was behind the congressional authorization of Loyalty Day (1958) and earlier helped develop VFW's congressional charter (1936). One of Van Zandt's greatest honors was to have a VA facility named after him — the James E. Van Zandt Medical Center located in Altoona, Pa.

In 1986, Commander-in-Chief John S. Staum said Van Zandt was an "inspiration to all Americans. He was a dedicated public servant, a man known for the courage of his convictions and a distinguished combat veteran of three wars." Few individuals did more to shape the VFW than James Van Zandt. He rests, most appropriately, in Arlington National Cemetery. He died Jan. 6, 1986, at 87, after a long illness.

A dream is realized when the first of 37 million Adjusted Service Bonds begin rolling off the presses in July 1936. Proud victors of the long, hard fight include, from left: Charles E. Weickardt, naval liaison officer; Joe D. Chittenden, director of the VFW National Service Bureau; VFW Commander-in-Chief James E. Van Zandt; Gen. Frank T. Hines, administrator of the Veterans Administration; Alvia W. Hall, director of the Bureau of Engraving and Printing; Harold W. Breining, assistant VA administrator; and Millard W. Rice, VFW legislative representative.

Chapter 2

Born of Battle

In 1931, four survivors met to commemorate VFW's founding. From left to right: James Romanis, Oscar Brookins, George Kelly, and John Malloy. Francis Dubiel's tailor shop at 286 East Main Street had become a restaurant during intervening years.

Thirteen Spanish-American War veterans — enlisted men all — gathered inside that Columbus, Ohio, tailor shop on Sept. 29, 1899. They were there to form an order that would last beyond their lifetimes to enfold veterans of foreign service in the coming decades.

Veterans of three units — the 17th U.S. Infantry, 1st Colorado and 28th Volunteer Infantry regiments — would return home to form separate veterans organizations in different states at varying times. But within 14 years they would all come together to create the Veterans of Foreign Wars.

On the evening of Sept. 29, 1899, 13 men gathered in a tailor shop at 286 E. Main Street in Columbus, Ohio. They were all veterans of the U.S. 17th Infantry Regiment who had fought on Cuba during the Spanish-American War. The war had formally ended 13 months earlier. This baker's dozen of veterans gathered to remember their comrades killed in action, to see what they could do for the living and to recall shared events of then the most popular war in America's history. After all, the 17th Regiment had a genuine claim to fame.

Approximately one-third of the Medals of Honor awarded to soldiers during the Spanish-American War went to members of the U.S. 17th Infantry Regiment, a regular unit stationed at Columbus Barracks, Ohio, before the war.

The 17th fought in the Santiago Campaign — specifically at the Battle of El Caney on July 1, 1898. As part of the 3rd Brigade, 2nd Division, V Corps, it assaulted the six wooden blockhouses, with a strong point at El Viso, known as El Caney. Initially held in reserve, it later dashed across the killing ground.

"From the grassy ridge, Chaffee ordered the 17th Infantry to advance up a slightly sunken road bordered with hedges on either side," wrote Ivan Musicant in *Empire By Default*. "No sooner did they break the cover of the ridge crest and deploy to the right through a gap in the hedges than they were struck by killing volleys from the trenches. The regimental commander was

Original founders of the Ohio AVFS were members of the 17th Infantry Regiment. At El Caney, Cuba, on July 1, 1898, the unit's members earned nine Medals of Honor. Among them was a VFW founder.

The 17th went on to the Philippines in 1899 where it served in seven of that war's campaigns.

The U.S. Army's Medal of Honor. VFW co-founder Oscar Brookins was awarded the coveted decoration for dragging a wounded comrade to safety under heavy fire during the battle for El Caney on Cuba in July 1898.

Veterans of Cuba were shipped to Camp Wikoff, at Montauk Point, Long Island, so as not to "infect" civilians with yellow fever. Thousands were transferred from the chaotic conditions at the 5,000-acre camp to hospitals on the Eastern seaboard. Others were prematurely discharged, ill and delirious. By the time Camp Wikoff was shut down in late 1898, 250 soldiers had died in a place where they were sent to recuperate.

COLLIER'S WEEKLY
AN ILLUSTRATED JOURNAL OF ART LITERATURE & CURRENT EVENTS

"HOME!"

hit three times, and his quartermaster was killed by his side. The 17th withdrew into a hollow and extended further to the right."

In his after-action report, Capt. L.M. O'Brien wrote: "The conduct of the men...compelled to receive fire without the opportunity to return it, is worthy of the highest praise for soldierly steadiness and courage."

The full extent of that courage was not known to O'Brien at the time. Nine men of Companies C and D displayed exceptional bravery in rescuing several comrades. Pvt. Oscar Brookins of Company C was one of the Medal of Honor recipients. His citation read: "Gallantly assisted in the rescue of the wounded from in front of the lines and under heavy fire from the enemy."

All told, the 17th sustained nine killed in action and 40 wounded on Cuba. In the spring of 1899, the regiment was dispatched to the Philippines where it ultimately served in seven of that war's campaigns.

That summer, some of those who had been discharged were presented with the Medal of Honor. Among them was Brookins who had been slightly wounded at El Caney. He had enlisted in Green County, Ohio, and was present that fateful evening in September 1899 when the VFW took root 100 years ago.

When the fighting had ended on Cuba in late July 1898, many warriors were scarecrows, shivering, glassy-eyed, stabbed with pain by malaria, typhoid and dysentery. They were dying at the rate of 15 per day. Then yellow fever invaded the camps, and the toll began to rise. Camps were evacuated too late.

"Most of them returned mere shadows of their former selves," wrote Dr. Nicholas Senn, chief surgeon of U.S. Volunteers, at the war's end. "The pale faces, the sunken eyes, the staggering gait and the emaciated forms show only too plainly the effect of climate and disease. Many of them are wrecks for life, others are candidates for a premature grave and hundreds will require most careful attention and treatment before they regain the vigor they lost in Cuba."

On Aug. 7, the first outbound detachment of the spent army boarded a transport waiting for them in the harbor at Santiago. The weary men were told that a splendid new camp awaited them at Montauk Point, Long Island, N.Y., where they would spend a restful summer recovering from the travails of campaigning in a hostile land.

When the first boatloads of Cuba veterans arrived at the eastern tip of Long Island on Aug. 14, 1898, they found themselves unloaded in the chaos of a 5,000-acre construction site called Camp Wikoff after Col. Charles A. Wikoff, killed on San Juan Hill. Among them were members of the 17th.

Conceived as a combination medical detention facility and hospital for the disabled, Wikoff became the focus of extensive press attention. Between Aug. 14 and Sept. 28, 20,000 veterans of Cuba were processed through the camp. Some arrived with a "deathlike pallor" on their faces, according to the *New York Tribune*. "Shrunken and ghastly white, their faces told a terrible tale of suffering and hardship," recalled an observer of their debarkation. Asked the *New York Times*, "What kindness of heart is that which lets brave soldiers who have served their country well die of malnutrition and neglect?"

New arrivals were shown tents without floors or bedding and were told to sleep on the ground. Sick men lay on blankets while a hospital was noisily erected around them. To relieve congestion, the War Department authorized surgeons to furlough convalescing soldiers. Hundreds were sent off, most of them sick, many to collapse in passenger cars and railroad stations an hour or two out of camp.

Camp Wikoff slowly became the recuperation center the War Department intended—but not before a public outcry had been raised over the treatment an inept government had handed its fighting men. By the time the last outfit

Mexican War Vets Earned Eligibility First

They were known as America's first gold stripe crusaders. Then-Pennsylvania VFW historian O.D. Lavan reckoned "a genealogist would describe their relationship to the organization as that of consanguinity, or relationship by blood, which is closer, of course, than by marriage, or that of affinity."

A quick scan of the membership eligibility list from the "Roaring 20s" would turn up an oddity. First on the list was the Mexican War of 1846-48. These aging vets of the nation's first foreign land war were welcomed with open arms into Posts from Paris, Mo., to Roanoke, Va. At least eight were mentioned by name in *Foreign Service* magazine.

In 1922, Post 107 in Brooklyn, N.Y., proudly displayed a Mexican battle flag and sword presented to it by the family of Emmanuel Oppenheim after he died. Other Mexican War veteran-members included Dan Gonder of Sioux City, Iowa; Uriah Gasaway of Brazil, Ind.; Amasa Clark of San Antonio, Texas; Uriah Rose of Roanoke, Va.; Bill Buckner of Missouri; and Owen Thomas Edgar of Washington, D.C. "Gran'pop" Nathan

Loar of Post 56 in Ft. Leavenworth, Kan., was, at age 101, the oldest active member of the organization in 1922.

When Edgar — the last surviving vet of that war — died Sept. 3, 1929, an era passed with him. Less than a week before his death, the "Dean of America's Foreign Service Veterans" was honored at the VFW's 30th convention in St. Paul, Minn. His symbolic stature, wrote *Foreign Service* Editor Barney Yanofsky, "clearly illustrated VFW's 'evergreen' quality...looking after the interests of the veterans of the past, the present and future."

Capt. William B. Krempkau, a veteran trail driver, brought one of the aging vets to San Antonio for care. For his deed, Krempkau was made an honorary member of Post 76. Perhaps 10 Mexican War veterans were among VFW ranks during the 1920s.

pulled out of Wikoff, 257 American soldiers had perished.

Veterans of what had been called the "Splendid Little War" were on their way home to an uncertain future. After discharge, several units paraded in their hometowns. A watcher recorded his impressions of the march of the 2nd Massachusetts Regiment in Springfield on Sept. 27, 1898. "On almost every face was the badge of the campaign against the pestilential fevers of Cuba and the sunken cheekbones and emaciated forms bore eloquent witness to the hardships and sufferings that had been undergone."

Vanguard of the 1st Colorado Volunteer Infantry Regiment crosses the Bridge of Spain leading into the heart of Manila on Aug. 13, 1898. "The taking of the trenches and fort at Malate by the 1st Colorado was the most brilliant and spectacular act of the day," wrote a *Chicago Record* reporter.

Meanwhile, the campaign for the Philippines had been waged in short order. As part of the second expedition, commanded by Brig. Gen. Francis V. Greene, the 1,086-man 1st Colorado Volunteer Infantry Regiment arrived in the Philippines on July 16, 1898. During the siege of Manila when the trenches were bombarded by the Spanish, the 1st Colorado moved to within 1,200 yards of the trenches and was held in reserve.

The Coloradans next extended their lines eastward to the Pasay Road, the easternmost approach to the capital city from the south. This was done under constant harassing fire and monsoons. "These hardships," Greene remarked,

"were endured by the men of the different regiments...with the finest possible spirit and without a murmur of complaint."

Greene's 2nd Brigade, led by the 1st Colorado, took Fort San Antonio de Abad when the actual battle ensued. "The Colorado infantry," wrote Ivan Musicant in *Empire By Default,* "streamed up the beach and forded the creek fronting the fort, which they found deserted, save for two dead Spaniards and one wounded. In a few minutes the U.S. flag was hoisted, its appearance accompanied by an exultant yell all along the line."

Among the attackers was a young second lieutenant named Rice W. Means. Reported a Denver newspaper: "He bears the distinction of having been the first American soldier to touch the walls of Manila. He swam the river and amid a hail of Spanish bullets proceeded to within 200 yards of enemy lines, which resulted in the fall of Manila. For his bravery, he was promoted to first lieutenant." Twice recommended for the Medal of Honor and cited three times in official orders, Means was later awarded the Distinguished Service Cross (DSC) for gallantry in action during the attack on Manila. (Following WWI, a Certificate of Merit became equal to the Distinguished Service Medal, which was later replaced by the DSC.)

According to Greene: "The Colorado Regiment, in particular, was extremely anxious to go to Manila, was always eager for duty, and performed enthusiastically whatever was required of them. They led the assault on August 13, and were justly proud of being the first to enter the Spanish Works." A reporter for the *Chicago Record* confirmed the action: "The taking of the trenches and fort at Malate by the First Colorado was the most

The 1st Colorado served for a full year in the tropical Philippines, fighting Filipinos from February through June 1899. Suffering 35 dead and 35 wounded, the unit helped wage America's first land war in Asia.

brilliant and spectacular act of the day." It even made the cover of the Aug. 17, 1898, issue of *Harper's Weekly*.

Reportedly, the yelling "drowned all other sounds with its strident savage note of victory." First to raise Old Glory over the walls of old Manila was Capt. Alexander M. Brooks, later a prominent member of VFW Post 1 in Denver, Colo. The founder of what became that Post was Irving Hale, who was cited for gallantry and promoted to brigadier general of the 2nd Brigade of the 2nd Division after Manila.

Brig. Gen. Irving Hale (left) with fellow officers in the Philippines in 1899. While commanding the 2nd Brigade, Hale was wounded in March of that year. Earlier, he had been cited for gallantry and promoted. After arriving back in Denver, he was instrumental in organizing one of VFW's parent groups.

Once over the Pasig River, the 1st Colorado occupied districts around San Sebastian and Sampaloc. Casualties for the 2nd Brigade were light — one killed in action and 54 wounded — while moving through the inner suburbs. Incidentally, the 1st's ranks already included well-known novelist and sports writer Damon Runyon who was serving as a private.

Taking Manila from the Spaniards did not end the combat in the Philippines — the real war would begin six months later. From February 1899 until July 1902, the U.S. waged a grueling campaign against Filipino guerrillas seeking independence. The 1st Colorado was right in the middle of the fray.

When the war against Spain ended in August, the 1st Colorado was among the regiments left occupying the Philippines. For five months, it bided its time on outpost duty. Then on Feb. 4, 1899, a 12,000-man Filipino army struck Manila. "In the Colorado regiment located next to the Nebraska camp, bullets poured into regimental headquarters," wrote William Sexton in *Soldiers in the Sun*. "One officer was wounded while standing by his bed getting dressed." When the fighting ended the next day, the Coloradans counted three dead and five wounded. Some 60 Filipino corpses were found in front of their lines.

The war was on — the 1st Colorado could look forward to eight months of duty in what one veteran described simply as "Hades." The 1st would join Gen. Arthur MacArthur's division in March in capturing the enemy capital at Malolos. Brig. Gen. Hale, who was wounded at Maycauyan some eight miles north of Manila on March 26, was then commanding the 2nd Brigade. The day before, Capt. John Stewart was killed — the first Post in Denver would later bear his name. The regiment's last major engagement at Laguna de Bay, southeast of Manila, occurred in June.

The Coloradans departed the islands July 18, 1899. They, like other state volunteer regiments, had borne the brunt of the heaviest fights, serving as "guinea pigs" in waging tropical warfare. They came in for high praise. "In the

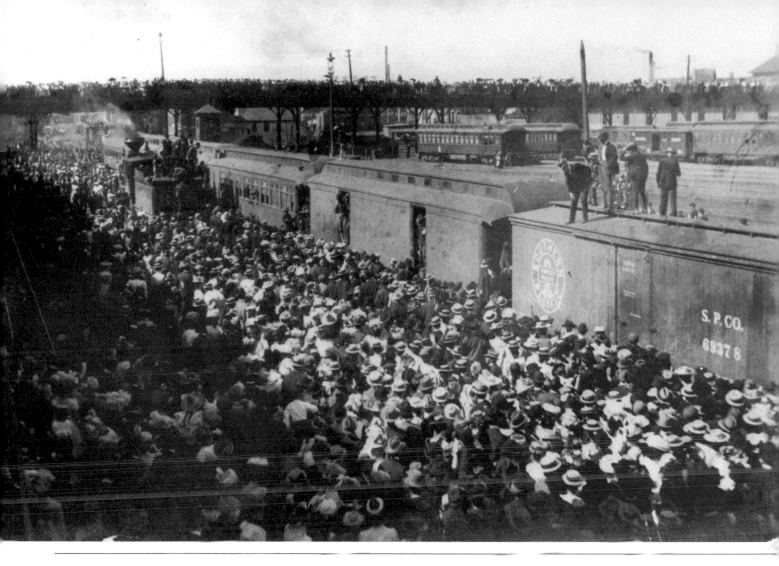

present war," reported Maj. J.S. Mallory, inspector general of MacArthur's division, "they proved themselves to be magnificent fighting men."

Casualties for the 1st had been relatively light — 12 killed in action, 23 dead from disease and 35 wounded. With two months additional pay for overseas service and travel pay for the return journey, unit members arrived home in Denver on Sept. 10 to a banquet, parade and 20,000 cheering fellow citizens. A special medal was struck in their honor and the names of the dead engraved on a flagpole base at the capital. Welcomed as heroes, these veterans would make their marks in both Colorado and American history.

Homecoming for the 1st Colorado was a riotous affair. Some 20,000 citizens gathered at Denver's Union Station in September 1899 to welcome the state's heroes. A special medal was even struck in their honor.

When state volunteers departed, they were replaced by federal volunteers recruited specifically for the Philippines War. These newcomers included the U.S. 28th Volunteer Infantry Regiment. Enlisted in Pennsylvania, the 28th was one of 25 regiments comprising 35,000 volunteers who signed up for two years to serve in the islands. Privates earned $15.60 per month and survived on abominable field rations. The 28th arrived in Manila in late November 1899 and by mid-1900 had 1,283 men in the field. Its first

Members of Company F, 28th Volunteer Infantry Regiment, pause before plunging back into a Philippine jungle in pursuit of elusive insurgents. The 28th served in the islands from November 1899 to March 1901. Compiling a fine war record, several of the regiment's veterans formed a group in Pennsylvania that would merge with associations from Ohio and Colorado to create the VFW.

campaign was waged on southern Luzon — "an awful region of known contagious and tropical diseases" — beginning in January 1900.

As part of Gen. Loyd Wheaton's Brigade, its three battalions fought near Imus and Binacayan, inflicting 245 insurgent casualties early on. "The 28th attacked so vigorously at Patol Bridge," stated the official report, "where they met entrenched insurgents on Jan. 7, the enemy was so completely defeated and demoralized that they hardly made another stand in Cavite Province."

July saw the 28th engaged in constant combat around Taal in Batangas Province. Early that month, 500 insurgents attacked the town, wounding six soldiers. Some 100 infantrymen in one 3 1/2-hour firefight killed 38 Filipinos. Regimental commander Col. William E. Birkhimer remarked, "The men were, as a rule, cool, aimed deliberately, and they made the shots count the result shows." Birkhimer, a Medal of Honor recipient, was henceforth known as the "champion insurrecto exterminator." Yet he later admitted, "We control within the line of our bayonets, but no further."

That fall, at Looc in Batangas, a mounted detachment of the 2nd Battalion made a gallant stand against 400 insurgents. In inflicting 75 casualties, each man of the 20-man detachment expended 130 rounds, but the unit sustained two killed in action and four wounded. "Each man did the work of a hero during the day," reported Capt. George W. Biegler. While every unit member was named for a Certificate of Merit, one in particular stood out. "I also specially recommend Pvt. George Metzger, Hospital Corps, for dressing the wounded under fire," wrote Biegler. Biegler himself was later awarded the Medal of Honor when "with but 19 men resisted and at close quarters defeated 300 of the enemy."

In early December, the regiment was ordered to Tagaloan in Surigao Province on Mindanao. Part of a three-month campaign lasting through March 1901, the 28th again distinguished itself despite adverse environmental conditions. Birkhimer observed that "the extraordinary roughness — mountain, canyon, deep rivers of the country — has made campaigning more than usually severe." But "…nothing could exceed the fortitude, pluck and endurance of the men of the regiment."

Company K's ordeal in February was a prime example. It had several encounters with guerrillas on the island, but kept on the move. "The movement of this company from Butuan to Placer was one of the most interesting in the history of the regiment," reported Birkhimer. "The incidents of this march through a country that rivaled the Everglades of Florida for difficulties…" were incredible. Among those who experienced this trial of endurance was Pvt. Herbert O. Kelley, a future VFW leader.

March marked the end of the 28th's time in the Philippines: It left Manila on the 16th. That month, Filipino insurgent leader Emilio Aguinaldo was captured. By mid-1901, the regular U.S. Army had assumed full responsibility for pacifying the islands of the archipelago. Arriving on the West Coast on April 14, the regiment was mustered out in San Francisco two weeks later. All told, the 28th Infantry lost 30 dead — mostly from disease — along with 55 wounded and injured in the Philippines.

Herbert O. Kelley, commander of the Pennsylvania AVFS, discovered that the Columbus AVFS was "no jest, but a stern reality." The two AVFS groups merged in 1905.

Veterans of three of units — the 17th U.S. Infantry, 1st Colorado and 28th Volunteer Infantry regiments — would return home to form separate veterans organizations in different states at varying times. But within 14 years they would all come together to create the Veterans of Foreign Wars.

It all began with that meeting in Columbus and a man on a bicycle. James C. Putnam, 31, pedaled through Columbus neighborhoods tracking down former members of the 17th Infantry Regiment to enlist them in a new cause — the creation of a veterans organization to look after their interests. Putnam's lean figure was topped with an angular face that beamed determination and good humor. He looked like a soldier, and he was.

James C. Putnam, descendant of a long line of Yankee warriors, fought Indians in the American West and treated wounded as a medic with the 17th Infantry on Cuba. Putnam wrote the AVFS constitution, paid for its charter and was elected first president of the organization.

Born in Ringgold County, Iowa, Putnam came from a long line of fighters. One of his ancestors was Maj. Gen. Israel Putnam, who served on George Washington's staff during the American Revolution. Another fought the British in 1812; another the Mexicans in 1846. The latest Putnam warrior enlisted in the 6th Infantry, then transferred to the 6th Cavalry and headed for the untamed American West to fight Utes, Zunis and Sioux.

In 1891, Putnam took a Sioux bullet in the leg while scouting along the White River in South Dakota. The wound was severe enough to have him medically discharged, but not daunting enough to divert him from the road to further adventure. He whooped and roared along with the rest of the Oklahoma Sooners during the great land rush of 1893. He stayed just long enough to become a deputy sheriff for Grant County.

Putnam's wanderlust took him back to the U.S. Army as a medic with the 17th Infantry. At El Caney, Cuba, he took a Spanish bullet in the neck and was evacuated to a stateside hospital. In bandages himself, Putnam spent the voyage caring for troopers hurt even worse.

Late in 1898, Putnam reluctantly accepted his discharge at Columbus Barracks. Despite a troublesome leg and a sore neck, he decided to become a fireman, and did. It was then that he met James Romanis who had been pained by the physical appearance of sickened vets in his pharmacy. The two ex-privates joined forces to right the wrongs inflicted by an apparently uncaring government. Romanis put a notice in the *Columbus Dispatch* calling for a gathering of vets.

Thus it was that the 13 veterans assembled at Francis Dubiel's tailor shop. Dubiel, a Polish immigrant fluent in five languages, had good reason to want rights secured for men who fought in pestilential climates: He was wasting away with malaria and had only a few years to live. Dubiel called the roll: George Beekman, David Brown, Oscar Brookins, John Clark, Charles Click, Bert DuRant, Andrew Grant, George Kelly, John Malloy, James Putnam, James Romanis, Walter Waddington — and a late arrival, Simon Heiman of the 4th Ohio Volunteer Infantry, which had served on Puerto Rico. Brookins was the same Medal of Honor recipient who had repeatedly risked his life under fire to drag wounded men to cover at El Caney in July 1898.

They were wary of repeating the mistakes of their predecessors. The Society of the Cincinnati, formed after the Revolutionary War, admitted only officers and came under critical fire as being elitist, a snub to enlisted men. The relentless toll on Civil War veterans — a Grand Army of the Republic (GAR) meeting hall had recently gone on the block because there weren't enough

Indian-Fighting Chiefs

What on earth do the Indian campaigns have to do with the VFW? More than you think — three VFW commanders-in-chief served in the wild West.

James C. Putnam, VFW's first leader, as an enlisted man of Troop F, 6th U.S. Cavalry Regiment, campaigned throughout the West against Utes in 1889, Zunis in 1890 and the Sioux in 1891.

While scouting along the White River in the South Dakota Badlands, he was wounded in the leg by one of Chief Sitting Bull's braves. That wound earned him a medical discharge on April 1, 1892. (He re-enlisted later.)

Gen. Lloyd M. Brett, commander-in-chief from 1923-24, began his military career in 1879 as a West Point graduate under Gen. Nelson A. Miles' command. As a second

Gen. Lloyd M. Brett, VFW Chief (1923-1924), spent 16 years on the Western frontier. He fought both Sioux and Apache.

lieutenant in the 2nd Cavalry Regiment, he earned the Medal of Honor. It was for "fearless exposure and dashing bravery in cutting off the Indians' pony herd, thereby greatly crippling the hostiles" at O'Fallon's Creek, Mont., on April 1, 1880.

On another occasion, Brett was cited in General Orders for gallantry after making a forced march of 26 straight hours *and* going 18 hours without water during the intense heat of summer in pursuit of hostile Indians.

During his 16 years on the frontier, he served against the Sioux in Montana (1879-80) and Geronimo's Apaches in Arizona (1885-86).

Gen. Charles King, an Army general who earned five distinct campaign medals, also counted Indian-fighting among his exploits on the frontier. The 1903-04 commander-in-chief of the Army of the Philippines, Cuba and Puerto Rico, spent a decade in the West from 1870 through 1879.

As a captain with the 5th Cavalry Regiment, he was so severely wounded that his "saber arm" became almost useless. Consequently, he was forced to retire — at least temporarily.

His experiences in the Sioux campaign of 1876 provided great material for the reading public. From the time he was wounded until the Spanish-American War, King wrote 20 novels about life in the West.

members left to keep it open—was a warning that this new organization would suffer the same fate if membership was limited to a single war against Spain.

Putnam wrote a constitution that laid the groundwork that exists to this day. Their organization would be called the American Veterans of Foreign Service (AVFS) and would welcome any U.S. soldier, sailor or Marine who had honorably served outside the continental limits of the United States, or would do so in future wars. When old fighting men of one war faded away, new warriors would arise to fill the ranks. It would be, in the parlance of the times, an "evergreen" association.

Putnam spelled out the purpose of AVFS: "To promote in all ways fraternal the general welfare of the men who have borne the brunt of battle, to foster true patriotism as true defenders of American principles, cooperating in celebrations of patriotic anniversaries and maintaining a status for the veteran, placing him in the front rank of American citizenship."

AVFS needed a symbol, and a historian among them reached back nine centuries to retrieve one. During the Crusades, a monk named Gerard founded the Order of the Hospital of St. John the Baptist, whose knights dedicated their lives to the care of sick and wounded. The new order fulfilled a need for those Crusaders trained to fight, but who longed for a religious

Gen. Francis V. Greene won out over Irving Hale as first commander of the National Association of the Army of the Philippines. Greene took office in 1900, presiding over one of the two major groups destined to found the VFW.

life. The Hospitalers moved across the scorching terrain of the Holy Land under banners emblazoned with the Cross of Malta. It was this cross, with appropriate additions, that was chosen to symbolize AVFS — crusaders in the cause of rights and recognition for a later breed of fighting man.

On Oct. 10, 1899, AVFS was granted a charter of incorporation as a non-profit entity in the state of Ohio. The fee was paid out of Putnam's wages as a fireman. Putnam was elected president, Kelly and DuRant vice presidents, Romanis secretary, Dubiel treasurer, Brown chaplain, Brookins, Clark and Malloy trustees, and Grant and Waddington sergeants-at-arms.

Headquarters Camp No. 1 was established in Columbus. Other camps were rooted in the Ohio towns of Hamilton, Marysville, Delaware and Marion. Reaching farther, a camp was founded in Portsmouth, N.H., and another in Sparta, Ill. It was slow going. Potential AVFS recruits were siphoned away by the rival United Spanish War Veterans, and thousands more candidates were still fighting in the Philippines. Romanis picked up pen and paper and began a letter-writing campaign to vets of the recent war wherever he could find them.

The fledgling organization earned favorable newspaper publicity, attracting new members by living up to Article I of its constitution, which promised to "assist worthy comrades."

AVFS discovered Myron B. Hall, a member and veteran of the assault on San Juan Hill, wasting away in a poorhouse. Hall came home with a lung disease that he could not afford to have treated; he was resigned to die among indigents. AVFS arranged Hall's transfer to the Soldiers & Sailors Home in Sandusky, Ohio, where he began to recover. His letter to the AVFS was reprinted in full in the *Columbus Dispatch*.

"I wish to thank my comrades for what they have done for me," he wrote. "As soon as I get well I shall do all I can for the benefit of the lodge" (as he called it). The paper noted that Hall was long overdue for his pension, small as it was. Pensions became a crusade for the AVFS from its inception.

As AVFS struggled in the East, organizing efforts were under way out West. One of the veterans who disembarked at San Francisco in 1899 to take the long train ride home to Denver was Brig. Gen. Irving Hale, the head of the 1st Colorado Volunteer Infantry Regiment. After the people of Colorado raised money to bring the regiment home in a special train, Hale knew his plans for a Colorado veterans organization would flourish.

Hale was a dynamic presence in the community. A West Pointer who had graduated with an enviable academic record, he was sought after as a lecturer on engineering and military science. He had no difficulty landing a job as general manager of a Denver electrical company.

Hale used his military drive and command presence to launch the Colorado Society of the Army of the Philippines. The first meeting was held in the state capital on Dec. 1, 1899. A constitution and bylaws were adopted on Feb. 3, 1900, when Gen. Francis V. Greene became the president. Dues were set at $1 a year. Membership was broadened to include sailors and Marines.

The founders in Denver voted to accept the sons of Philippine veterans as a hedge against the eventual demise of the Society. But men who had fought on Cuba and in the 1900 Boxer Rebellion in China, as well as those who had seized Guam and Puerto Rico, were excluded.

More than 1,000 Philippines veterans descended on Denver for the first reunion on Aug. 13, 1900. Men from every state in the West and from as far away as Tennessee and Pennsylvania attended. Hale told them the organization was going national and would henceforth be called the National Association of the Army of the Philippines.

Camp No. 1 was established in Denver; the second camp was formed in St. Paul, Minn., in May 1900. Within six years, the Society numbered 1,314 veterans of the Philippines. Maj. Gen. Arthur MacArthur was elected president in 1906.

Maj. Gen. Arthur MacArthur was among many who strongly supported the aims of veterans organizations. He, along with Secretary of War William Howard Taft and Brig. Gen. Frederick Funston — nemesis of Filipino insurrectionists — were prominent guests at the 1904 reunion of veterans of the Philippines campaign held in St. Louis, Mo.

Back in Ohio, the itinerant Jim Putnam was once again overcome with wanderlust. Explaining that he had always led a "roving and dare-devil existence," he took a job with the Pennsylvania Railroad. On Jan. 1, 1900, he turned over the leadership reins of AVFS to Will White, once a captain in the 4th Ohio Volunteer Infantry. Putnam kept his residence in Columbus, using his railroad pass to travel the country, spreading the word about AVFS.

In 1901, there arose in Pittsburgh the Philippine War Veterans under the leadership of G.H. Smith. Yet another organization appeared with the same name in Altoona, Pa., that July. It was initially formed by veterans of the 43rd Volunteer Infantry. Its first chapter was named after James L. Noble who was killed in action on Leyte on Sept. 30, 1900, while attempting to rescue a fellow soldier of Company C.

On July 24, 1902, the American Veterans of Philippine and China Wars was formed in Philadelphia by Capt. Robert S. Hansbury, who had served with the 28th U.S. Volunteer Infantry Regiment. It had the following objectives: "To preserve and strengthen the fraternity among the membership; to assist worthy comrades and their widows and orphans; to perpetuate the memory and history of our dead and to maintain true allegiance to the United States of America and fidelity to its Constitution and laws."

In 1903, the three groups from Philadelphia, Pittsburgh and Altoona

In 1903, Robert S. Hansbury became the first commander of the American Veterans of Foreign Service, headquartered in Altoona, Pa. Neither the Columbus nor the Altoona group knew of each other's existence until 1904.

merged to form the American Veterans of Foreign Service, identical in name to its counterpart in Ohio. Unflagging efforts by Jim Romanis, through hard-hitting editorials in his magazine, *American Veterans of Foreign Service,* brought order out of the chaotic name changing and dispersion of effort. In September 1905, the two AVFS groups united at the Eastside Theater in Altoona.

Herbert Kelley was then head of the Pennsylvania AVFS; James Romanis led the Ohio group. George Metzger was chosen to ramrod the newly united Pennsylvania and Ohio outfits. Both Kelley and Metzger had served with the 28th Volunteer Infantry in the Philippines War during 1900-01.

In keeping with its military heritage, the AVFS altered the titles of its elected officers to national commander, senior vice commander, junior vice commander, adjutant general, quartermaster general, judge advocate general and inspector general, while retaining chaplain on the roster. Romanis had helped untangle most of the knots in the East, but the Denver-based Army of the Philippines would prove a tougher nut to crack.

By 1910, AVFS numbered 1,203 members scattered among 34 camps. Executives knew that two separate veterans organizations could never have the same political weight as a single outfit, even if both had the same goals. The AVFS made fresh overtures to the Army of the Philippines, but was rebuffed.

During the 1911 annual meeting of the Philippines vets in Detroit, a resolution made their opposition clear: "This organization must and shall not amalgamate, affiliate, become part of, or enter into any agreement of whatsoever nature with any other organization of any description, except upon the individual consent of every member of this organization. This amendment, after its adoption, shall not be amendable to reconsideration or be repealed except upon the individual consent of every member of this organization." The amendment passed by a landslide; only three farsighted men voted against it. Two of them were Gus E. Hartung, 32, and Rice W.

Rice W. Means led the newly named VFW in 1914. Means served in the Philippines and later fought with the 4th Infantry Regiment, 3rd Division, during the 1918 Meuse-Argonne campaign. He became a U.S. senator from Colorado (1924-27) and in the early '30s published *Stars and Stripes.*

Means, 35. Hartung was a New Yorker who moved to Colorado as a youngster and served with the 1st Colorado during early campaigning in the Philippines. Means enlisted in the unit while still in school and served in the islands as a first lieutenant. His heroism under fire earned him the respect of the men he fought with, as well as the citizens of Colorado.

Hartung invited AVFS's commander-in-chief, Robert G. Woodside, to hold its 1913 encampment in Denver at the same time the Philippines veterans would meet. Woodside, a 37-year-old Brooklynite who had served with the 10th Pennsylvania Volunteers, saw advantage in proximity. The invitation was accepted.

The two clans assembled in Denver in August and verbal combat ensued. Opponents cited the "unrepealable" amendment voted on two years earlier; proponents pointed to the undeniable benefits of unification. But the sticking point was the name.

Hale threw his weight into the argument and proposed an interim tag: "The Army of the Philippines, Cuba and Puerto Rico." Though cumbersome, it temporarily satisfied the fierce pride of those Westerners who wanted their deeds remembered by place name. On Aug. 20, 1913, the joining of the two groups became a reality, but a name remained to be chosen. Rice Means was elected the first commander-in-chief.

A few diehards still questioned the legality of it all. A Philippine Society camp in Boston disavowed the proceedings. Members of the Luzon Camp in Chicago became renegades, distancing themselves from the parent organization for another 13 years.

General Order No. 6, dated April 15, 1914, put the choice of a permanent name to a referendum. The three options: "Veteran Army and Navy of the U.S.," "Veteran Army and Navy of the Republic" and "Veterans of Foreign Wars." The latter said it all and took the honors. Then-Judge Advocate General Martin J. O'Donnell of Kansas City reportedly was instrumental in the selection of VFW as the new name.

On Aug. 1, 1914, General Order No. 10 publicized the referendum's results and the Veterans of Foreign Wars came into being.

Members of the still-identified Army of the Philippines, Cuba and Puerto Rico pose for a panoramic picture in front of Heinz 57 Varieties Company in Pittsburgh on Sept. 17, 1914. That August, the new name had already been decided by referendum: Veterans of Foreign Wars.

Chapter 3

A Gold Chevron Order

America's involvement in World War I proves pivotal to VFW's growth and development. Returning Doughboys infuse the ranks with youthful energy and enthusiasm.

Thomas Crago, a captain in the 10th Pennsylvania Infantry Regiment, became VFW commander-in-chief in 1914. Crago is credited with VFW's greatest achievement of the time: the pension bill for widows of Spanish-American War veterans.

World War I convulsed Europe in the summer of 1914 — the same summer the VFW was officially born. U.S. involvement in the "Great War" would, in many ways, virtually make the organization. Returning Doughboys (WWI soldiers) filled the ranks, transforming the VFW from an obscure society to a well-known order recognized and respected by the American public.

A gold chevron on the lower left sleeve of a Doughboy's uniform meant only one thing — he had been overseas during World War I, often in the trenches of France. "The gold chevron has become a traditional emblem of overseas service," offered *Foreign Service*, VFW's official publication, "one that is familiar to the American people and requires no explanation." Because VFW was exclusively made up of vets with foreign duty, the organization quickly became known as the "Gold Chevron Order."

When the VFW national encampment convened in Detroit on Aug. 16, 1915, the opening gavel was held by Commander-in-Chief Thomas S. Crago, 49, representative-at-large of Pennsylvania's 23rd Congressional District. Crago, who had fought in the Philippines, steered the proceedings toward the VFW's primary concern of urging the nation to prepare for war. If not with Mexico, then almost certainly with Germany, whose depredations soared to new heights with the sinking of the *Lusitania*.

Adjutant General Robert G. Woodside stood at the lectern knowing that Europe was emptying its treasuries to field armies numbered in the millions. Meanwhile, the U.S. was spending less than 1 percent of its gross national product to meet the threat of approaching war. Woodside concurred with Maj. Gen. Leonard Wood, who declared that the U.S. Army was "just about equal to the police forces of Boston, New York and Philadelphia."

Woodside called for an active veterans reserve corps, men who had already "met the elephant" (been in combat), to form cadres and to pass along experience gained on the battlefield. Crago reminded veterans of the woeful lack of equipment with which they had embarked to fight Spaniards

Opposite page:
To wear a gold chevron was to be eligible to join VFW ranks. Each chevron represented six months service overseas. By the time the Armistice was signed on Nov. 11, 1918, more than 2 million uniformed Americans had served in France.

17 years earlier. He called for a first line army of 100,000, a second line of another 100,000, and enough war materiel to supply an eventual force of a million armed men.

VFW adopted a resolution pledging "instant response to the call of duty," while noting that "peace at any price is the swan song of the decadent and the virtueless. Preparedness will prevent the enormous sacrifice of human lives that has characterized every war in which the United States has been engaged throughout its history. We dare not indulge ourselves in the enjoyment of the blessings of peace while turning deaf ears to cries of distress or to the summons of a righteous cause."

Editorials in *Foreign Service* encouraged members to organize preparedness meetings wherever a VFW Post was located. These meetings were designed to "crystallize and concentrate the sentiment of this nation to a true understanding of our duties to other nations as well as to ourselves." The "other nations" signified VFW's recognition that Europe's problems with the German juggernaut were rapidly becoming our own.

Membership was also a priority. Delegates voted to recruit active-duty personnel. A new initiative was necessary. VFW's annual encampment began in Chicago on Aug. 13, 1916, with nine national officers and 130 delegates and alternates representing 5,000 VFW members in Posts scattered from Maine to the Philippines. Attempts to revive the defunct McIntyre Post in Washington, D.C., were met with indifference, leaving the nation's capital without VFW representation at a time when it was needed most.

The organization also needed visibility and a new fixed address — VFW headquarters was located in Pittsburgh, which was a bit removed from the center of social activity. Thus, when member Walter I. Joyce offered rent-free office space in a building he owned in lower Manhattan for a new national headquarters, the offer was quickly accepted in late 1918. The building was at 32 Union Square, on the edge of Greenwich Village. Union Square seemed an unlikely place for a conservative veterans organization dedicated to flag and country, but it proved a godsend to VFW.

At the 1916 encampment, Rep. Crago, now chairman of VFW's Legislative Committee, reported on the snail's-pace progress of the Key Pension Bill for Spanish-American War widows and orphans, which had been shunted back and forth in Congress since 1912. The bill finally made its way through the House with little opposition and was reported favorably out of the Senate committee, but then died. Crago explained that both Houses were so involved in wrangling over how to reorganize the Army and raise funds to expand the Navy that the pension bill was pigeonholed.

Meanwhile, the world war was coming ever closer to America's shores. It arrived April 6, 1917, when Congress declared war on Germany. One of the nay-sayers was Minnesota Rep. Ernest Lundeen of Post No. 7 in Minneapolis. When Lundeen refused to resign, VFW convened a court-martial. He became the first VFW member to be ousted by court-martial, which found that he had "violated the objects and purposes of the VFW to foster patriotism, to maintain and extend the institutions of American freedom, and to preserve and defend the United States from all her enemies whomsoever."

Others, however, made up for Lundeen's lack of enthusiasm. Among them was Theodore Roosevelt who was the first President to become a VFW member. He signed up in Pittsburgh on July 26, 1917, at the William Penn Hotel. Another was a onetime Missouri farm boy, Maj. Gen. John J. Pershing, 55, a paid-up member of VFW Post 27 in Manila, who would lead the American Expeditionary Forces (AEF) to France.

On the home front, VFW rallied to the cause. D.R. Sullivan of Post 92 in New Kensington, Pa., set aside part of his real estate office as a recruiting station and sent more than 200 volunteers off to training camps. Robert Woodside organized the U.S. Veterans Reserve for the Allegheny County VFW to be used for home guard duty. He then volunteered himself and was soon on his way to Camp Gordon, Ga., to begin a second wartime tour of duty. Some VFW members, despite their age, again volunteered for the colors. For instance, 25 men of Post 45 in New York joined the regular Army or were mobilized through the National Guard.

VFW steered clear of wartime hysteria. An early VFW historian, J.I. Billman, explained: "There were no more patriotic men in the country than the veterans who wore the Cross of Malta on their lapels, but they felt that the work of enforcing municipal, state and national laws belongs to duly constituted authority and not to a fraternal society. It would have been easy to court newspaper notoriety by calling out local posts whenever there were industrial disputes or other disturbances, but the VFW believed that every comrade should stand squarely behind constituted authority."

The only nod by VFW to the wave of anti-German sentiment was passage of a resolution calling for a halt to publishing newspapers in the language of the Central Powers for the duration of the war.

Both wartime encampments, the first in New York City and the second in Minneapolis, centered on the problems at hand and those that would arise once the war ended.

One of the problems facing national officers was VFW's primary news outlet, *Foreign Service,* the struggling monthly magazine edited by Junior Vice Commander-in-Chief William E. Ralston, who received no salary for what

Former President Theodore Roosevelt, the nation's most famous Spanish-American War veteran, was a vociferous advocate of preparedness. He joined VFW on July 26, 1917, in Pittsburgh at the William Penn Hotel.

Gen. John J. Pershing stubbornly refused to allow soldiers of the American Expeditionary Forces in France to be thrown away piecemeal. A member of Post 27 in the Philippines, he was named "Honorary Commander-in-Chief of the VFW" in 1920 while visiting Kansas City. He was a Missouri native.

seemed to him a thankless task.

Delegates at the 1917 encampment in New York wondered if *Foreign Service* should be given a decent burial. Ralston's financial statement was not encouraging. Subscriptions brought in $1,218; advertising $2,375. Printing costs alone amounted to $1,989, which left little for expansion.

But with a war on, the magazine could become a priceless recruiting tool. New bylaws were drafted that made all members of the armed forces overseas eligible for membership. The magazine was saved by raising the per capita tax to $1 a year, which guaranteed an uninterrupted forum for VFW needs, goals and accomplishments. Bundles of the magazine were included with troop mail handed out at training camps in muddy fields near Gondrecourt and Soulaucourt in France.

Editor Ralston addressed a ready audience: "You are now somewhere 'Over There' in America's vanguard of democracy, and we most heartily and cordially extend the right hand of comradeship and urge you to join the veterans organization that does things. This you can do by filling in and signing the application blank that appears elsewhere in these columns. You will be carried on our membership rolls absolutely free of charge until you muster out of the United States service at the close of the present war."

Pvt. W.C. George signed up first. He was enrolled in Post 92 in New Kensington, Pa. On Dec. 30, 1917, he wrote from France: "I felt mighty proud the day I put on my uniform, but since I have become a member of the Veterans of Foreign Wars my chest has a tendency to stick out a few inches more."

Also quite obvious was governmental indifference to the welfare of fighting men and the families they left behind. The *War Risk Insurance Act* covered merchant sailors, but not members of the armed forces. This inexplicable oversight was corrected late in 1917 by amendments that provided insurance, allotments and death and disability benefits previously administered haphazardly by the Treasury Department. VFW was instrumental in securing these amendments.

In Chicago, Gen. Loyd Wheaton enlisted the aid of the Illinois Bar Association to use Post 74 as the site of a VFW legal aid board. Free counsel was dispensed to families of men overseas who were not available to protect their property rights.

Other wartime necessities were met by VFW, too. Ambulances were in short supply. So a nationwide drive for contributions was announced through *Foreign Service.* Money was donated by Posts and Auxiliaries, ranging from $4 to $337.05. It came from communities — large and small — across the country. The first Ford ambulance was presented to the U.S. Army on

Aug. 29, 1917; the second on July 15, 1918. *Foreign Service* listed each contribution under the headline: "Veterans Striving to Demonstrate They are 'In It.' "

Indeed, they were. On the evening of July 14, 1918, Capt. Bob Woodside — recently adjutant general of VFW — was in a fighting hole along the brushy southern bank of the Marne River waiting for the Germans. To his left and right were 3,500 men of the 38th Infantry Regiment of the newly formed 3rd Division. Woodside and the men of the 38th lined a two-mile stretch of the gently flowing river, ready to repel the enemy's last great offensive of the war. The Germans' goal was Paris, less than 60 miles away.

The 38th was green, but filled with regulars and eager volunteers from Ft. Slocum, N.Y., and Columbus Barracks, Ohio, just down the street from the birthplace of VFW. The division had been trained in Pershing's method of waging war — in the open, with the briefest orders and maximum individual initiative. The training that had been hammered home was about to pay dividends.

The Germans sent the best they had at that bend in the river, including the Kaiser's favorite 5th Grenadiers. They believed themselves unstoppable. Woodside's regimental commander, Brig. Gen. Ulysses Grant McAlexander, believed otherwise.

At 12:10 a.m., July 15, 1918, German artillery opened fire. Regimental Sgt. Maj. Joseph E. Cornaccione recalled: "A veritable hell had been let loose. Shells came so thick and fast it was a continuous, tremendous roar. High-explosives, shrapnel and gas swept our entire sector. We huddled in our tiny splinter proofs or open slit trenches for hours that seemed like weeks. The barrage lifted. We waited for the second shock — the shock of material bodies that we could see, feel and fight."

The Grenadiers, wearing new leather and uniforms, started across the river in pontoon boats and ran into heavy automatic weapons fire and showers of grenades.

To support the troops in Europe, VFW presented a much-needed ambulance to the U.S. Army on Aug. 29, 1917, in Union Square, N.Y.C.

"You are now somewhere 'Over There' in America's vanguard of democracy, and we most heartily and cordially extend the right hand of comradeship and urge you to join the veterans organization that does things."

William Ralston, Editor of *Foreign Service*

The Rock of the Marne by Mal Thompson. Near Mezy, France, July 1918. When the German army launched the last great attack of WWI along the Marne River, the 30th and 38th regiments of the U.S. 3rd Infantry Division held fast, checking the assault. After the war, 3,000 veterans of the 38th Regiment formed the "Rock of the Marne" Post in Europe.

Twenty boatloads of Germans wound up as corpses floating downstream before they gained a bridgehead on the other side of the river. They were met by yelling Doughboys who charged into them firing from the hip until the ammo was gone, then clubbing and bayoneting until they were killed or swallowed up by the mass of field gray.

Sgt. Dave McMiun was wounded in both legs. He ordered his men to carry him to the river's edge where he lay firing into the German ranks with his Springfield until killed.

One of Woodside's fellow company commanders, Capt. William "Wild Bill" Morrison, observed an American walking along the railroad embankment. Morrison wrote in his war diary: "I hollered, 'Get down, you damned fool!' He started to come my way, and it looked as though he would draw fire. So I yelled at him again and called him a damned idiot. He came down and damned if it wasn't Col. Alexander. I felt mighty foolish and started to apologize. He laughed and said, 'When you get to be a colonel you can go where you please.'"

Thinned American companies and platoons launched impromptu counterattacks. At the end of the day, the wreckage of the Grenadiers was crowded along the American edge of the Marne looking for reinforcements that never came. From that time forward, the 38th Infantry proudly bore the title "Rock of the Marne."

In speaking of the 38th Infantry, Pershing would say: "A single regiment wrote one of the most brilliant pages in our military annals. The men of this one regiment, firing in three directions, succeeded in throwing two German elite divisions into complete confusion, capturing more than 600 prisoners."

Pershing opened the Meuse-Argonne campaign on Sept. 26. It was a grueling 45-day test of American endurance. Bob Woodside was in the thick of it. His men moved up to battle, tangled in a nightmarish traffic jam behind the lines with roads choked by miles of transport drawn by exhausted, starving mules. Sometimes they were immobilized end-to-end for 16 hours at a time.

They marched at night in glutinous mud and drenching rain. They subsisted on thin slabs of hardtack and the last drops of water from canteens. Desperate men dipped canteens into polluted, corpse-smelling water at the bottom of shell holes and became violently ill, many to die.

Woodside was among the 100,000 casualties of the First Army during the first two weeks of the Meuse-Argonne offensive. Hit on Oct. 9, he was recuperating in a hospital when the guns fell silent along the Western Front on Nov. 11, 1918.

Every inch the soldier, Capt. Robert Woodside proved his mettle during the epic stand of the 38th Infantry Regiment along the Marne River in 1918. Serving with the Army of Occupation, he lost no time in recruiting new VFW members in Germany. Woodside formed Rock of the Marne Post 138, which later moved to New York. He became VFW commander-in-chief in 1920.

'Rock of the Marne': A Premier Post

In 1919, his duties with the Army of Occupation in Germany ended, Capt. Bob Woodside, adjutant of the 38th Infantry Regiment, 3rd Division, transferred his VFW activities to Paris. It was the city his unit had helped save during the battle on the Marne.

Woodside had written a letter to VFW Adjutant General Walter I. Joyce in New York, saying he wanted to recruit members-at-large while there were still thousands of Doughboys in Europe. He was discharged before Joyce could reply, but he still made his way across the Rhine River to rejoin the 38th.

"On my way up to the Army of Occupation about the first of February, 1919," he recalled, "I met a VFW member from San Francisco. We began talking about VFW on the train to Coblenz. Every officer in the compartment was interested. I decided to try to bring about the organization of a Post of the VFW in the 38th Infantry."

Woodside, wearing the ribbon of the Distinguished Service Cross and a wound stripe, was an impressive spokesman. There were 15 rifle companies in the regiment, and he addressed them all. "We swore into the Rock of the Marne Post 138 more than 3,000 members. I was made first commander of the Post," recalled Woodside.

That May, Woodside arranged a Memorial Day ceremony in Neidermendich to honor comrades who now lay buried in French fields.

The speaker was Maj. Gen. Robert Alexander, known as the "soldier's general," who stood before a huge floral arrangement shaped like the Cross of Malta. As each company's letter was called, the first sergeant stepped forward. Then he slipped a card in a cup at each arm of the cross bearing the names of those killed in action or died of wounds or disease. By war's end, the 38th had suffered 598 KIA and 2,669 WIA. Those casualties were divided almost evenly between the Battle of the Marne and the Meuse-Argonne Offensive.

Woodside planned a permanent foreign Post. He obtained 1,728 signatures for a charter to make it possible. The "Rock of the Marne" Post was founded in France on March 16, 1919. Part of the motivation was expressed in the October 1919 issue of *Foreign Service*: "Remember the daily mail call behind Montfaucon? For every name that was answered with 'Here,' the silence of the grave greeted the majority of names called by our mustering officer. Our losses were great, our bereavement real, the scenes of battle vividly before us. We would never forget our missing comrades."

The 38th Infantry Regiment was among the last to be disbanded in Europe. Woodside and his comrades returned long after other Doughboys, who had been met by cheering New Yorkers. They came down the gangway to step onto American soil after 89 days on the line and more than a year overseas. Few people were at the docks, however, to welcome them home. Woodside looked in vain for a VFW contingent. To his everlasting chagrin, VFW's commander-in-chief had forgotten to send a delegation to meet the unit's survivors. Yet their commitment to VFW remained intact.

Members who returned to civilian life and resumed activities at their original Posts could remain on the rolls of the Post in Paris. They would be non-resident members as long as they paid dues of $1 a year. The Post was given its own space in each issue of *Foreign Service*. A roster was published so "all members of the 38th Infantry will be able to maintain regimental association as part of the larger veteran body and reunions can be held at the stated conventions of the Veterans of Foreign Wars."

Woodside and the others decided to erect a vivid reminder of the 38th's courage in World War I. It was a stone-and-bronze monument in Syracuse, N.Y. — birthplace of the regiment. Survivors contributed $25,000 to its construction. The Rock of the Marne Monument still stands in that city's Billings Park today.

On July 15, 1920, veterans gathered for the dedication and to hear Brig. Gen. Ulysses G. McAlexander deliver the address. He stood in front of a life-sized bronze Doughboy poised at the top of the central edifice — Springfield and bayonet ready, harking back to the stand along that red-tinted river in 1918.

The Rock of the Marne Monument in Syracuse, N.Y., is dedicated to men of the 38th Infantry Regiment who gave their lives. In WWI, nearly 600 men of the 38th were killed in action. Bronze tablets list their names. The monument was paid for by donations from regimental survivors.

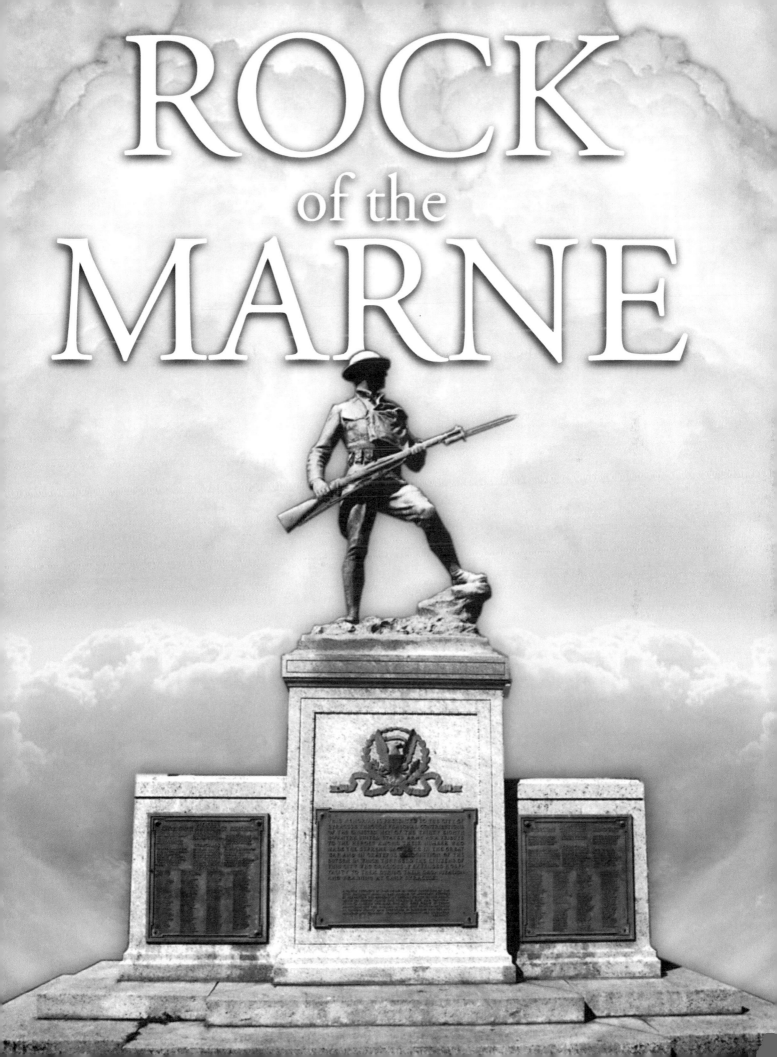

Chapter 4

A Name to be Reckoned With

The "Roaring Twenties" produce several VFW socio-economic accomplishments — a National Service Bureau, Legislative Committee, Buddy Poppy, National Home, the first World War I Bonus and the official national anthem.

More than 2 million men of the AEF returned from France eager to pick up their lives in peacetime America. Among them, of course, was Bob Woodside and his fellow vets of the 38th Infantry Regiment. Despite the tough social and economic times that confronted them, post-World War I America proved a boon to VFW's explosive growth and expansive development.

Doughboys came home at the beginning of an economic slump with prices of almost everything doubled and the country in turmoil. Strikes were epidemic. In January 1919, 35,000 shipyard workers in Seattle, Wash., downed tools and walked off the job. They were soon joined by more than 60,000 other industrial workers in the country's first general strike. The city was all but shut down. Some 500 veterans put their uniforms back on and patrolled the streets to cut down on widespread looting.

Veterans who wanted their old jobs back in the steel industry were out of luck. When U.S. Steel refused demands for raises and an eight-hour day, 350,000 workers in nine states left the mills. Mounted cops with heavy night sticks waded into crowds of demonstrators and cracked skulls. State and federal troops were called out to break up picket lines. Eighteen strikers were killed before labor unions gave in. But other strikes kept occurring.

On Sept. 9, Boston policemen walked away from their beats and disappeared from station houses. Criminals had a field day. Massachusetts Gov. Calvin Coolidge achieved national recognition when he said, "There is no right to strike against the public safety by anybody, anywhere, anytime." He recruited a new police force from the large pool of unemployed veterans — many of them wartime MPs experienced at dealing with hard cases — and the striking cops were left out in the cold.

The United Mine Workers came out of the pits in November. Before the year was out, labor would generate 2,665 strikes of varying magnitude — only a few hundred less than the number staged during wartime when the American war industry was pressed to the limit.

Blame for violent confrontations between labor and management was placed on the "Reds," home-grown Bolsheviks who had cheered the

Opposite page:
Hundreds of thousands lined the streets of Washington, D.C., in 1918 to welcome back the men who fought to make the world safe for democracy. Some 2.5 million Doughboys served in France, many of whom would join the "Gold Chevron Order."

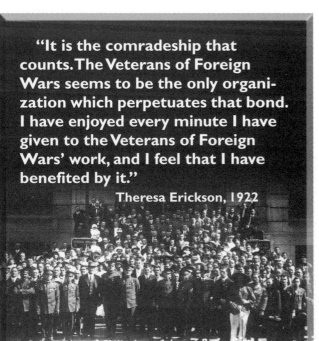

Communist agitators had long used Union Square as a rallying point. A Red leader urges his followers to march on New York City Hall on March 6, 1930. Two months later, the VFW commandeered the square for patriotic purposes.

overthrow of Russia's Czar Nicholas II and the murder of his wife and children in 1917. The American Communist Party and the Communist Labor Party were recent offspring of the Socialist Party. U.S. Bolsheviks were dedicated to bringing the Soviet form of government to America by whatever means.

Package bombs exploded on the doorsteps of Attorney General A. Mitchell Palmer, Supreme Court Justice Oliver Wendell Holmes and Assistant Secretary of the Navy Franklin D. Roosevelt. Palmer went on the warpath in November. Federal agents swept through a dozen American cities to round up suspected Communists — 249 of them, all aliens, were put aboard a ship dubbed the *Soviet Ark* and shipped to Russia. This so-called "Red Scare" prompted involvement by veterans, too.

Anti-communism quickly became a tenet of the VFW creed. Many seasoned veterans of the trenches did not take kindly to this particular brand of radicalism. Before long, VFW would be in the midst of the ideological struggle, publicly calling for the outlawing of the Communist Party.

As 1920 began, the nation welcomed a new man in the White House, President Warren G. Harding, whom Republican Party bosses had chosen as a candidate over the fire-eating VFW member Leonard Wood. "What America needs," Harding said, "is not heroics, but healing. Not nostrums, but normalcy. Not revolution, but restoration. Not surgery, but serenity."

"It is the comradeship that counts. The Veterans of Foreign Wars seems to be the only organization which perpetuates that bond. I have enjoyed every minute I have given to the Veterans of Foreign Wars' work, and I feel that I have benefited by it."
Theresa Erickson, 1922

But normalcy was not in the cards for VFW. Quite the contrary, the organization was on the membership fast track. Bob Woodside's vigorous enlistment campaign — begun in France — continued when the "Rock of the Marne" moved to New York City as Post 138, the largest of them all. In 1920, Woodside was elected commander-in-chief. VFW then numbered 20,000 members in 500 Posts nationwide. Assets exceeded $25,000 — nearly 10 times that of 1919.

Membership climbed to 60,000 during the following year. VFW was restructured to handle the swelling rolls and to implement new programs. The National Council of Administration was increased from three to 10 members-at-large, including the senior and junior vice commanders-in-chief, quartermaster general, judge advocate general and inspector general. Posts within each state were organized into Departments (the first was the District of Columbia) headed by state commanders elected by Post delegates.

In addtion, new VFW committees were created to help veterans regain normal lives. A committee headed by Edward H. Hale looked into the federal vocational training program. It came across the dismal fact that since the war only 32 veterans had been given rehabilitation assistance.

Out of this committee grew the VFW's National Service Bureau (NSB) with an office in Washington, D.C. VFW was the first veterans group to establish a permanent service bureau in the nation's capital.

At the 1919 national encampment in Providence, R.I., VFW addressed postwar problems facing veterans. In October of that year, a committee was formed to settle claims against the War Risk Insurance Bureau. Another committee acted on veterans complaints against the bureau in charge of vocational training and other benefits administered by the Treasury Department. Claims presented by veterans to Post welfare committees were relayed to the national committee for action.

In 1920, NSB set up shop at 3913 Kansas Ave., N.W., in the hub of political activity. The pioneering bureau represented claimants with service overseas before various government departments that dealt with veterans affairs.

Edward Hale, wounded in France with the AEF, was the first NSB director. But a disabling accident forced him to resign. His successor, Robert B. Handy, Jr., took over the bureau on March 1, 1921. His dedication to the organization was exemplary — he once personally borrowed $3,000 to help pay VFW bills during lean times.

Eventually, NSB would evolve into the VFW's National Veterans Service, today a highly respected institution on Capitol Hill.

VFW's Legislative Committee was headed by Junior Vice Commander-in-Chief Bertram E. Snodgrass. It promptly launched an investigation into the War Risk Insurance Bureau. Within the first

Member of Congress

ROYAL C. JOHNSON
"...much injustice has been done."

A past VFW judge advocate general and member of Post 17 in Aberdeen, S.D., Royal C. Johnson, wounded in the 1918 Meuse-Argonne offensive, would play a key role in assuring justice for WWI vets.

First meeting of the House Committee on World War Veterans Affairs in 1924. Chairman Royal C. Johnson, a prominent VFW member and decorated WWI veteran, is seated center wearing glasses.

Buddy Poppy: 'Flower of Remembrance'

In 1915, Col. John McCrae of the Canadian infantry picked up his pen and began, "In Flanders fields the poppies blow, Between the crosses, row on row." The poem would long outlive its author.

In Paris, Anna E. Guerin chose the poppy as a symbol of the wartime dead, the "flower of remembrance." In 1920, she and a host of volunteers made bright red artificial poppies. They distributed them to raise money for hundreds of thousands of French orphans and others made destitute by the war. She approached the American Legion to handle sales in the U.S. When the Legion Auxiliary seized on her idea to sponsor it for themselves, Mme. Guerin felt deceived. When the Legion confused horticulture with history and jettisoned the poppy for the daisy because it was "more American," she became angry.

The "Poppy Lady" approached VFW and found a warm reception. In May 1922, VFW began its first distribution of poppies made in France. Demand exceeded supply, so florists in New York made up the shortage. At the national convention in 1923, a plan was adopted to have disabled veterans assemble the poppies. A factory was set up in Pittsburgh for that purpose. Doughboys, Marines and sailors called their friends "Buddy." So the paper flowers with green-taped wire stems were called Buddy Poppies. They were sold by the thousands on Memorial Day.

In 1924, VFW was granted the trademark on Buddy Poppies and has owned the rights ever since. That same year, assembly and distribution branched to regions all across the country. Poppies are still put together in VA hospitals and veterans homes.

Buddy Poppies have enjoyed broad popular support since their inception. American presidents have had poppies pinned to their jackets by girls from the National Home. During the 1940s and 1950s, leading Hollywood actresses became "Buddy Poppy Girls," including Jane Wyman, Doris Day and Natalie Wood — all representative of the American ideal "girl next door."

Distribution of poppies remains a staple of Veterans and Memorial Day activities. One extraordinary Buddy Poppy donation was made in New Jersey in 1997. An anonymous donor gave $13,640 in cash and checks to Post 2294 in Jersey City, according to member Carlbert Heard. By any measure, that display of generosity is unique in the annals of the program.

More than a billion Buddy Poppies have been distributed since 1922. Under VFW bylaws, the proceeds are funneled to Post Relief Funds for distribution to disabled veterans, maintaining the National Home or similar facilities dedicated to the care of veterans. Funds also perpetuate the memory of America's war dead in the form of memorials.

Visitors today can still find poppies waving gently in soft breezes among the crosses row on row in Flanders' peaceful fields in Belgium.

Babe Ruth, the N.Y. Yankees' champion slugger and popular American hero, presented President Warren G. Harding with the first official Buddy Poppy of 1923.

In 1930, Buddy Poppy distribution reached 4 million for the first time. Poppies continue to be distributed by VFW volunteers throughout the country.

Beginning just prior to United States entry into World War II, famous stars of the stage, screen and TV were selected to promote Buddy Poppies. Through cooperation with Warner Brothers Studios, tremendous publicity and prestige were brought to the program. Later, children from the National Home were chosen as Buddy Poppy Girls.

Here's a list of those actresses.

Year Selected	Actress
1940	Ellen Drew
1941	Joan Leslie
1942	Jane Wyman
1943	Irene Manning
1944	Alexis Smith
1945	Jean Sullivan
1946	Eleanor Parker
1947	Margaret O'Brien
1948	Jeanne Crain
1949	Janis Paige
1950	Doris Day
1951	Virginia Mayo
1952	Ginger Crowley
1953	Kathryn Grayson
1954	Joan Weldon
1955	Dorothy Malone
1956	Lori Nelson
1957	Natalie Wood
1958	Venetia Stevenson
1959	Louise Wynn
1961	Elaine Edwards

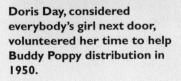

Doris Day, considered everybody's girl next door, volunteered her time to help Buddy Poppy distribution in 1950.

Natalie Wood helped boost donations in 1957. From 1940 through 1961 (except 1960), promising movie actresses were regularly chosen as Buddy Poppy Girls.

A wounded Marine is given care in a trench in the Toulon sector on March 22, 1918. He returned home to face a nation undergoing social discord. Labor strikes and radical agitators made post-war America crave for a return to "normalcy."

six months of the inquiry, more than $300,000 was recovered and turned over to discharged veterans who otherwise would have been denied their hard-earned benefits.

Still, veterans needed standing committees at the heart of the federal government and this was initiated at the urging of VFW. The House Committee on World War Veterans Affairs was the first, with Rep. Royal C. Johnson of South Dakota named as chairman. Johnson had opposed the declaration of war against Germany in 1917, but months later he was in the thick of infantry combat in France. He enlisted as a private with the 313th Infantry, 79th Division. For his mettle during the Meuse-Argonne offensive, he was awarded the Distinguished Service Cross, the *Croix de Guerre* and a wound chevron. Also, he was among VFW's most prominent members.

In 1925, the Senate formed a Subcommittee on Veterans Affairs as part of the Senate Finance Committee. Veterans now had active representation in both houses of Congress.

A past VFW judge advocate general and a committed member of Post 17 in Aberdeen, S.D., one of Johnson's first moves was an effort to equalize the sacrifice. He introduced the "Tax the Profit Out of War" bill that would have drafted labor and capital, as well as men, during any future conflagrations. The bill was not passed, but Johnson had made his point.

Without waiting for the government's ponderous machinery to produce results, VFW and American Red Cross teams took to the field to find out-of-luck and out-of-touch veterans. The bird dogs of these "clean-up squads" poked into the dark crannies of the nation, including city tenements and small rural towns, to find men who had no idea of their veterans benefits. Many were immigrants unable to read government forms, and could have perished through sheer ignorance. They were steered toward what amounted to financial and medical aid stations.

VFW also learned that many veterans locked up in the federal prison at Leavenworth, Kan., were suffering unnecessarily harsh treatment for offenses committed after the fighting ended. The Gold Star Mothers of America, whose sons were killed in the war, joined the VFW in a petition drive. More than 2.5 million signatures were gathered — enough to persuade Secretary of War John W. Weeks to launch a case-by-case investigation of unjust sentences.

Vets of WWI now totaled 4.7 million (both overseas and stateside). They strained government resources to the limit, especially when it came to health care. The Public Health Service had only 7,200 hospital beds under its direct administration—hardly enough to accommodate the overwhelming number of men who returned with missing limbs, disfiguring burns and still coughing up bits of lung. To meet the demand, *Public Law 326* transferred nine military hospitals to the Public Health Service, which added 10 new hospitals to the 20 it already operated.

The country was equally unprepared for the load of psychiatric cases brought back from France. For lack of a better term, "shell shock" was used to describe acute psychosis and neurosis inflicted on men. Their bodies — but not their minds — had survived German shelling and the mordant fear of being ripped to shreds. More than 158,000 of Pershing's Doughboys were rendered incapable to one degree or another — 36,000 of them permanently unhinged by Western Front combat.

Eleanor Roosevelt began her lifelong concern for veterans welfare with a visit to the mental ward of St. Elizabeth's Hospital in the nation's capital. She came away almost shell-shocked herself at the sight of some men "chained to their beds, others unable to stop shouting of the horrors they had seen."

There were five separate agencies to handle these and other veterans problems: Bureau of War Risk Insurance, National Homes for Disabled Volunteer Soldiers, Bureau of Pensions, Public Health Service and the Federal Board for Vocational Education. The last two were originally created for the general population and industrial workers. To handle the cascade of new responsibilities, the federal government realigned its resources.

Widespread and unwelcome publicity about the sorry treatment of yesterday's heroes forced President Warren Harding's hand. He appointed a presidential commission to look into the maze of bureaus and agencies. The commission made the sensible recommendation that three should become one as far as veterans were concerned. Congress agreed, and in August 1921, the Veterans Bureau came into being with an annual budget of $500 million. Only the National Homes and the Bureau of Pensions remained separate agencies.

Creating the Veterans Bureau was a step forward. But of paramount importance to the VFW was securing a bonus for the men who had spent part of their fleeting youth serving their country on land, sea and in the air. Privates and apprentice seamen were handed $60 in cash upon discharge and headed home to confront the realities of life in an unsettled nation.

The experience of Sgt. Robert Merrill, a future VFW commander-in-chief, of Great Falls, Mont., was not extraordinary. Merrill was 23 when a boat load of Air Service veterans arrived from England in the winter of 1919. They were told to take the train to Seattle where they would be discharged and receive their government stipend.

This was hard news — the men of the 306th Aero Squadron had not been paid for seven months and were without rations for the long, cold journey across America. Merrill was not a sergeant for nothing. He got hold of the conductor and secured a list of the stops along the way. Then he sent telegrams to the Red Cross. At each stop, the famished airmen were given sandwiches,

Robert T. Merrill, part of the 306th Aero Squadron, returned home with friends in 1919 after seven months without pay. He saw to it that his men were fed along the route from Boston to Seattle. The lesson was not lost: "I learned early you've got to fight for your own and take care of each other."

Merrill became VFW commander-in-chief in 1942. He received praise from Gen. "Hap" Arnold for VFW's Aviation Cadet Program that prepared young Americans for flight training during WWII. Merrill is seen here, right, at the 1990 convention. He died at age 102 in January 1999 in Escondido, Calif.

Sen. Hiram Johnson on the Capitol steps in 1919 with the first WWI bonus petition. The California Republican entered the Senate during the World War.

candy, tailor-made smokes and pocket money to last them until the next station. "I learned early," Merrill said, "that you've got to fight for your own and take care of each other."

Merrill's bunch was lucky. Instead of thanks and good cheer, Pvt. Harry Zander boarded a train for the trip home to Atlanta to find civilian attitudes grown cold. Eighteen months earlier, "waiters and civilians had fallen all over themselves to give me a chair, now the car was filled with brusque businessmen no longer concerned with the man in uniform," he recalled.

That attitude was put into words by renowned economist Thorsten Veblen who complained that the nation was saddled with a "legion of veterans organized for a draft on public funds and the cultivation of warlike distemper."

If Pvt. Zander could not find work before his $60 was exhausted, what would his mustering out pay purchase? For $4.20 he could buy a pair of work shoes; denim overalls would set him back $1.85; and a work shirt $1.49. If he were seeking white-collar employment, he could buy a two-piece suit from Sears Roebuck for $12.65, and an Elgin pocket watch to get him to the office on time for $7.43. To look neat for the boss and secretaries, one of the new Gillette safety razors and a dozen blades in a nickel case could be purchased for $3.74.

To rally public support for men like Zander, a large parade was put together for a march called the "Petition in Boots." On Oct. 16, 1920, 100,000 New Yorkers jammed the sidewalks to watch 75,000 men head down Fifth Avenue in a 4 1/2-hour procession behind a steam Calliope, to the beat of drums and brass bands. Marchers were interspersed with about 600 trucks filled with 2,000 of the war's victims. Some had only one arm or one leg; some had no legs at all; some were blind; many wore grotesque facial wounds still pink from grafts and other surgeries.

More than 100 VFW Posts participated in the Bonus parade, including members of Lt. Quentin Roosevelt Post 12. New York Mayor John F. Hylan summed up the march this way: "The Bonus parade was perhaps the greatest event in the history of the city of New York."

The crusade was taken up by *Foreign Service* in an editorial that pointed to the cavernous gap between soldiers' pay and those who stayed at home to work in war industries. The editorial reminded the public it was the government that decided which draftees "would fight for a dollar a day and which would work at occupations that paid 15 times as much. Economic readjustment for those whose lives were disrupted and are suffering from financial distress is not charity, but justice."

VFW's bonus offensive covered many fronts. Liaison deputies were appointed in each state and legislative district to pressure congressmen whose political lives depended on the votes of millions of veterans. The public was enlisted in the fight through letter campaigns and applications (available in *Foreign Service*) to join the "Committee of 10,000."

To put the matter in perspective, the magazine reminded readers the British had yet to pay a dime on American billions borrowed during the war. Yet the U.S. Treasury had quickly paid a debt to the British of $35 million. British transports brought the AEF to England in its time of need.

Bill after bill — more than 200 before it was over — was submitted to Congress and passed, and just as quickly vetoed by the man in the White House. President Harding told Congress a bonus would establish the "dangerous precedent of creating a Treasury covenant that puts a burden of four or five million dollars on the American people — not to discharge an obligation, which the government must always pay — but to bestow a bonus that the soldiers themselves did not expect." Harding vetoed the bill; the Senate failed to override his veto.

His successor, Calvin Coolidge, was just as firmly against any bonus. He vetoed the bill the first time it hit his desk. In one of the longest speeches of his career, "Silent Cal" explained his veto: "We owe no bonus to able-bodied veterans of the World War. The first duty of every citizen is to the nation. The veteran of the World War performed this duty. To confer on them cash consideration or its equivalent for this first duty is unjustified." Coolidge concluded with the judgment that "Patriotism that is paid for is not patriotism." But VFW's relentless campaign finally paid off where it counted. The House overrode the President's veto by a vote of 313-78. And as a VFW report noted, "On May 17, 1924, the tranquility of the Senate was interrupted when the bill passed that body by a vote of 59-26."

The *Adjusted Compensation Act*, as it was finally called, granted World War veterans a

On Oct. 16, 1920, New Yorkers turned out to cheer the "Petition in Boots" parade down Fifth Avenue. Commander-in-Chief Bob Woodside led more than 75,000 marchers to draw public attention to the need for a serviceman's bonus. Mayor John F. Hylan called it "perhaps the greatest event in the history of the city of New York."

Public interest in the bonus drive was elicited by such tactics as driving a truck loaded with a million signatures through major cities. Americans overwhelmingly favored a bonus — a sentiment not shared by a majority of senators.

While able-bodied veterans with jobs could fend for themselves, widows and orphans of American servicemen could not. In 1922, a young Michigan woman named Amy Ross decided to do something about it. "Why not hire out-of-work veterans to build a home for orphans?" she asked.

Thanks to the World Series baseball game played at the Polo Grounds in New York on Oct. 5, 1922, the dream took a giant step toward reality. Proceeds were donated to charity — the VFW received $20,000 and invested the money in the name of the "VFW Baseball Trust," courtesy of Commander-in-Chief Tillinghast L. Huston.

The second step was made during the 1923 National Convention. VFW's Military Order of the Cootie backed Amy Ross's idea and promised full support. The Cooties, formed in the fall of 1921, distinguished themselves from all others by an outlandish uniform: tasseled red overseas caps worn sideways, white ruffled shirts, white slacks and red vests trimmed in lace with a stylized bug — the infamous trench louse — on the back. Despite the costume, Cooties devoted themselves to good works in the community.

The final step was taken when a millionaire cattleman, Corey J. Spencer, donated a 472-acre farm near Eaton Rapids, Mich., for the home. The first family—a widow and her six children—moved into the National Home on March 9, 1925. Brick cottages began to blossom on the farmland, and by 1929 there were 60 orphaned children studying, working and being cared for by the staff of the VFW National Home. The Ladies Auxiliary raised $25,000 toward a new hospital. Departments and Posts contributed funds to dam a creek for an outdoor swimming pool. The kids helped plant hundreds of trees to start a fruit orchard and pitched in to feed the chickens on a new poultry farm.

The National Home survived the Depression. Some members suggested VFW turn the operation over to another organization because there were so many state and federal agencies already in existence that could handle the Home's benevolent work. But such ideas were vetoed.

The Home grew to 629 acres, 36 houses, a community center, guest lodge, chapel, nursery school and museum. On its 50th anniversary, the Detroit News headlined its story about the home, "VFW's Happy Home for Veterans' Children." The Home received a wonderful boost with a generous gift from R. Robert Dale of Post 5036 in St. Charles, Ill. He donated $870,000 and later an additional $83,000, which funded a scholarship program beginning in 1987.

Home facilities served 108 children and 26 single-parent families in 1998. (Since its inception, 1,611 children have resided at the Home.) Contributions from VFW Departments, Posts, Auxiliaries and individuals provide food, upkeep of the facility and medical care plus monies for an assortment of other needs. Children learn responsibility through community service and household chores. Funding from the Military Order of the Cootie recently allowed refurbishing of the Cootie Field House, including an 18-by-24-foot expansion and the purchase of an eight-passenger van.

National Home residents are raised with traditional values that our nation's veterans fought so hard to protect—moral principles, personal responsibility, self-worth, spiritual growth, community involvement, educational achievement and love of country.

Today, the Home's board of trustees and management are planning for the 21st century. They will assure that this privately funded home is ready for future generations of children who will need a place to live. Moreover, the National Home will continue serving as a living memorial to the VFW and to all veterans.

Theresa Erickson: Pioneer Female Member

Theresa Erickson of Owatonna, Minn., epitomized real service to the country and VFW. She was the first regular Army nurse to set foot on the Philippine Islands in 1898 and served there for three years. At this time, the islands had not been purged of fever and garrison life broke the health of a great many strong men.

Erickson kept the Red Cross flag, one of her most valued possessions, which flew over her makeshift hospital in the Philippines. It was later presented to the State Historical Society of Minnesota.

After returning from the Philippines, Erickson engaged in private nursing for several years and when it seemed there would be war with Mexico in 1916, she entered the service

again and was sent to the border. After several months' work there under conditions far from favorable, she suffered a nervous breakdown which confined her to her quarters for a considerable period.

She had just returned to duty when war with Germany became a certainty and she volunteered to go to France with one of the first complete hospital units to take the field. She served in France until long after the Armistice, then returned to the U.S. and accepted a position as county nurse.

Erickson brought cheer and happiness to the bedsides of several thousand American fighting men. Of her valiant service, she said it was her duty. She did not consider that she had done anything out of the ordinary and once quietly admitted she would return to the Army Nurse Corps in a heartbeat if the corps were in need of nurses.

She was an enthusiastic member of A. R. Patterson VFW Post No. 7 in Minneapolis. She was active in organizing a Post in her home town, Owatonna, as well. A VFW enthusiast, Erickson worked hard to further the growth of the organization in Minnesota.

Her war record, which includes the Philippines, Mexico and World War I, was commented on by the media throughout the country.

Her years of service brought her in contact with many of America's most famous fighting men and she said she knew more soldiers than civilians. Erickson's life was an interesting one, and she had an inexhaustible fund of stories. She could recall the trying days in a base during the Chateau Thierry drive, then give a vivid description of the trials and tribulations of the men who went to the Philippines.

Erickson always believed the VFW as a national organization could do great work. "It is the comradeship that counts," she once said. "The Veterans of Foreign Wars seems to be the only organization which perpetuates that bond. I have enjoyed every minute I have given to the Veterans of Foreign Wars' work, and I feel that I have benefited by it."

She felt service to one's country during a period of national emergency is something we should be willing to accept without complaint. A glimpse at her service record will show that she believed in practicing what she preached.

An unfortunate circumstance in connection with Erickson's service is the fact she was not entitled to a pension nor any form of compensation, even if she were disabled.

(After WWI, membership was granted to women vets, but was closed in 1944.)

A REAL SERVICE RECORD

By JOHN K. LEACH

MISS THERESA ERICKSON, A VETERAN OF THREE WARS

MISS ERICKSON, NOW COUNTY NURSE FOR STEEL COUNTY, MINNESOTA, SERVED IN THE PHILIPPINES, ON THE MEXICAN BORDER AND IN FRANCE DURING THE WORLD WAR

RED CROSS FLAG USED BY MISS ERICKSON IN THE PHILIPPINES

Theresa Erickson nursed American troops during three conflicts: the Philippines (1898-1901), Mexican Border (1916) and France (1917-18). A member of VFW Post 7 in Minneapolis, Minn., she helped organize a Post in her home town of Owatonna, Minn.

Erickson said: "It's the comradeship that counts. Men who have suffered together have a great common bond. The VFW seems to be the only organization that perpetuates that bond."

Reprinted from the February 1922 issue of Foreign Service.

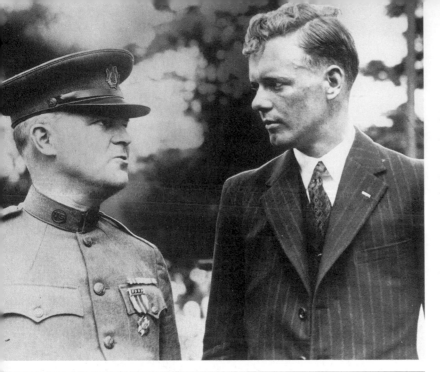

20-year paid-up endowment policy at the rate of $1.25 a day for overseas service and $1 a day for service in the States. Interest was compounded at 4 percent. Service certificates would be worth $3.5 billion at maturity — and there was the rub.

Men had waited six years, and now, when money was needed the most, they learned with bitter disappointment that the maturity date was sometime in 1945 — 21 years in the future. Cynical veterans called it the "Tombstone Bonus," with many believing they would not be alive to receive their checks for $1,000 when the notes came due.

Commander-in-Chief Theodore Stitt conferred honorary VFW membership on Charles A. Lindbergh during the national encampment of 1927 in Providence, R.I. That May 20-21, "Lucky Lindy" became the first man to make the long solo flight across the Atlantic in *The Spirit of St. Louis*.

The bonus battle was being waged in the middle of a major move of VFW headquarters, debated during the 1923 encampment in Norfolk, Va. Proposals came from Detroit, Minneapolis and Kansas City, Kan., whose city fathers offered enticements to lure the VFW away from lower Manhattan.

Detroit offered space in the General Motors Building with a year's free rent — but no guarantee that an annual fee of $38,000 would not be levied afterwards. The Minnesotans offered free facilities in an existing structure and $75,000 with which to help erect a new building in the future.

Not everybody, however, wanted to move from Union Square from where so many successful campaigns had been launched. Also, it was a place the VFW

The "Roaring '20s" were known for more than Prohibition. That decade was also a golden age of adventure and exploration. Charles Lindbergh's famous flight across the Atlantic was followed by momentous news at the South Pole. All of America cheered when this other historic aviation milestone was achieved.

As was the case in every other form of human endeavor, VFW members were prominent in this headline-making event. Two members, in fact, played important roles in exploring Antarctica.

Harold I. June is introduced to President Herbert Hoover by Rear Adm. Richard Byrd at a White House reception for Antarctica expedition members on June 20, 1930.

Byrd's expedition made history when it reached the South Pole on Nov. 29, 1929. June, 33 and a WWI Navy vet, was co-pilot and radioman on the exploration.

He doubled as cameraman for Paramount Pictures. One of the most highly respected members, he was regarded as among "the heart of the expedition."

A member of Post 133 in East Brunswick, N.J., he wrote before the trip: "We both hope to carry the emblem of the VFW into the Antarctic."

His fellow VFW member from Post 427 in Washington, D.C., was Charles E. Lofgren who served as Byrd's secretary. Lofgren, 34, and also a WWI Navy vet, accompanied the famed explorer on a cross-country lecture tour after the expedition.

could keep a watchful eye on radical agitators who gathered every May Day to preach communism. An argument was made for proximity to the heavy membership base in the East. The reasoning was irrefutable, but not persuasive.

Kansas City extolled the new $500,000 Veterans Memorial Building due for completion in August 1924. VFW could occupy the 20,000-square-foot top floor for $1 a year; light and heat included. Other tangible benefits included a busy rail system with 14 trunk lines serving 400 passenger and freight trains daily, three-day mail service anywhere in the nation and a growing interest in Kansas City as a hub for the fledgling airline industry.

The choice was put to a vote and Kansas City won handily. VFW put out a flier announcing within a year "The Heart of the VFW" would be in "The Heart of the U.S.A."

Shortly afterward, the entire national headquarters staff boarded a train at Pennsylvania Station for the 1,500-mile journey to Kansas City. They were welcomed by the new commander-in-chief, Lloyd B. Brett, a 40-year-veteran of the U.S. Army. His service included the Kansas frontier in 1879 and as a brigade commander with the 80th Infantry Division in France. Brett walked the New York delegation through the two-story brick building VFW headquarters would occupy until the Veterans Memorial Building was done.

Headquarters staff moved into the new building in October 1924 and within a year 30 new Posts were established in neighboring states — proof, it seemed, that the move had been a wise one. But the honeymoon with the Kansas side of the border would be short. Eight months later, VFW started looking for a new home.

On Jan. 1, 1930, VFW moved across the river to a new headquarters building at Broadway and 34th Street in Kansas City, Mo. (Previously, it was headquarters for the Jackson County Medical Society.) This photograph was taken in 1961.

Trouble began in June 1925 when the Memorial Building was placed under a board of trustees. Its first move was to demand VFW pay for part of building maintenance and give up office space — contradicting the original agreement. Insult was added to injury when trustees ordered the VFW symbol removed from the base of the flagpole in front of the building. This unseemly confrontation ended when VFW struck a deal with the city council in Missouri. This Kansas City, first settled by white pioneers in 1821 on Wyandotte Indian land, was once the eastern terminus for goods from Santa Fe. Whiskey, groceries, prints and sundries were sent to New Mexico; wool, buffalo robes and jerky, Mexican silver coin, gold and silver dust and ore came in return.

Between 1900 and 1920, Kansas City, Mo., doubled its population to more than 167,000. The city offered rolling hills interspersed with graded tracts turned into green parks. It seemed ideal as a permanent site for national headquarters. On Jan. 1, 1930, it moved into a 12-story building on the corner of Broadway and 34th Street where it has remained ever since.

As the decade closed, it became painfully clear President Harding had blundered in appointing political crony Charles R. Forbes to head the Veterans Bureau. The results were disastrous. Forbes had no idea how to weld the disparate agencies into an effective organization. But he knew how to dip into the till. He was indicted for squandering and embezzling more than $200 million during his first year in office. The Veterans Bureau credibility was at rock bottom.

Harding forced him to resign. Forbes' criminal

VFW officials call on President Calvin Coolidge on Nov. 24, 1927, to again press for bonus legislation. Congress passed the 1924 bonus bill, but "Silent Cal" vetoed it. He said, "We owe no bonus to able-bodied veterans of the World War." From left to right: Edwin S. Bettelheim, chairman of the VFW National Legislative Committee; Commander-in-Chief Frank T. Strayer; and Veterans Bureau Director Frank Hines.

instincts proved infectious. When a Senate investigating committee delved deeper into the books, the bureau's legal advisor committed suicide. Forbes was convicted of defrauding the government and sentenced to serve a two-year prison stretch.

Brig. Gen. Frank T. Hines filled Forbes' post. As his first step, Hines went out of his way to build smooth working relationships with Congress, VFW and other veterans organizations. He tied up loose ends, gathering in the Bureau of Pensions and the National Homes for Disabled Volunteer Soldiers to create the Veterans Administration (VA). The executive order signed on July 21, 1930, officially established the VA as an independent agency, but its most trying challenges lay ahead.

Creation of the VA was a victory it took the VFW five years to achieve. Beginning in 1925, VFW had urged consolidation of the agencies dealing with veterans programs. Then-Commander-in-Chief H.N. Duff personally explained to President Herbert Hoover the reasons for unification. Hoover included VFW's recommendation in his 1930 State of the Union address. Meanwhile, Edwin S. Bettelheim, chairman of VFW's National Legislative Committee, had lobbied extensively for passage of the bill embodying VFW's position.

Bettelheim was the only veterans organization representative present when Hoover signed the bill establishing the VA. This was only appropriate — VFW was the sole group that worked for the bill's passage. George E. Ijams, a VFW member, became assistant VA administrator. He resigned years later to become director of VFW's National Rehabilitation Service.

VFW Makes Star-Spangled Banner National Anthem

VFW vigorously took on the fight to make *The Star-Spangled Banner* this country's national anthem. In 1928, the United States was the only modern nation in the world without a sanctioned national anthem — a flagrant lapse the VFW was determined to set right. It was Walter I. "Daddy" Joyce, director of the National Americanization Committee, who led the crusade.

The *Star-Spangled Banner* had been played and sung with varying degrees of success for more than 100 years. The uplifting words came from the pen of Francis Scott Key, a 35-year-old lawyer who had watched from Chesapeake Bay, Md., the night the British bombarded Ft. McHenry in 1814.

Next morning, the sight of the tattered flag still flying over the shelled fort inspired Key to put his feelings to words. They were published as a poem in the Sept. 20 issue of the Baltimore *Patriot*. Set to the music of an old English drinking song, "To Anacreon in Heaven," it became an instant favorite. President Woodrow Wilson proclaimed it the national anthem in 1916, but Congress had yet to legislate it as the nation's patriotic musical signature.

Joyce, with the endorsement of Commander-in-Chief Frank T. Strayer, energetically pursued his goal of securing an overwhelming number of petition signatures with which to bombard Congress. Posts and Auxiliaries pitched in against opposition by pacifist groups that objected to its alleged "militaristic" tone. But at the national encampment in St. Paul, Minn., in 1929, Joyce reported 4 million signatures in hand. A Gold Star mother collected 12,000 signatures; a New Jersey VFW member, 9,000; and another in Troy, N.Y., 5,000.

Musical purists said, with justification, the music was in too high a register to be sung by all except operatic sopranos — the score was rewritten in the key of A flat to bring it within reach of more American vocal cords.

Joyce persuaded Rep. Hamilton Fish of New York to introduce a bill before Congress, but it never got out of committee. Nor did it during the next session. Then, on Jan. 30, 1930, representatives of more than 60 patriotic organizations gathered in Washington to press for another version of the bill introduced by Maryland Rep. Charles Linthicum. It went before the Judiciary Committee the next day, where Joyce presented 5 million signatures and endorsements from other organizations representing another 15 million citizens. Among the signatures were those of 26 governors. *Foreign Service* proudly proclaimed it "a feat without parallel in the history of any veterans organization."

The climax came when VFW Auxiliary member Elsie Jorss Reilly stood and sang Key's words to the accompaniment of the Navy Band. The bill came out of committee by a vote of 16 to 2, but stalled on the floor of the House because of the objection of a representative from Mississippi.

It finally passed on April 21, 1930, and was sent to the Senate Library Committee, where it again lay fallow until March 31, 1931. On that date, it passed unanimously a day before the 71st Congress adjourned. President Herbert Hoover signed the bill the following morning. *The Star-Spangled Banner* was now this nation's national anthem by law, as well as in fact, thanks to the little-known campaign waged by VFW.

In recent years, the *Star-Spangled Banner* has been under assault. Media mogul Ted Turner and company have waged a campaign to replace it with something other than a "war song." Public opinion, however, appears to be on the side of tradition.

VFW waged a determined campaign to make the *Star-Spangled Banner* the official national anthem. On Jan. 31, 1930, officials presented petitions to the House Judiciary Committee — bearing more than 5 million signatures— urging passage of the measure. The bill was enacted in March 1931.

Left to right: Rep. Leonidas Dyer, Mo.: Elsie Jorss Reilly; Maryland Rep. J.C. Linthicum, who authored the bill; and Walter I. Joyce, VFW director of Americanism. Elsie Reilly sang the anthem during presentation of petitions.

Chapter 5

Mission to North Russia

Three "Polar Bears" are interred at Arlington National Cemetery. VFW Washington, D.C., Department Commander Harvey L. Miller decorates each casket with the Cross of Malta in 1929.

VFW members return to a distant battlefield to recover the remains of American soldiers who died in a forgotten campaign after WWI.

While the fight for the bonus and creation of the Veterans Administration took center stage, a battle of another sort was brewing in diplomatic circles. VFW's concern for war dead was always a priority. The organization was destined to undertake a humanitarian mission of the noblest kind. In so doing, it established a tradition entrenched to this day — one that has spanned four wars.

In the early spring of 1929, Commander-in-Chief Eugene Pendleton Carver, Jr., was approached by the Polar Bear Association in Detroit, and asked for VFW help in a strange and difficult mission. The Polar Bears were survivors of a campaign that was little-known while it was being waged — and quickly forgotten afterward. That is, except by those Americans who had fought in the snows of Russia in a hopeless cause months after World War I ended. Some 5,000 members of the 339th Infantry Regiment and attached units had been sent there by President Woodrow Wilson during the Russian civil war to counter Bolsheviks around Archangel. The mission lasted from September 1918 through June 1919.

The Association, formed in 1922, was uncomfortable with the knowledge that only about half of those who died in that alien and frozen wasteland had been brought home. The thought of sons and brothers still lying under the soil of an atheist nation was a source of anguish to the dead men's relatives.

To mount a search and recovery mission, Michigan Sen. Arthur H. Vandenberg secured $79,592 from Congress to add to the $15,000 appropriated by his state legislature. But there the project stalled. The U.S. had never recognized the Soviet Union, so the State Department could not help American citizens enter Communist Russia. The Polar Bears turned to the VFW as the only outfit willing and able to get the job done.

Carver knew it would be no easy task: northern Russia was thousands of

The U.S. 339th Infantry Regiment ("Detroit's Own") found itself embroiled with Bolsheviks in North Russia in late 1918. Few knew why. Fighting lasted well into 1919, long after the war in Europe ended. These men of Company G pose with a British Vickers machine gun at Pinega, south of Archangel, near the top of the world.

miles away under a suspicious and politically fanatic dictatorship. But Carver, a lieutenant with the 5th and later the 56th Pioneer Infantry in France, relished challenges. He and the rest of VFW were determined to bring home the first Americans to have fought Bolsheviks — revolutionaries going forward under red banners in the name of communism.

Ninji Gora. Shenkursk. Seltso. Pinega. Bolshie-Ozerki. Ust-Padenga. Toulgas. These were all obscure battle sites. But they were remembered by Americans who fought through the winter and spring of 1919, many still unaware that the war in Europe was over. Fresh British troops arrived, and by the end of May 1919 the Americans were back in Archangel.

The ragged Americans took part in a Memorial Day parade down the streets of Archangel and stood at attention in the town cemetery while a bugle sounded taps over American graves. By June 28, the last U.S. soldiers had sailed away from northern Russia still baffled at why they had been sent there in the first place. They also left wondering why 232 of their own lay buried in scattered graves in soil retaken by the Bolsheviks.

In August, a long procession of carts drawn by shaggy Russian ponies trundled through the streets, each cart bearing a long wooden box. They were filled with the remains of American soldiers bound for home. U.S. Army Graves Registration Service (GRS) teams scoured the battlegrounds until early 1920, when Bolsheviks occupied all of Archangel Province and closed it to foreigners. Boxes with 105 remains were shipped home, but there were still 127 graves somewhere in the tundra. It was across this daunting terrain that the VFW team would have to make its tortuous way.

To gain the organization entry into the Soviet Union, Carver, in 1929, approached Secretary of War Patrick J. Hurley, a logical move in that Hurley was a former national officer of VFW. Despite Hurley's Cabinet rank, Moscow turned him down. Then Hurley and Carver tried another tack: They approached the Soviets as private citizens acting on behalf of a fraternal organization with no political affiliations. That did the trick, and the People's Commissariat for Foreign Affairs of the Union of Soviet Socialist Republics granted VFW the right to enter Soviet territory to fulfill its mission.

The chairman of the VFW National Legislative Committee, Edwin S. Bettelheim, Jr., volunteered to lead the recovery team soon assembled. Walter C. Dundon, John C. Evans, Michael Macalla, Roy Derham and Gilbert T. Shilson, all Polar Bears from Lansing, Mich., joined Bettelheim's small group of military archaeologists. Equipped with old campaign maps, they sailed from New York harbor on the first leg of what would become a 13,000-mile journey.

In France, they were joined by Paris Post 605 Commander Russell H.

In 1929, surviving Polar Bears asked Commander-in-Chief Eugene Carver for VFW help in finding and bringing home their fellow unit members. The remains of 127 "Polar Bears"— as 339th veterans were known—remained buried in Communist soil long after the misbegotten campaign ended.

Dutcher and Capt. Stuart D. Campbell along with three experienced men of the Army's Graves Registration Service, all VFW members. They boarded a train and headed for Germany, pausing in gloomy Berlin only long enough to get aboard another train. It rocked its way through Poland and across the endless Russian steppes to put them in Moscow.

It was now the first week of August, and the Americans had until only mid-October to finish their task. After that, the winter would close down operations. Its sub-zero horrors and deep frost would make digging almost impossible. The Polar Bears among them knew the Russians were not exaggerating. "Every possible aid was given us by the Russian officials," Bettelheim recalled. "Time was so short that we had to buy metal and construct the zinc coffins in Russia."

The Russians suggested the Americans pack away their good clothes, so obviously foreign, and outfit themselves in Russian peasant garb. This would

Fighting against Bolsheviks leaves 232 U.S. dead in the frozen wastes of an alien land. An Allied cemetery on the outskirts of the Russian port city of Archangel held many of the dead. On May 22, 1919, 1st Lt. Clifford F. Phillips and Pvt. James H. Lynch of Company H, 339th Infantry Regiment, are buried side by side.

Search party members dressed in Russian peasant garb to appear inconspicuous.

They are, from left: Russell H. Dutcher, Capt. Stuart D. Campbell, interpreter Stephan Pokitonow, Orlando Overstake, Edwin S. Bettelheim, Jr., chairman of VFW's National Legislative Committee and Walter C. Dundon, president of the Polar Bear Association and past commander of VFW Post 436 in Detroit.

prevent drawing attention to themselves while in the northern province. When outfitted in the native costumes, VFW members resembled the Bolshevik soldiers Doughboys had fought all those years ago. The expedition was attired in baggy pants and blouses, long coats with a belt around the middle, calf-length boots and fur caps. They boarded the train bound for Archangel 370 miles away.

Bettelheim divided the group into two teams that set off for the inhospitable wilderness. He remembered the tough going, a journey little less arduous than the campaign itself: "We traveled up the Divina, the Vaga, the Onega, the Penega and the Yemptze Rivers, along the railroad fronts, through deep forests. We climbed cliffs, scrambled over sand dunes and waded knee-deep through marshes and swamps searching for bodies.

"We made our way up the rivers in wood-burning, flat-bottomed boats, drawing about a foot of water, a red-and-yellow VFW pennant flying from the mast. A number of times we slept on the banks of the river where we built bonfires — it was better to sleep on the banks of the river than it was to attempt to sleep in the vermin-infested houses in the villages or cramped in our small boat.

"We found remains in swamps, in deserted cemeteries along the line of our trenches that still remained in front yards of peasant houses, along the sides of cliffs, and some whose graves were covered with a forest of underbrush. In some instances we had to make two or three separate expeditions to the same locales, offering rewards to peasants before we could get any information as to where American soldiers might be lying."

Peasants often pointed to graves that when excavated revealed British remains. The grave would be refilled, and the team would move on to the next beet field, river bank or forest.

Ten years of alternating heat, rain and deep freeze left very little of the men underground. "Nothing remained," said Bettelheim, " but skeleton bones and the skull, with here and there small pieces of decayed flesh attached to joints. When we attempted to lift the uniforms, they would crumble in our hands or rip to pieces when we touched them."

Weeks of this grisly work proved too much for two of the expedition members: One simply disappeared for two weeks and returned without explanation; another stayed up all night singing hymns.

One by one the remains were gathered, identification made from odds and ends — here a monogrammed cigarette case, there a class ring — because most of the dog tags had crumbled to rust-colored dust. Two months of exhausting field work produced the remains of 86 American soldiers. The bones were washed in Lysol, wrapped in linen and placed in the zinc coffins.

On Oct. 27, the team boarded a Soviet steamer with the zinc boxes and sailed away from Leningrad. At the French port of Le Havre, the boxes were put inside regulation coffins, the excess space filled with blankets. A French military honor guard stood watch over the flag-draped caskets. A memorial service was held on Nov. 18, attended by French and U.S. officials, as well as VFW members from Paris.

The remains of 11 of those brought back from North Russia, at the request of relatives living abroad, were turned over to Graves Registration for burial in one of the many U.S. military cemeteries in France. The other 75 sets of remains were taken up the gangway of the SS *President Roosevelt* and stowed in a hold below decks for the trip across the Atlantic.

In November 1929, zinc coffins are placed aboard the SS *President Roosevelt* at Cherbourg, France, for the long voyage home as VFW mission members watch.

Two months of exhausting field work uncovered the remains of 86 American soldiers.

VFW Member Finds Long-Lost MIAs

In 1927, a VFW member of what was then Post 1269 in Camden, N.J., was camping in the Pocono Mountains of eastern Pennsylvania. While there, area residents told him four Revolutionary War veterans were supposedly buried nearby, although no one knew where.

After much searching, VFW member James J. Burke and his friend, George R. Anschutz, stumbled across an old cemetery. It was "overgrown with trees, small shrubbery and undergrowth," said Burke in the March 1927 issue of *Foreign Service* magazine. The men in the graves were regulars in Gen. John Sullivan's army and had died of starvation during a retreat after a battle in 1779 with Iroquois Indians allied with the British.

In the first of many such efforts to come, the VFW or its members helped resolve the fate of some long-lost missing in action from a distant war.

The funeral train makes its way in foul weather across America. Public officials and members of the VFW Allegheny Council pay tribute when the train halts in Pittsburgh. A VFW firing squad stands by to render honors.

When the ship docked at Hoboken, N.J., on Nov. 28, it was greeted by a 17-gun salute and triumphant music from the 16th Infantry Band. VFW Commander-in-Chief Hezekiah N. Duff and Senior Vice Commander-in-Chief Paul Wolman headed a delegation waiting on the docks. Duff placed a red Buddy Poppy on each casket.

Remains of 17 men were shipped to relatives in various states for private burial. Three more were buried in Arlington National Cemetery, and the remaining 56 were put aboard a special nine-coach funeral train draped with black crape. VFW members stood guard during the long journey to Detroit.

The train stopped in every city and town of any size in New York, New Jersey, Pennsylvania, Ohio and Michigan. Taps was played at each station even in the dead of night, the plaintive notes registering on silent crowds of citizens and VFW honor guards. Nothing like it had been seen since the train bearing the body of assassinated President Abraham Lincoln made its sad journey to Illinois in 1865.

Michigan Gov. Fred W. Green (center), of Post 701 in Lansing, stands in the snow with four members of the recovery team. From left: Ray Durham, Walter Dundon, Gov. Green, John C. Evans and Gilbert Shilson. They were all on hand when the train made its final stop in Detroit on Dec. 1, 1929.

It made its last stop on Dec. 1, 1929, where thousands gathered in front of Detroit's Union Station under a steady fall of snow. Duff turned to the mayor, Fred W. Green, a VFW member from the Spanish-American War. "Mr. Mayor, the bodies of these heroes are now before you," he said. "They belong to the state of Michigan. The VFW is proud to have participated in this labor of love. The Polar Bears are home."

(However, 41 *Amerikanski* remained in Russia. Of those, 14 would be recovered by the GRS in 1934. But 27 Americans' remains were never found.)

It was an experience Bettelheim never forgot. "As the mothers and fathers of these heroes stood silently in the bleak, snow-driven cold at Detroit, our responsibilities in discharging a most arduous task were again emphasized with a deeper and more penetrating significance," he said. "We forgot weeks of weary effort, seeing and thinking only of those bereaved, their prayers at last answered by the loyalty and energy of comrades who recognize their obligation to the memory of the nation's soldier dead as a sacred duty of the Veterans of Foreign Wars of the United States."

"Crowds lined Ford Street, braving the snow and cold to pay tribute to the last remnants of the 85th Division [the 339th was part of it]," reported the *New York Times*. "After the City Hall ceremony, 3,500 members of veteran and allied organizations marched to Cass Park."

Citizens watched 56 flag-covered caskets loaded inside as many hearses for the slow drive to White Chapel Cemetery at Troy, outside the city. They were placed in a mausoleum known as the Temple of Memories to await Memorial Day 1930. On that spring morning, the soldiers who had traveled so far were laid to final rest, watched over by a defiant polar bear of white stone.

"They [those killed in North Russia] recognized and proved anew it is better to die that the spirit of freedom may live than to live in a world from which liberty has departed."
Michigan Gov. Fred W. Green

A massive stone polar bear stands eternal guard over 56 American soldiers (24 not identified) who gave their lives in North Russia. All are buried in a special plot at the White Chapel Cemetery at Troy, Mich. The monument, sculpted by Leon Hermut, was dedicated on Memorial Day 1930.

Chapter 6

Battling for the Bonus

The Bonus Expeditionary Force (BEF), thousands strong, arrives in Washington, D.C., on May 30, 1932. VFW's leadership was leery of the mass demonstration, fearing it would prejudice Congress against pending VFW-sponsored legislation.

During the Depression decade, VFW presses for veterans rights. Limelight shines on veterans as they march on Washington, D.C. A full Bonus finally becomes reality.

Recovering the remains of Doughboys killed in North Russia was but a brief — yet sacred — interlude in the VFW's greater crusade of ensuring the rights of World War I veterans during the dark days of the Depression. To that end, a steady stream of legislation was presented to Congress. When President Herbert Hoover took office, he discovered that more than 40 veterans pension bills had been introduced during the preceding session and most languished there.

The Veterans Administration (VA) came into being during the first year of the Great Depression — a lingering economic cancer that ate at the vitals of the nation, destroying industries and wrecking lives. In Washington, VA Administrator Frank Hines and his staff wrestled with chaos. A summary of veterans legislation passed over the years astonished Hoover, who condemned "conflicts and injustices....tremendous numbers of discordant and unequal treatments."

For instance, disabled vets of the 1917-1918 war were admitted to VA hospitals whether the disability was service-connected or not. This was a privilege denied those whose actions dated to Gettysburg or San Juan Hill, unless there happened to be a bed available. In 90 percent of the cases there was not.

Hoover's irritation grew in May 1930 with the passage of an expanded pension bill for veterans of the war with Spain, the Philippine Insurrection (1899-1902) and the Boxer Rebellion of 1900. The bill provided nearly $12 million each year to increase disability pensions for these graybeards who had served 70 days or more. There were no disability pensions for the Doughboys of 1917-1918. This was clearly discrimination. Hoover exercised his first veto, insisting on raising time of service to 90 days and a "means test" (eligibility based on income),

Persistent efforts by VFW pushed through the WWI service disability pension. On July 3, 1930, President Herbert Hoover signed the measure known as *Public Law 522*.

Secretary to the President Walter Newton (left) presents Hoover's pen to Edwin S. Bettelheim, chairman of VFW's National Legislative Committee. Newton told Bettelheim:

"This pen should be of unusual significance to the Veterans of Foreign Wars, knowing your long-standing interest in establishing a pension system for veterans of the World War."

August 1930   FOREIGN SERVICE

A Pension for Disabled World War Veterans

Statute Books Now Carry Legislation Conceived and Championed by the V. F. W.—Adoption of Pension Principle an Exclusive V.F.W. Victory

Secretary to the President, Walter Newton, in the presence of General Frank T. Hines, Administrator of Veteran Affairs, presents the pen with which President Hoover signed the disability pension bill making it a law, to Edwin S. Bettelheim, Chairman of the National Legislative Committee of the V. F. W. "This pen should be of unusual significance to the Veterans of Foreign Wars," declared Secretary Newton on behalf of President Hoover, "knowing your long standing interest in establishing a pension system for veterans of the World War."

By

Edwin S. Bettelheim, Jr.
Chairman, Nat'l Legislative Committee, V. F. W.

The world war service disability pension is now an established fact, thanks to the persistent efforts of the Veterans of Foreign Wars. President Hoover signed the measure, which became Public Law 522, on July 3, 1930. All during the campaign to put the idea of a world war service pension across, the name of the V. F. W. stood out prominently over and above all other veteran organizations and our organization can proudly look every world war veteran in the face and say to him, "Comrade, after practically a lone fight over a period of five years, the Veterans of Foreign Wars has brought about legislation whereby every World War veteran will be entitled to either compensation or a pension in at least some amount of money."

The following is an extract from the report of the V. F. W. Legislative Chairman made at the 28th Annual Encampment of the Veterans of Foreign Wars at Providence, Rhode Island, September, 1927:

"The Chairman of your Legislative Commit-

have been honorably discharged therefrom and who are not receiving compensation or pension and who are now, or may be hereafter, suffering from any mental or physical disability incapacitating them for the performance of manual labor. Your Chairman sounds the opening gun that this will ultimately become a law."

This is quoted from page 190 of House Document of the 69th Congress 2nd Session. And as the result of this plea, the National Encampment adopted Resolution 35, in 1927, calling upon the Congress to pass a measure.

Our road was beset with difficulties. The Chairman of the Legislative Committee of the American Legion ...ing made, without authority that we could find, a ...ment before the Finance Committee of the Senate ...the bonus bill was being discussed, that the Ame... Legion would never ask for a pension for World Veterans. The Legion's strenuous opposition ...brought right down to the present time. The ...sent out a memorandum to its various depa...

which critics called a "pauper's affidavit" that would shame veterans.

Hoover relented on the means test and came up with a bill that had the backing of VFW, but of no other veterans organization. Royal C. Johnson, chairman of the House Committee on World War Veterans, stood solidly behind Hoover and his version of the *World War Disability Act* that cut through the tangle of qualifications. Veterans with non-service-connected disabilities were granted $480 a year. Veterans totally disabled by wounds received in action could receive as much as $2,400 annually —a handsome sum at a time when 65 percent of Americans earned less than $3,000 a year.

The Senate added its own amendments and passed the bill on July 1, 1930. But the amendments were tossed out, and Hoover signed the bill as he had originally written it. More than 407,000 World War I veterans with non-service connected disabilities were added to the rolls. Newspapers were outraged at the $73 million a year to be drained from the federal treasury. Hoover was castigated by various groups for favoring veterans as a special class of Americans at a time when the economy was snowballing downhill and millions of ordinary citizens were headed for the poorhouse.

The *Disability Act* added a victory streamer to the VFW banner, but provided nothing in the way of funds for a veteran's daily existence. There was neither social security nor unemployment benefits—unlike Britain. So a fresh offensive was launched to collect on the "Tombstone Bonus," now crumbling while in its sixth year.

From his strategic congressional command post, Johnson enlisted the aid of Reps. Isaak Bacharach and Hamilton Fish, both from New York, Sen. Arthur Vandenberg of Michigan and Rep. Wright Patman of Texas. They put together the *Bacharach Amendment* that would allow veterans to borrow up to 50 percent of the maturity value of their

bonus certificates — IOUs issued by the government — at 3 percent compound interest.

The amendment was hurried into committee and onto the floor before the 71st Congress could adjourn. It made it before the deadline, and on Feb. 27, 1931, *Public Law 743* sailed through both Houses and was signed by Hoover.

The stampede began. In Washington, VFW borrowed the ground floor of the Tower Building. It was staffed with volunteers to handle applications from thousands of threadbare veterans, standing in a serpentine line surrounding the building.

In Kansas City, printers worked overtime to print cartons of application blanks. The demand was so heavy that a week later the local VA office called on VFW for help in supplying another 20,000 forms for distribution to needy men. One grateful applicant told a VFW volunteer that he had lost his business, then his home to the Depression, and was down to his last 5-cent piece. The $800 check would enable him to retrieve his wife and child from her parents and start again.

By 1932, the country was in desperate shape. More than 12 million Americans were jobless, wandering from one place to another looking for work that was not there. In the big cities, veterans — some wearing campaign medals on ragged coats — stood on street corners trying to peddle apples. Men shuffled in long lines toward cauldrons filled with hot soup. Shanty towns grew haphazardly around city dumps, where the jobless picked about for scraps of food. Things were equally bad in the countryside.

In Le Mars, Iowa, a local judge was dragged out of his court by angry farmers when he issued a flock of foreclosure notices. Harry Terrell remembered: "The people were desperate. They took him to the fairgrounds with a rope around his neck, and they had the rope over the limb of a tree. They were gonna string him up in the old horse-thief fashion, but somebody had sense enough to stop the thing before it got too far. When you took a man's horses and his plow away, you denied him food and convicted his family to starvation. It was just that real."

To some veterans, desperate times demanded desperate measures. Walter W. Waters of Portland, Ore., decided to lead an army of jobless veterans to Washington to plead their case for immediate cash payment of the bonus. The former cannery superintendent had been out of work for 18 months and had a wife and two children to support. Waters had been a sergeant with the AEF in France. He was still lean and carried himself like a soldier.

Hundreds joined Waters, and in early May of 1932 they set off to cross the nation. They called themselves the Bonus Expeditionary Force (BEF).

Pro-bonus newspapers ran cartoons reminding wartime profiteers of obligations owed to the men who "made the world safe for democracy."

BEF Slogan: "Cheered in '17, Jeered in '32."

Waters warned his followers: "No drinking, no panhandling, no radicalism."

They climbed aboard empty boxcars and headed east, fed along the way by sympathetic citizens who gathered at the stops to cheer them on. At almost every halt, the BEF was joined by other out-of-work veterans. Waters' small army began to grow as word spread fueled by media publicity.

On May 21, the BEF reached East St. Louis and ran into trouble. Railroad cops barred them from climbing aboard a B & O freight train, whereupon the vets uncoupled the cars and soaped the rails. The governor of Illinois sent in the National Guard — in the ensuing mêlée some heads were dented. The public outcry caused the governor to rethink his tactics — he ordered state-owned trucks to ferry the veterans safely out of his state.

Other freight trains converged on the nation's capital. A Southern Pacific locomotive hauled more than 200 men across Nevada, rations supplied by merchants and county officials in Sparks and Reno. In New Orleans, 300 bonus-seekers were routed by railroad cops when they tried to climb aboard empty cars. Veterans route-marched into Mississippi where they were fed and driven across the state line in Packards, Buicks and Pierce Arrows confiscated from bootleggers. Authorities in Alabama helped the men on their way to Washington board box cars headed north.

District of Columbia Metropolitan Police Superintendent Pelham Glassford, a VFW member, donated $1,000 of his own money to buy food for his fellow WWI veterans. "They're my boys," he said.

National officers at VFW headquarters in Kansas City were leery of the BEF and the march on Washington. The descent of a mob, however orderly and well-intentioned, could only prejudice Congress against pending legislation designed to give veterans what they were seeking. Nonetheless, state Departments and individual VFW Posts along the line of march opened their doors to the marchers, fed them and gave them a place to sleep.

The first BEF contingents arrived in Washington on Memorial Day, May 30, 1932. Others poured in from all points of the compass. Finally, there were some 20,000 homeless veterans, wives and children camped on the Anacostia Flats and in downtown buildings slated for destruction. Waters' deputy, George Kleinholz, told reporters: "Most of these men are married and have been out of work for two years. Just take a look at these fellows. If you offer any of them a job at a dollar a day they will take it."

The superintendent of the metropolitan police was Pelham D. Glassford, who had been the youngest AEF brigadier general. Glassford, the son of a career cavalry officer, had spent his youth on Army posts in the West. He was tall, lean as a whip, and a few minutes in his company revealed why cadets at West Point called him "Happy."

Glassford, an early member of the VFW, put out the welcome mat for the

BEF by providing a pair of rolling kitchens serving up hot chow for the marchers. Secretary of War Patrick J. Hurley, not to be outdone, ordered 2,000 bed sacks and two tons of straw to make beds. Cruising the streets of the capital aboard a dark blue motorcycle, Glassford became a familiar sight. He frequently stopped to share wartime experiences with the other men.

Waters had no trouble meeting Wright Patman, whose energy was responsible for the cash-now bill then making its way through Congress. Waters said, "We intend to stay here until the bonus is paid — whether it is next week, next year, or in 1945." Patman told him he would try to force a vote within two weeks.

The issue was in doubt. A senator from Illinois, J. Hamilton Lewis, raised the specter of terrorism where none existed. He stood before an overflow crowd at the National Soldiers Home and said, "I warn you as a fellow soldier that you risk defeat by placing yourselves where the charge can be made against you that you have come here to terrorize the public servants and force their surrender."

Patman was as good as his word. His bill cleared the House on June 15, and would be voted on by the Senate two days later. Thousands of BEF men gathered around the Capitol Building and waited through the afternoon of June 17. Sen. Elmer Thomas of Oklahoma came out and approached Waters

Thousands of bonus marchers gather on the Capitol Building steps on June 17, 1932, to await the outcome of a bonus bill submitted by Sen. Wright Patman (D-Tex.). The bill failed to pass. So thousands of bonus marchers departed, but thousands more stayed in the capital.

Bonus marchers and their families erected tents and shacks on Anacostia Flats, living in filth. Members of local VFW Posts visited the squalid encampment, bringing meals and fresh water to veterans and their families.

83

Hollywood Supports Buddy Poppies

When George Hill returned from World War I, he had a great vision for the motion picture industry. A cameraman prior to the war, Hill wanted to create the drama of the war for the silver screen. Thus, in the 1920s, he directed *Tell it to the Marines*, a film that first placed Marines in motion pictures with celebrities like Lon Chaney.

A member of MGM Studio Post 1476, he became a successful director because of this movie. While serving in Italy, Hill captured the very essence of the war and preserved it in memory. He caught the spirit of the war as only a veteran could and turned it into a cinematic masterpiece.

VFW stormed Hollywood to recruit members from the film industry. Many actors, directors and cameramen had seen service overseas during WWI.

In the top photo, director George Hill stands surrounded by associates at a lectern emblazoned with VFW logo denoting Post 1476 at MGM Studios in 1927.

In the center photo, left to right: Post Commander Dave Friedman, Louis G. Mayer, past Department Commander Col. D.J. Brady and Department Judge Advocate Leo Daze.

The bottom right picture shows Lon Chaney, star of ***Tell it to the Marines.***

VFW was already a familiar organization in Hollywood at the time. Attending the screening of *Tell it to the Marines* were members of Post 1476, as well as those from Universal City Post 1267.

Louis Mayer, executive head of Metro-Goldwyn-Mayer Studios, presented Post 1476 with its set of colors. Mayer was made an honorary VFW member.

In 1929, the Department of California took on a recruiting campaign for 5,000 new members. Post 1267 served as a strong force in Department Commander Darold DeCoe's recruiting efforts.

Former VFW Commander-in-Chief Frank Strayer also was active in DeCoe's plan. The film industry warmly opened its arms to Strayer as he made his way through the Golden State seeking recruits.

Post 1267 entertained Strayer Hollywood style. Carl Laemmle, president of Universal Pictures Corporation and an honorary VFW member, spearheaded the events which included a tour of Hollywood and various movie sets.

John Boles, a Universal film star and World War I veteran, was obligated as a member of Post 1267 by DeCoe. The event was captured on film and later presented to VFW.

Since its inception, VFW has taken the lead in preserving American traditions and ideals. With this in mind, it jumped at the chance to sponsor an exhibition of patriotic films produced by Warner Brothers in 1939.

The organization felt showing of the films in local theaters would be ideal for its patriotic message. Also, it saw the films as a way to combat un-American propaganda. The 16-minute films included *The Man Without a Country, Give Me Liberty, Lincoln in the White House* and *The Song of a Nation.*

Each included an original musical score consistent with the research for the movie and was recorded with a full ensemble of more than 60 musicians. VFW was acknowledged at each viewing with ceremonies, including musical units, color guards and guest speakers.

waiting at the top of the marble steps and gave him the bad news: The bill failed to pass the Senate.

Defeated members of the BEF drifted out of Washington by the hundreds, but thousands remained, and what happened next would shame the nation.

Diehards threw together ramshackle dwellings of scrap lumber and tin on the muddy Anacostia Flats, dug latrine pits and lived in the squalor they called "Hooverville." A lucky few crawled under pup tents supplied by Glassford, determined to wait it out

because they had nowhere else to go. Waters instilled military discipline, ordering the area policed however possible. A bugle sounded reveille and taps, men marched to chow in formation. The food was terrible — rotting vegetables and meat scraps cast aside by grocers.

D.C. police become involved in the fray along Pennsylvania Avenue where one vet is killed. Bricks and rocks are hurled at police and photographers alike during the mêlée on July 28.

Appalled by the squalor, Glassford reached into his own bank account for $1,000 to buy fresh food for the hopeless marchers and their families. "They're my boys," he explained, "many fought with me in France."

By July, conditions in the camps were appalling. The place gave off an odor of rotting food and excrement — it was a playground for rats. Many veterans left, but thousands stayed.

Communists infiltrated BEF ranks, precipitating on July 20 the first of two violent confrontations with police in an abortive attempt to storm the White House. The clashes were a prelude to the final showdown between the government and the BEF, now estimated by Glassford to number 8,300 men, women and children.

The District of Columbia Board of Commissioners ordered Glassford to evict the veterans from the buildings they had occupied since May. Glassford warned of serious trouble, and it came. On July 28, the veterans were ousted from the vacant buildings and milled around outside. Communist agitators hurled bricks at the cops and a riot erupted. One rattled officer stumbled and fell. He got to his knees, pulled his service revolver and fired blindly. The round struck a veteran named William Huska, from Chicago, who fell dead in the rubble. General firing broke out, answered by a shower of bricks, one of which cracked a police officer's skull. Glassford told the cops to holster their weapons and pull back.

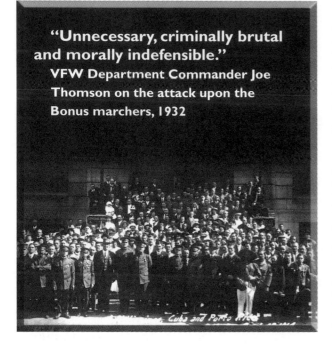

Hoover now had to act. Secretary of War Hurley told Chief of Staff Gen. Douglas MacArthur to form a battalion. His orders: drive the BEF from occupied buildings and raze the squatters village at Anacostia. Hurley also instructed MacArthur to accord "every consideration and kindness" to women and children; to "use all humanity consistent with due execution of the order."

At 4:30 on the afternoon of July 28, MacArthur's combat-equipped troops, 843 infantrymen and cavalrymen behind a vanguard of six light tanks commanded by Maj. George S. Patton, waded into the BEF. Tear gas drove the veterans out of the buildings. Resistance was met by blows from the flats of cavalry sabers.

Mounted regulars herded a mass of BEF members down Pennsylvania Avenue toward Anacostia Flats. There, MacArthur gave the inhabitants one hour to clear out. They frantically scurried around gathering their possessions, but before they could get everything together a rain of tear gas bombs fell among them. MacArthur and his aide, Maj. Dwight D. Eisenhower, watched Red Cross and VFW volunteers treat women and children whose faces streamed with tears.

Soldiers lit their kerosene soaked torches and went among the shacks. Flames and smoke roiled up in the evening sky as the camp burned to ashes, the fires visible from the White House. By midnight, it was finished and so was the BEF.

Peggy Terry, wife of an Oklahoma veteran, said it all when she remembered: "My husband went to Washington to march with the Bonus boys. He was a machine gunner in the war. He'd say them damn Germans gassed him in France. And he come home, and his own government stooges gassed him and run him off up there with the water hose, half drowned him. My husband was bitter — and that's puttin' it mild."

The occupation that had lasted just under two months was dramatically ended in a day and set off a chain of lasting repercussions.

At the VFW's 1932 National Encampment, former Department Commander Joseph C. Thomson submitted a lengthy resolution condemning the rout of a "pitiful and inoffensive crowd of ragged and unarmed bonusers." He shamed the government for the use of "charging cavalry, drawn sabers, fixed bayonets with rifles ready to fire, and with tanks against men with no arms — men loyal to the United States — men, women and children weakened by hunger and unemployment." To Thomson, it was "unnecessary, criminally brutal and morally indefensible." The resolution passed with a unanimous vote.

Hoover's political career went up in smoke with the burning of the BEF camp. Franklin D. Roosevelt swamped Hoover in the November 1932 election to become the nation's 32nd President and moved into the White House. VFW would soon discover that his budget ax was sharper and his veto pen more fluid than that of his predecessor.

But VFW's first battle was with the National Economy League (NEL). A goal of the League was to reduce government expenditures by killing the *Disability Act* so recently enacted.

NEL's prime mover was Archibald Roosevelt, son of Theodore. Archie, himself a highly decorated WWI and seriously wounded veteran, called the Act a "vast legalized racket foisted on the people" and set out to have it expunged from the books. He enlisted the aid of some of America's most illustrious names: Adm. Richard E. Byrd, Gen. John J. Pershing, Maj. Gen. James G. Harbord and Adm. William S. Sims, among others.

Archie Roosevelt and his "Saviors of the Republic" opened offices in the National Press Building in Washington, D.C. Duncan Hassell, Jr., one of the watchdogs for *Foreign Service*, visited the office and found Aubrey Taylor seated behind a new mahogany desk as the public relations director. Taylor had been fired as the *Washington Post's* managing editor and confessed his new salary was "admittedly attractive."

Hassell wrote: "Taylor's principal job is collecting handout statistics and prowling the corridors of the House Office Building where he tags congressmen with petty trades and inducements to vote down veteran measures."

The big guns of the League leased a dozen suites in a New York skyscraper and hired more than 80 staff members at inflated salaries — strange behavior for an economy-minded organization. They opened branch offices in all 48 states. Thousands of dollars were poured into radio and newspaper advertising to promote a campaign aimed directly at veterans benefits. In a pure public relations move, the League created a front organization called the American Veterans Group (AVG) that existed only on paper.

Rep. Wright Patman looked into the status of the major players. For the benefit of VFW members, the editors of *Foreign Service* published findings that outraged veterans and non-veterans alike.

Archie Roosevelt, as part owner with financier J. Pierpont Morgan of the Roosevelt Steamship Company, had secured a lucrative contract with the government to haul mail across the Atlantic. The contract price was $6 per mile. Within the first 10 months, Roosevelt and Morgan had been paid $807,000 — other steamship companies would have charged $28,000. "Thus," observed the magazine, "Roosevelt's company received a gift from the government of $779,000."

Robert E. Coontz led VFW from 1932-33. He was commander-in-chief of the U.S. Fleet in 1925 and earlier was chief of naval operations. A veteran of the Spanish-American War, he was the last of that conflict to serve as VFW Chief. Famous for saying, "men fight, not ships," he helped lead the battle against the National Economy League and defended the Bonus Marchers.

In 1958, the first guided missile frigate built on the West Coast was named in his honor. Coontz had served as commandant of the Puget Sound Navy Yard at Bremerton, Wash., during World War I.

President Franklin D. Roosevelt's Civilian Conservation Corps (CCC) siphoned off millions of dollars while disabled WWI veterans were denied their benefits. These CCC workers from Chicago arrive in Washington in 1933 to clear burned-over areas in a national forest.

Even more flagrant was the discovery that Archie Roosevelt and his banker cohorts charged taxpayers $20,000 for delivering two pounds of mail from New York to London. The statutory price was 80 cents per pound, or $1.60 total.

Adm. Byrd postponed his plans for another expedition to the South Pole to take over chairmanship of the NEL. The salary plus his annual $5,000 pension would see him through the campaign to divest veterans who could not prove service-connected disability for their $40 a month. Byrd wanted to recruit 20 million Americans to "fight this out to a finish."

Pershing's retirement pay, that is, his pension, amounted to $21,500 a year. Harbord was guaranteed $6,000 annually for life, along with a handsome corporate salary that elevated the general above financial worries. As for other League members: Elihu Root was one of the highest paid corporate lawyers in the country and Cal Coolidge suffered not at all as a retired President. But the greatest threat came from FDR.

VFW had little time to mobilize against the bill designed to eliminate veterans benefits. On March 20, 1933, President Roosevelt signed it into law disguised as the "Act to Maintain the Credit of the United States Government."

Two extracts from this infamous bill reveal its severity:

• *To do away with the payment of all disability allowance benefits for non-service-connected cases, except where a veteran, having served 90 days or more in an enlistment which occurred during wartime, is found to be permanently and totally disabled not the result of misconduct. The amount of the pension in such cases is $20 monthly.*

• *The withdrawal of presumption of service connection for disabilities and the necessity of showing direct service-connection in line of duty, except in the case of certain chronic diseases which become manifest to a degree of 10 percent within a year following discharge from the service.*

Reaction was swift. Sen. Arthur R. Robinson called it the "most brutal act ever passed by a cowardly Congress." He noted the provisions made it next to impossible for Civil War veterans to eke out an existence in their old age. "Spanish-American War veterans gave us an empire," Robinson said, "and made the United States a world power. Now their sacrifices have been forgotten. Disabled veterans of the World War have been ruthlessly cut off and abandoned to their fate by a country for which they offered their lives."

The senator saved his most scathing remarks for the League, "created by millionaires and near millionaires in the shadow of Wall Street. Donors to the campaign to vilify disabled veterans were among the wealthiest citizens of the Republic." Robinson pointed to the fact that Archie Roosevelt's henchman, J.

Pierpont Morgan, "has not paid a cent of income taxes in the past two years—nor has any of his 19 partners."

The stated purpose of the bill was to save the government $450 million in veterans benefits. Yet right after its passage, another bill was proposed that would put 250,000 Americans between the ages of 18 and 25 to work in a massive reforestation program. The "Tree Planter's Bill," as it was called, was the first of many to keep Roosevelt's new Civilian Conservation Corps (CCC) busy in the coming years. More than 1,300 camps would be set up.

CCC members would be paid $1 a day and live in barracks, just like soldiers. Robinson answered the question as to where the money was coming from. "There was $148 million still on the books for emergency public housing — money appropriated for the building trades to guarantee a decent standard of living, money now diverted to the tree planters.

"To keep this small army of 250,000 able-bodied men in the camps for a year will require an outlay of at least $500 million — almost all of it taken from disabled veterans and their families. The net result is the gravest sort of injustice. As for a balanced budget, it is not balanced now, will not be balanced next year, nor the year after that."

Those damaged the most were veterans whose records were fouled up — sometimes at company level, or in the labyrinth of VA files. Who has worn the uniform who has not spent months or years trying to get his service records straight? The system was even more fallible in the 1930s when Hines and others grappled with the chaos they inherited during the formation of the VA.

Rep. Wright Patman, staunch supporter of the VFW and often called the "father" of the Bonus Bill, confers with James E. Van Zandt (right).

The energetic Van Zandt, commander-in-chief in 1933, swept the country, drumming up support for the Bonus Bill. Relentless newspaper and broadcasting campaigns drew national attention to the plight of veterans affected by the Economy Act.

Defeated by the *Economy Act* — at least for the moment — the VFW swung its guns toward the obstacles in the way of a cash bonus payment. More than 407,000 World War veterans had been added to the disability rolls before the congressional ax fell and money was needed more than ever.

VFW witnessed a sudden spurt of growth from 76,669 members in 1929 to 165,540 in 1933 when an energetic new commander-in-chief was elected at that year's national encampment in Milwaukee.

James E. Van Zandt, 35, was a native of Altoona, Pa., and a member of Post 3, one of the earliest in the VFW. He left the Pennsylvania Railroad and joined the Navy on April 30, 1917. Van Zandt spent two years aboard a destroyer in the Atlantic war zone and rose to chief quartermaster by the time he was discharged in 1919. He stayed in the Naval Reserve and was active in

Carl Sandburg Joins VFW Staff

One of America's great literary figures, Carl Sandburg, was appointed VFW national historian in 1938. Sandburg was famous all over the world as an author, poet and biographer — his biography of Abraham Lincoln was considered a historical masterpiece.

Sandburg served with Company C, 6th Illinois Volunteers, during the Spanish-American War, taking part in the seizure of Puerto Rico in 1898. He was an active member of Post 1459, Benton Harbor, Mich. He often drove 20 miles back and forth from his home in Harbert to attend meetings.

Sandburg, born on Jan. 6, 1878 in Galesburg, Ill., began his writing career with *System* magazine in Chicago. Of Swedish extraction, he moved to Stockholm as correspondent for the Newspaper Enterprise Association.

He returned to America and wrote editorials for the Chicago *Daily News,* the salary enabling him to pursue his real craft: writing about America's soul.

Sandburg's world fame grew from a body of literature that included *Chicago Poems, Corn Huskers, Smoke and Steel* and the outstanding work, *Abraham Lincoln — The Prairie Years.*

His Viking roots urged him out of city grime and to a wooded estate overlooking Lake Michigan, where he raised rare breeds of goats for relaxation. The poet and historian lived until 1967.

Commenting on his appointment, *Foreign Service* magazine observed: "Steeped as he is in this nation's history and as an authority on the days of the Civil War, our new national historian is confident of America's destiny."

Noted Author Named National Historian

Carl Sandburg Ranks Among Nation's Great Literary Figures

IN the appointment of Carl Sandburg, distinguished author, poet and biographer, as National Historian, the Veterans of Foreign Wars of the United States, includes among the ranks of its leaders an outstanding American figure and personality, and one of the nation's great men of letters.

Carl Sandburg is recognized as the greatest authority on Abraham Lincoln in the country today. He is at present engaged on a life of Lincoln, which he expects to complete within the year, and which will be a distinguished addition to the works he already has published on the subject, which include "Abraham Lincoln—The Prairie Years" and "Mary Lincoln, Wife and Widow."

The National Historian, who succeeds in that office Comrade Robert E. Kernodle, of Kansas City, recently resigned, is a member of Twin City Post No. 1459, Benton Harbor, Mich., to whose meetings he often drives 20 miles from his home at Harbert, Mich. He is a veteran of the Spanish-American War, in which he served...

Among his books are Chicago Poems, 1915; Corn Huskers, 1918; The Chicago Race Riots, 1919; Smoke and Steel, 1920; Slabs of the Sunburnt West, 1922; Rootabaga Stories, 1922; Rootabaga Pigeons, 1923; Abraham Lincoln—The Prairie Years, 1926...

In 1938, Carl Sandburg — renowned poet, author and biographer of Abraham Lincoln — was appointed VFW's national historian. He wore a uniform during the Spanish-American War and was a member of Post 1459 in Benton Harbor, Mich.

veterans affairs from the beginning.

Under Van Zandt, national headquarters organized against the well-heeled opposition. An eight-page set of "Battle Orders" was drawn up and sent to every Post, County Council and Department in the country. The document outlined the Bonus Bill, guided publicity procedures that would get newspaper and radio attention and spelled out ways to draft petitions to Congress.

To finance the drive, a call went out nationwide for contributions. When ready cash was lacking, the Ladies Auxiliary pitched in to raise funds through ice cream socials, raffles and rummage sales. More than $9,000 came in to hire fiscal and public relations consultants. A second publication resulted, *Bonus Campaign Ammunition,* containing a dozen custom-written speeches designed to win public favor. The grass roots campaign paid off: A Gallup poll showed the number of Americans in favor of the Bonus on the rise.

Jimmy Van Zandt was joined in the Bonus crusade by two stalwarts: Wright Patman and the irrepressible Marine Maj. Gen. Smedley Butler. Butler, twice a

Medal of Honor recipient and member of Post 1086 in Harrisburg, Pa., was a character even by Marine Corps standards.

He addressed VFW gatherings at every opportunity, chiding members for forgetting how to fight now that the peacetime cards were stacked against them. After the *Economy Act* passed, he told one group: "I notice that you are getting a little old, but you are the same lovable class of Americans — dumb though you are. Anybody can put anything over on you.

"America is divided into two classes: the Tories who believe that the whole of this country was created for their sole benefit, and the other 99 percent of us — the soldier class, the class from which all of you came. That class hasn't any privileges except to die when the Tories tell them. Every war that we have ever had was gotten up by that class — they do all of the drum beating and away the rest of us go."

Butler had their attention, and he reminded them of how it was 16 years earlier: "We march down the street with all the Sears-Roebuck soldiers standing on the sidewalk, all the dollar-a-year men with spurs, all those who call themselves patriots, square-legged women in uniforms making Liberty Loan speeches. You go down the street, and they ring all the church bells. They promise you the sun, the moon, the stars and the earth — anything to save them. Then the looting commences while you are doing the fighting. This last war made over 6,000 millionaires. Today, those fellows won't pay the bill."

Butler laid it out in economic terms: "Don't you realize that when this country started out it wasn't worth more than 25 cents and that every damned bit of land we have we took at the point of a gun? The soldiers took it, and now this nation is worth $320 billion through their sacrifices. So don't let anyone bluff you. Stand by your own kind. There is a bond among fighting men who have slept in the mud together that nothing can supplant.

"It's human nature to despise a sap, and as much as I love you boys, you sure have been acting like saps the last few years. Congress fixed up some promissory notes and dated 'em ahead 20 years and gave 'em to you with a pat on the head and a benevolent smile and our poor, dimwitted lovable chumps took 'em and said, Thank you kindly, Uncle Sam — and went right on starving.

"You're all acting as if you've never been in a fight before in your lives. You're waiting for someone to take your hand and lead you safely through enemy lines. All right, here's *my* hand. Let's go!"

Butler, an old China hand, raised the *gung ho* — work together — cry. "*If* every veteran in this country will forget his own little personal affairs and think of veterandom as a whole — *if* you will get it through your dear, dumb heads that nobody's going to do anything for you, that it's up to you to do

Smedley D. Butler

THE simple funeral services characteristic of the Quaker faith were held at West Chester, Pa., on Monday afternoon, June 24, for Major General Smedley Darlington Butler, beloved officer of the United States Marine Corps and veteran of 30 years' active service in many distant parts of the world.

General Butler—affectionately known as "Old Gimlet-Eye"—died June 21 at the Naval Hospital, Philadelphia, after an illness which became acute only during the last month. His health had been failing somewhat for the last year or two. He underwent an operation shortly prior to his attendance at the 40th National Encampment, Boston, Mass., last August.

General Butler was an active member of Private Earl E. Aurand Post No. 1086, Harrisburg, Pa. His home was at Newtown Square, Delaware County, Pa. He is survived by his widow, the former Ethel C. Peters, of Philadelphia, whom he married June 30, 1905; a daughter, Mrs. John Wehle, wife of Lieutenant Wehle, U. S. Marine Corps, and two sons, Thomas Richard and Smedley Darlington Butler, Jr.

"Old Gimlet Eye" in a characteristic defiant pose.

tested the regard in which General Butler was held by all who knew him. Past Commander-in-Chief James E. Van Zandt, United States Congressman, represented Commander-in-Chief Otis N. Brown at the funeral. Representatives from V.F.W. units in approximately 20 states, also, were

TORN FROM the PAGES of VFW MAGAZINE

The irrepressible retired Marine Maj. Gen. Smedley D. Butler, highly decorated, fought apathy among veterans and opponents of the Bonus Bill.

Butler, a member of Post 1086 in Harrisburg, Pa., hit the campaign trail as a VFW crusader for veterans rights in 1933. He reminded a VFW audience: "There is a bond among fighting men who have slept in the mud together that nothing can supplant."

Butler's vociferous demands for action in Congress and renewed zeal among veterans for righteous causes were long remembered.

whatever it is that needs to be done — and *if* you will stick together for even a little while and hammer away like you used to do in the war — I tell you you'd be there before you know it."

After delivering the shock treatment, Butler told his audience to regain the discipline they once had and to educate themselves on the issues. He reminded them of the power of the vote — in other words, wise up and go to the polls. Veterans would have taken the chewing out only from Smedley Butler — and only Smedley Butler would have delivered it.

Van Zandt took to the road using planes, trains and automobiles. He crisscrossed the country, adding a million miles to his travel log. He was as indefatigable as he was enthusiastic: He averaged four cities, 10 speeches and a radio address every 24 hours. He talked Bonus from train platforms, front porches and from a rancher's fence in New Mexico.

Rep. Wright Patman joined Van Zandt, and they stormed through the Midwest. The pair teamed up in front of microphones at radio stations, addressed businessmen's luncheons and women's clubs and filled school auditoriums.

Van Zandt's most ambitious plan was to pack Madison Square Garden in New York. To assure a huge turnout, Smedley Butler and the Rev. Charles E.

A Chartered Organization

By 1936, the VFW numbered 199,199 members and legislative accomplishments that year were significant. During Commander-in-Chief Jimmy Van Zandt's third term in office, the World War I bonus bill was passed, widows and orphans were granted pensions and strides were made toward achieving uniform pensions through *Public Law 788*.

VFW's solid reputation and demonstrated ability to look after veterans needs and rights laid the groundwork for *Public Law 630*, which granted a congressional charter of incorporation to VFW. The bill, sponsored by Rep. Francis E. Walter of Pennsylvania and Sen. Matthew M. Neely of West Virginia, passed on May 28, 1936.

Granting of a congressional charter not only gained prestige for the VFW, but protected it against infringement of name and insignia. It also granted legal benefits in certain states — benefits not available to groups lacking a charter. A certificate showing that the law was filed with the Department of State was issued June 8, 1936.

An article in *Foreign Service* that July proclaimed: "Today, VFW occupies an enviable position among the powerful and influential organizations of the country."

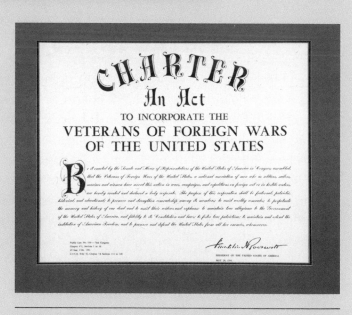

On May 28, 1936, Congress passed *Public Law 630*, granting a congressional charter of incorporation to the VFW. The charter, signed by President Franklin D. Roosevelt, provided congressional recognition and protected VFW's name and logo.

Coughlin flanked the VFW Chief on the platform. Coughlin, the Irish-Catholic rector of the parish of Royal Oak near Detroit, was known as the "radio priest." He operated the Shrine of the Little Flower Radio Station. More than 10 million Americans tuned in to such observations as: "Gold was the root of all evil and New York bankers the devils." Coughlin was a risky choice. His reputation for intolerance often overshadowed his emotional appeal.

Van Zandt's unbridled enthusiasm, Butler's unvarnished castigation of the Economy League and Coughlin's Irish witticisms drew cheers from 20,000 New Yorkers still weighted down by the Depression.

VFW's attention was temporarily diverted by fresh assaults from unexpected quarters — college undergraduates and members of the League's "Junior Committee." They were still in grade school when bloody combat was being waged across the deadly fields of France.

The League had made inroads at Princeton University where students formed a facetious organization called "The Veterans of Future Wars." The college boys petitioned for immediate payment of a $1,000 bonus due in 1965. "Payment now," they said, "will lift the country out of the Depression and will enable the beneficiary to enjoy it before he is slain in some future war." Its leader, Lewis J. Gorin, Jr., died at age 84 on Jan. 1, 1999.

Girls at Vassar College, one of the most expensive private schools in the nation, created the "Gold Star Mothers of Veterans of Future Wars," demanding paid passage abroad to "view the prospective graves of their future sons."

This travesty drew fire from Senior Vice Commander-in-Chief Bernard W.

The Bonus Bill underwent numerous amendments to make it palatable to both Congress and President Franklin D. Roosevelt. The bill sailed through both Houses. But Roosevelt addresses a joint session of Congress to state his objections — then promptly vetoes the measure in 1935.

Kearney. "The sarcastic attack on veterans and the Gold Star Mothers," he wrote, "demonstrates the insidious results of the National Economy League propaganda and the vital need for a defense fund that will protect veterans against these students when they take their places in the civic affairs of the country later in life."

The Junior Committee, not surprisingly, maintained a suite of offices in the Fidelity Trust Building in Philadelphia. The chairman, who graduated from college 12 years after the war ended, wrote Van Zandt: "Don't forget that we are still paying pensions to widows of veterans of the War of 1812 —widows who as girls of 13 or less married aged veterans on their death beds merely to secure pension benefits." Van Zandt could have stopped reading right there, but he went on to the final paragraph.

"If the test of all benefits which you seek is to be service-connected we will be in agreement. Otherwise, we will brand your efforts as another attempted steal." Van Zandt considered the source of these insults and ludicrous claims, moving on to serious business.

The classic cartoon of the two donkeys straining at opposite ends of a tether unable to reach a tempting pile of hay just out of their reach characterized the relationship between VFW, American Legion and Disabled American Veterans (DAV) in the 1930s. The Legion shifted uncertainly during the long battle for cash payment of the Bonus, and the DAV remained largely on the sidelines. To get the job done, political leverage would have to be brought to bear. Disparate veterans organizations would have to pull together as the donkeys did to reach the prize.

The familiar *Patman Bill* was resubmitted in 1935 and sailed through the House and Senate. Now it was up to Franklin Roosevelt. Instead of a quick slash of his veto pen, he chose to appear in Congress and address both Houses to deliver the bad news.

"I hold that the able-bodied citizen because he wore a uniform and for no other reason," he began, "should not be accorded treatment different from that accorded to other citizens who did not wear a uniform during the World War. To argue for this bill as a relief measure is to indulge in the fallacy that the welfare of the country can be generally served by extending relief on some

Three major veterans organizations worked in concert to get the Bonus Bill passed. Ray Murphy (left), national commander of the American Legion; James E. Van Zandt (center), VFW commander-in-chief; and Thomas Kirby (right), legislative representative of the Disabled American Veterans, confer on strategy.

On Jan. 24, 1936, the Senate and the House deliver a stunning blow to Roosevelt by overriding his veto.

basis other than actual deserving need.

"The core of the question is that a man who is sick or under some special disability because he was a soldier should certainly be assisted as such. If a man is suffering from economic need because of the Depression — even though he is a veteran — he must be placed on a par with all other victims of the Depression."

So saying, FDR then put pen to paper and vetoed the bill. Whereupon the House overrode the veto by an overwhelming majority — but the Senate did not by the narrow margin of 54-40.

Patman and some others tinkered with the wording to Van Zandt's satisfaction so that the bill, by then known as the *Steiwer-Brynes Bill,* could be reintroduced at the opening of the 74th Congress in January 1936. Another roadblock was thrown in the way when the Steering and Policy Committee of the Democratic Party majority in the Senate met and decided that no further Bonus action would be taken during the upcoming year.

Other senators dismantled this blockade by threatening to filibuster pending legislation known to be particular favorites of the man in the White House and his advisors. Opponents caved in, and the modified bill was scheduled for priority consideration.

So Van Zandt got together with Ray Murphy, the new national commander of the American Legion, in order to get at the hay on the same tether. Van Zandt called Murphy "one of the finest men I have worked with on a project."

To keep the Economy League and its henchmen from getting wise and making counter moves, however, VFW and Legion officers met secretly on Nov. 10, 1935, and agreed on tactics. The coalition was strengthened when the DAV came aboard. For the first time since the end of the war, the three largest veterans groups were working in concert toward a common goal.

Reps. Wright Patman, Fred M. Vinson and John McCormack sponsored the amended bill. It was swiftly reported and passed by the House on Jan. 10, 1936, by a vote of 346-59. It reached the Senate on Jan. 20 and went through 74-16. Roosevelt promptly unscrewed the cap on his pen and vetoed the measure for the second time.

Back it went to the House on Jan. 24 for a 325-61 override, then to the Senate on the following Monday for the grand climax. This time, the issue was never in doubt: The senators destroyed FDR's veto with a 76-19 vote. The cash-now Bonus was a reality.

Things moved swiftly. At 4:50 that same afternoon, Frank Hines handed the first printed application forms to a jubilant Van Zandt. Fifty minutes later, the forms were aboard DC-2s of the U.S. Air Mail Service headed for VFW Departments, Councils and Posts all over the country.

Hundreds of thousands of veterans began filling out forms that would have government checks in their hands before the year was out. A little more than $2 billion was ultimately distributed to 3.5 million World War I vets.

Joseph A. Kane receives his bonus bond at Camp Wawayanda in upstate New York, where he worked for the Civilian Conservation Corps.

Chapter 7

Rallying the Home Front

VFW waged a tenacious battle to see the GI Bill enacted into law. Final enactment was owed to a wild ride through the night by a Georgia representative who burst into the House of Representatives conference room and declared: "I'm here to lick anyone who tries to hold up the GI Bill of Rights. Americans are dying in Normandy." On June 22, 1944, President Franklin D. Roosevelt signed S.1767 into law.

VFW's WWII Aviation Cadet program qualifies 100,000 recruits. The landmark GI Bill triumphs in Congress in 1944.

After the bonus victory of 1936, VFW turned temporarily to restructuring its internal departments in preparation for battles ahead. Those fights would be mostly on the foreign affairs front. War raged from Ethiopia to Spain to Manchuria. VFW, like most of the nation, was in no mood for foreign entanglements.

A "Neutrality Code" was drawn up and submitted to Congress. It demanded an arms embargo on all belligerents, withdrawal of U.S. ships from their waters, release of government responsibility for protecting private financial interests in warring nations and a ban on federal and private loans to any country at war. Strong measures, but in keeping with public sentiments.

In November 1937, VFW launched a "Keep America out of War" campaign through a massive petition drive. In charge was VFW's publicity director, Barney Yanofsky, whose exuberance equaled that of Van Zandt's.

"We sent petition blanks to every VFW Post and news releases to 2,000 daily newspapers and 10,000 weeklies and magazines," Yanofsky said. "We sent letters to more than 200 of the nation's outstanding patriotic leaders asking for endorsements. We sent releases to every radio station in the country and followed up with progress reports. Our campaign received the greatest measure of press support ever given any one project sponsored by VFW or any other veterans organization. Newspaper clippings received at national headquarters measured more than 10,000 column inches — about a tenth of the space [media coverage] actually devoted to this campaign."

On April 27, 1938, VFW's Americanization Day, a delegation arrived on the steps of the Capitol Building bringing with it the fruits of the five-month campaign — carton after carton of petitions bearing the signatures of 3,640,980 citizens determined to keep America out of another European war. The petitions were accepted by Sen. Key Pittman of Nevada, chairman of the Senate Committee on Foreign Relations, and by the flamboyant speaker of

By early 1938, war clouds were gathering over Europe. VFW was determined to keep the U.S. out of another European blood bath.

At national headquarters, Adjutant General Robert B. Handy, Jr., examines a sheaf of "Keep America Out of War" petitions. He holds a handful of the hundreds of thousands signed by citizens supporting the VFW campaign.

The clipping-filled wall behind Handy testifies to the nationwide backing newspapers gave to VFW's stance.

the House, Rep. William B. Bankhead of Alabama.

On hand were VFW Commander-in-Chief Scott P. Squyres, National Auxiliary President Laurie Schertle and the Vice President of the United States, John Nance "Cactus Jack" Garner, who invited Sen. Pittman and VFW legislative representative Millard Rice inside to "strike a blow for liberty." To Garner, that meant only one thing — a jolt of bourbon and branch water.

The timing seemed right to once again introduce a measure to "take the profit out of war" through steeply graded income taxes. It landed on the floor as *Senate Bill 3912* backed by 55 senators. A companion piece of legislation was sponsored by more than 100 representatives. But munitions lobbies still held the upper hand — both bills died. Even so, VFW's campaign was a signal success: The number of petition signatures was unprecedented; the publicity phenomenal.

The nation was sharply divided over foreign affairs into two camps: Those who supported the America First Committee (AFC) and those who backed the Committee to Defend America by Aiding the Allies. "America Firsters" included isolationists and others who felt no threat to America. AFC also represented the views of many patriotic Americans — including VFW members — embittered by the post-war consequences of WWI.

However, arguments dissolved in a cloud of Japanese high explosives that destroyed most of the U.S. Pacific Fleet at Pearl Harbor on Sunday morning, Dec. 7, 1941. War with Japan was declared the next day; three days later Germany and Italy declared war on the U.S.

Members of VFW Post 1865, Kenosha, Wis., formed the Veterans Emergency Defense Unit in 1943. Armed with '03 Springfields, the vets of WWI were ready for any emergency if summoned by the Sheriff's Department of Kenosha County.

On the day Pearl Harbor lay in ruins, VFW numbered 240,000 members. VFW, preempting a thought expressed years later by a future President, turned its attention to what the organization could do for the country— not what the country could do for its members.

Volunteer activities in the field were directed by the VFW War Service Commission. The home front was rich with opportunity. For example, VFW provided civilian auxiliaries — recruited and trained at many of its 3,400 Posts across the country — to replace thousands of firemen and policemen destined for the military.

Security was uppermost in the minds of Americans during the dark, early months of the war. There were more than 600,000 Germans residing in the U.S. Who among them was loyal to the Stars and Stripes? The VFW's Department of Americanism, headed by Victor E. Devereaux, worked with the FBI to uncover subversives and saboteurs in cities where war factories rolled out tanks, bombers and heavy artillery around the clock.

Victor E. Devereaux, head of VFW's Department of Americanism, worked with the FBI to uncover subversives and saboteurs.

The Department of Michigan joined forces with the Michigan State Police to weld the Wayne County Council's 47 VFW Posts into investigative teams. Agents raided a pro-Nazi cell in Detroit and confiscated a small arsenal of short-wave transmitters, high-powered rifles and loaded handguns, along with a 6-by-8-foot swastika flag. Germans who owned this small truckload of destruction were arrested, adding to the eventual bag of 4,000 espionage suspects apprehended by the FBI.

Hundreds of wooden observation towers sprouted along the U.S. coastline, many manned by VFW volunteers equipped with binoculars and aircraft recognition charts. Known *Luftwaffe* bombers barely had the range to reach the north of England and back, let alone to cross the Atlantic. But who knew what might appear in the skies next month, next year?

VFW war bond drives were carried out with unmatched vigor. Examples were legion, but here are a few. In Cleveland, Post 2926 had spent four years raising $10,000 for its Post home. When war came, members dedicated the entire amount to bonds. Working six days a week, Ladies of the Auxiliary to Post 589 set up a Victory Center Bond Booth in Hazleton, Pa., and sold $25,000 worth of bonds and stamps. Not to be outdone, Post 952 and its Auxiliary in Huntington Park, Calif., sold more than $65,000 worth of bonds in two weeks in 1943. In Dearborn, Mich., Post 1494 brought in $1,135,625 worth of bonds — 84 percent from one school board. VFW National Headquarters certainly did its share, too. By early 1945 in the 6th War Loan Drive, $1,020,000 had been invested in war bonds by the organization.

VFW members manned watch towers along the Eastern seaboard against the threat of enemy air raids. Men of VFW Post 3148 in Towson, Md., scan the sky for the approach of *Luftwaffe* bombers.

On the tower, left to right: Frank J. Thurston, Harry C. Kirsh and Walter Dewees. On the ground, left to right: Post Commander Charles G. Garrison, Joseph Knight, William A. Garrison, Robert W. Stouffer and Quartermaster William F. Dawson.

Manpower for the war effort was the most pressing need in 1942. More than a quarter of those eligible for enlistment or the draft were high-school dropouts. A third came before examiners with only a grade school education. VFW's Americanization Department branched out from its primary purpose of promoting the American way of life to helping the U.S. Office of Education. Volunteers tutored functional illiterates — there were a million Americans who could neither read nor write — and enabled a good number of them to enter the armed forces.

Many draft-age men were only marginally physically fit — growing up during the Depression had robbed them of good nutrition and some kids lacked proper exercise. VFW and the American Legion joined forces to whip youngsters into shape under the guidance of Robert A. Higgins of Post 321 in State College, Pa. Higgins coached varsity football at the University of Pennsylvania and knew what to do. Flaccid youths were rigorously drilled in exercises they would face during basic training — side-straddle hops, push-ups, duck walks, chinning on the bar and exhausting laps around the track. The program made it possible for the formerly unfit to make it through wartime boot camp or basic training.

But VFW's efforts didn't end there. Materiel was needed as well as men. So VFW collected $150,000 and turned it over to the government for the purchase of 15 training planes for men destined to fill cockpits.

Direct contributions to the war effort included sales of war bonds and stamps by the Ladies Auxiliaries. This booth was manned by women of the Auxiliary to Post 589 in Hazleton, Pa. Working six days a week, they sold some $25,000 worth of bonds and stamps by January 1943.

VFW contributed $150,000 to buy these 15 PT-19 training planes. Pilots sit in cockpits, ready for takeoff to ferry the new aircraft to flight training centers across the country.

...no mental standards prescribed before enlistments closed. ...dent Marie C. DeWitt, ...arter General Luther S. ...mander-in-Chief Robert T. Merrill and Alan Clarke, at the Allegheny County Municipal Airport.

Lined up to take off "into the wide blue yonder" are seven of the 15 PT-19s donated to the Army Air Forces by the V.F.W. at a total cost of $150,000. At the controls are the pilots, ready for departure to the various training centers throughout the country where the V.F.W. gift planes will help train aviators to beat the Axis.

FEBRUARY, 1943

An even more ambitious program was created by VFW at the behest of Lt. Gen. Henry H. "Hap" Arnold, chief of the U.S. Army Air Forces. Arnold was committed to fielding the largest strategic and tactical air force in history. When the war began, he commanded only 152,125 airmen. Aircraft production was below the 48,000 mark. But Arnold looked ahead to a force of more than 2 million and a production rate of

96,000 planes a year. He needed student pilots by the tens of thousands — about half of whom would wash out of training.

VFW Department commanders of a dozen Midwest states met with Arnold's representatives in Chicago in April 1942. A VFW Aviation Cadet Committee was formed, headed by Mark Kinsey of the Department of Iowa. Volunteers for the "glamorous" life of a combat aviator were not the problem — ability to pass stringent qualification exams was. Eager young men had the lightning reflexes and hand-eye coordination needed to make a pilot, but many were academically deficient.

Kinsey and his technically minded VFW colleagues worked out a curriculum of instruction to tutor aspirants. It covered those who lacked the two years of college traditionally needed to get into the cadet program. They could enter flight training by passing a stiff entrance exam demonstrating if they had the inherent ability to decipher problems in mathematics, physics and mechanics.

Kinsey's men set up 1,400 Aviation Cadet committees in 46 states and went to work. A preliminary test uncovered glaring weaknesses in math, science, history, geography and English. Aspirants were provided with study manuals and coached without charge. VFW provided 150,000 booklets, 200,000 applications and 10,000 posters. With these materials, men from ages 18 to 26 were alerted that the Army Air Forces wanted them. Moreover, the VFW stood ready to help them achieve the dream of flying against the enemy.

One VFW district reported that 83 percent of those who had failed the Army Air Forces entrance exam the first time had, under the tutoring program, successfully passed the second time around. Now, if they made it through flight school, they could write history over Europe or the Pacific.

The program lasted seven months, feeding 65,000 men into the cadet instruction cycle. On Dec. 4, 1942, Gen. Arnold wrote VFW Commander-

VFW's Aviation Cadet recruiting program had the active support of the Army, Navy and Marine Corps.

VFW Posts 156 and 1837 sponsor a recruiting booth at a picnic held by the Oak Cliff Chamber of Commerce in Dallas.

Left to right: Adjutant J.C. Kemp of Post 1837, Auxiliary District President Tula Smith, Army Cpl. Kline, Pat Kevton, Navy Yeoman Prade, Marine Sgt. Bruer, Auxiliary (1837) President Beth Kevton and two interested onlookers.

Altogether, VFW committees examined, selected, coached and recruited more than 100,000 men for the armed forces. Some 65,000 became Army Air Forces pilots, bombardiers and navigators. Another 35,000 went into Navy aviation and other technical jobs.

"The War Department has long appreciated the generous and patriotic assistance given by the VFW in recruiting aviation cadets. Your collaboration has been an important factor in enlargement of our air forces."

Gen. "Hap" Arnold
Chief, U.S. Army Air Force

Dedicated members of the War Service Committee of the Auxiliary to Post 112, Wichita, Kan., contributed to morale by spending long hours in kitchens. The Ladies averaged 1,400 cookies each month, destined for the local servicemen's canteens and for sons and daughters in uniform.

Left to right: Mrs. Earl E. Dedman, Mrs. Roy Jones, Mrs. O.G. Brickler, Mrs. W.A. McKenna and Auxiliary President Mrs. Edward L. Kline.

in-Chief Robert T. Merrill: "The War Department has long appreciated the generous and patriotic assistance given by the VFW in recruiting aviation cadets. Your collaboration has been an important factor in enlargement of our air forces."

Few VFW wartime-related endeavors were undertaken without the assistance of the Ladies Auxiliary. No group worked harder on the home front than the Ladies. By the beginning of 1942, there were 2,510 local auxiliaries with 96,000 members. These women opened canteens for servicemen, worked on blood drives, operated booths to sell war bonds, collected pots and pans for scrap metal drives and contributed heavily to fill the greatest needs of fighting men overseas — mail and chow from home.

They kept the home fires burning in their kitchens, baking mountains of cookies and chocolate cakes, boxing them to withstand the rigors of maritime shipment. Hundreds were sent to APO and FPO addresses. They became adept at writing on the new V-Mail forms — single sheets folded twice and microfilmed by the hundreds of thousands to at last be delivered as 3-by-4-inch sheets to some foxhole, Quonset hut or ship's mail room.

The Ladies learned to drive trucks for the Transportation Corps, too. Some taught the basics of first aid; nurses among them instructed others in medicine. Many put on white World War I helmets of the Civil Defense organization and dutifully served as air raid wardens.

As victories on European and Pacific battlefields grew, the painful cost was evident to those women who entered hospital wards to provide solace to the wounded. What they saw was searing— Marines blinded by Japanese grenades, soldiers with missing legs from German mines, sailors looking like charred meat from shipboard conflagrations, airmen with faces shredded by razor sharp flak and Coast Guardsmen with metal plates in their skulls. Wounds were of every conceivable description. Other men were encased in plaster from head to foot from dreadful accidents that always accompany war.

By 1943, several million uniformed Americans had served in war zones overseas — an invaluable reservoir of candidates

VFW home front support for men fighting overseas included a flow of goods from the U.S. Frank L. Barnett (left), commander of Post 857 in Ft. Wayne, Ind., and past Department Commander, William H. Lace stand behind a wall of Christmas boxes to be shipped to Post members serving in the armed forces in 1944.

for VFW ranks. Victory lay somewhere over the horizon after what would seem endless months of bloody combat. A vastly enlarged VFW would be needed to meet the peacetime demands of those who made it home.

So in September of that year, the organization created an extension department to begin an all-out recruiting drive. The new commander-in-chief, Carl J. Schoeninger, a veteran of the AEF's 16th Engineers, appointed a committee of a dozen men from various parts of the country to whip the department into shape.

Nearly a quarter of a million blank cards were printed and distributed to Posts all over the country — each member was asked to write the names and wartime addresses of men overseas. These in hand, the Extension Committee mailed application forms and an invitation to join VFW. When the forms and dues payments flooded in, new members were sent membership cards, a VFW service ribbon and a letter of welcome.

Meanwhile, VFW members on active duty prowled through rear areas and ships' compartments looking for recruits. Their brochures listed postwar plans and cited VFW's legislative victories.

For instance, on the day after Pearl Harbor was bombed, VFW's Rehabilitation Service drafted an amendment to the National Service Life Insurance Act to cover the one-third of American servicemen who had no coverage. The amendment was made retroactive to Oct. 8, 1940, providing $5,000 to survivors of men killed in the line of duty, survivors who otherwise would have suffered. The Legislative Committee applied pressure that raised

In 1945, Commander-in-Chief Jean Brunner visits men at the 101st Evacuation Hospital in Regensburg, Germany.

1st Lt. Audie Murphy, America's most highly decorated WWII soldier, is inducted into Dallas VFW Post 1837 in his home state in 1945. He also receives a 15th Infantry Regiment flag from Gen. W. A. Collier, Eighth Service Command. To Murphy's right stands B.L. Adams, commander of Post 1837. At far left is Judge Al Templeton of Dallas.

the pay of privates and seamen from $21 to $30 a month, and that granted free postage to men and women overseas.

A vigorous campaign was waged at home, too. Billboards appeared illustrating VFW wartime activities on the home front. A fleet of sound trucks cruised main streets carrying VFW's message. VFW also beamed spot announcements via radio into American living rooms. And it featured professionally scripted narrations during the weekly "Calling All Veterans" and "Speak Up for Democracy" programs. Themes of comradeship and other benefits of VFW membership were echoed in each issue of *Foreign Service*.

To catch the attention of troops coming back from overseas, the Extension Committee printed 500,000 "Information Please" cards. They were sent to discharge centers to be handed out along with the sheaf of paperwork that would usher servicemen into civilian life. Those who had, of necessity, joined as members-at-large were urged to transfer to a Post near their homes. Public outreach paid handsome dividends. A year of relentless effort resulted in 100,000 new members.

Fighting still raged on two continents, but VFW looked ahead to when the guns fell silent and millions of WWII vets returned home.

After two years of global war, many American servicemen, wounded and emotionally unhinged, had already returned. Marine Bill Smith came back from Guadalcanal in 1943 to a government ill-prepared to care for his wounds. A Japanese grenade destroyed part of his brain, leaving his left side paralyzed. Released from the hospital and handed an honorable discharge, Smith found his pay stopped and his mother's allotment cut off. At that time there was no mustering out pay.

No one guided Smith through the tortuous channels leading to his disability compensation of $100 a month, free hospitalization and vocational training. When the paperwork was finally submitted, it took four months for government bureaucrats to approve it — meanwhile Smith and his mother lived on the charity of friends and neighbors.

Congress seemed unaware of this national shame until exposed by daily broadsides in Hearst newspapers. Sen. Edwin Johnson of Colorado admitted: "I never realized anything approaching this situation existed. It is almost unbelievable that this nation should permit boys to go for months without

food, without money or clothes, except what they can beg.

"You can't explain a situation like this. You can't brush it off or forget it. We must put money in the hands of every man who is discharged — and we are discharging as many as 75,000 men a month." Johnson demanded mustering out pay upon discharge, when vets "feel lost and alone, when their need is greatest."

Clamor over mustering-out pay increased at a time when U.S. infantrymen were attacking through acres of Italian mud to reach the Volturno River, when the 8th Air Force had 60 four-engine bombers shot out of the sky in a raid over Schweinfurt (600 airmen lost in one afternoon), and when 1,081 Marines were killed in a bloody assault on Tarawa. For those who survived, the pay was clearly justified.

On Dec. 1, 1943, Sen. Alben Barkley, the majority leader from Kentucky, introduced a bill calling for $300 per veteran immediately upon discharge. It was not enough. Two weeks later, the Senate Finance Committee reported out an amended version calling for a payment of $500 for those who had served overseas for 18 months or more. It decreased to $200 for those with less than 12 months of Stateside service.

The Senate passed it Dec. 17 — only to have the Administration balk because the bill "diluted the basic principle of equal treatment for all." The

In less than 72 hours after the muster out pay bill became law on February 3, District Service Officer Kenneth Rhoades, Omaha, was ready to serve applicants. This picture, published in the Omaha World Herald on February 6, shows Alexander H. Loomer, discharged Sd... ....cific Navy veteran, filling out his applica....... ....mony was ....n and Dista....... ....y Hood.

Public Law 225, which provided mustering-out pay for veterans with honorable discharges, was passed Feb. 3, 1944. Just 72 hours after passage, VFW District Service Officer Kenneth Rhoades (right) in Omaha, Neb., was ready for business.

Pacific Navy vet Alexander H. Loomer signs his application for a $300 government check. His fiancee, Ardith Anderson, and District Commander Harry Hood watch as Loomer signs on the dotted line.

bill stalled — there would be no merry Christmas for several hundred thousand vets.

VFW's chief Capitol Hill fighter was Omar B. Ketchum, director of VFW's National Legislative Service. Ketchum's career crossed many territories — special investigator for the Internal Revenue Service, a champion of labor as staff representative of the Bituminous Coal Commission and president of the Topeka Typographical Union. As a VFW member, he had served as national chief of staff, first director of the Extension Service, Post commander and on the Kansas VFW Council of Administration.

Ketchum made as many as 50 appearances a year before congressional committees in pursuit of veterans rights. As the war gained momentum, he and his staff helped engineer the passage of these measures:

• *Public Law 10* — granted domiciliary care and burial expenses to veterans of World War II on the same basis as the 1917-1918 war.

• *Public Law 312* — increased awards to all beneficiaries by 15 percent, excepting those awards that were statutory.

• *Public Law 313* — boosted disability compensation from $40 to $50 a month for permanent non-service connected disabilities.

Preference in federal hiring was another key achievement. Preference for veterans re-entering civilian life was extended in 1876, 1912 and 1919. But an overhaul was needed to codify these measures under one law. VFW along with other vet groups supported the *Veterans Preference Act of 1944*.

Its major provisions added to civil service exams five points for veterans; 10 points for veterans with service-connected disabilities; 10 points for wives of veterans who were unable to work because of service-connected disabilities; and 10 points for widows of veterans until they remarried. Furthermore, if a veteran were passed over by an appointing officer, his action would have to be justified in a written report to the Civil Service Commission.

Next on the agenda was the most far-reaching veterans legislation in U.S. history. The Legion and VFW differed in their approach to what became known as the *Servicemen's Readjustment Act of 1944,* or the *GI Bill.* Fearing a single package of benefits would never make it through Congress, VFW favored handling various benefits one at a time and routing them through separate congressional committees.

At the national encampment in 1943, *Resolution 374* was adopted, calling for the nation to "provide college or trade education at government expense for those veterans of World War II and those veterans whose education was interrupted, interfered with, or delayed by war service."

This proposal was sponsored by Sen. Bennett Champ Clark of Missouri as the first education bill put forth by a veterans organization. It was put into the hopper loaded with other wartime measures to await its turn.

Meanwhile, the American Legion crafted its own legislation — an omnibus bill including every benefit believed due WWII vets. No such omnibus bill had ever gotten through Congress, but the Legion was determined to try.

The first draft was put together by Henry Colmery, an Army Air Service flying instructor during WWI and the Legion's national commander in 1936. Released on Jan. 8, 1944, the draft included the most urgent need — mustering-out pay. It sailed through the House 370-0 and became law on Feb. 14 of that year.

Other provisions of the Legion bill came under a barrage of criticism. An open letter signed by VFW's Omar Ketchum, Millard Rice of DAV, Frank Haley of the Military Order of the Purple Heart and W.M. Floyd of the Regular Veterans Association was sent to every member of Congress.

"All that glitters is not gold," it began. "Our nation's first responsibility should be to those who have suffered physical and/or mental handicap by reason of military or naval service. Any legislation that grants entitlement to four years of college training at government expense to any able-bodied veteran who had *90 days service* [emphasis added] should be carefully examined in the light of our tremendous war debt and the ability of the nation to adequately care for its war disabled....Let us not have another example of "act in haste, repent at leisure."

Ketchum and the others feared that the broad scope of educational benefits proposed by the Legion would consume funds needed for other

A cartoon in the June 1947 issue of *Foreign Service* compares civil service veterans preference to the old shell game. "Now you see it, now you don't," wrote Omar B. Ketchum, director of VFW's National Legislative Service.

VFW waged a relentless battle to keep intact the law guaranteeing qualified veterans preference when applying for federal jobs.

On hand when President Roosevelt signed the GI Bill were (at extreme left) Paul C. Wolman, VFW National Legislative Committee chairman; Commander-in-Chief Carl J. Schoeninger (to the right of Wolman); and Omar B. Ketchum, National Legislative Committee representative (standing behind Wolman).

programs, especially hospitalization. In their minds, it could result in another 1933-era *Economy Act*, as Michael J. Bennett aptly pointed out in his 1996 book *When Dreams Come True: The GI Bill and the Making of Modern America.* Proponents of the bill were dismayed — the joint letter provided an opportunity for congressmen who were against it, but were afraid to say so, to turn thumbs down when it came to a vote.

An intermediary coordinated a meeting between the planning committees of the Legion (1,250,000 members) and VFW (457,000). Ketchum was joined by the head of VFW's Legislative Committee Paul G. Wolman, VFW commander-in-chief during 1930-1931 and a member of the Jewish War Veterans (founded in 1896).

They sat down in a Washington hotel room with the Legion's John Stelle and discussed the GI Bill point by point. Ketchum now saw speed and logic in an omnibus bill. When the rewriting was done, the Legion's 1 1/2 page draft grew to 13 1/2 pages that included $500 million for VA hospitals. This was enough, it was hoped, to allay DAV's fears. Wolman said that "in uniting these two great organizations we have made history here."

DAV's Millard Rice, however, renewed his assault on the education component. Then he lambasted the "52-20 Club" proposal that would give veterans $20 a month for 52 weeks if they were unable to find work. Rice's cynicism surfaced when he claimed that the "lazy and chiseley types of veterans" would reap more benefits then the resourceful and the conscientious among them. Rice told Congress that he did not believe "the Veterans Administration should have any responsibility as to the postwar adjustment of able-bodied men." He overlooked the fact that it was able-bodied men who had fought for the welfare World War I's disabled veterans.

Exasperated committee members of VFW and the Legion were reminded of the fairy tale of Penelope, who labored throughout the day to weave a web of fine cloth, only to have it unraveled by mischievous spirits at night.

Two months had passed since the draft version of the bill emerged from the Statler Hotel. Unable to reason with DAV, Sen. Champ Clark introduced *S.1767* on March 13. Endorsed by 81 other senators, it sped through the Senate and passed on March 24. Celebrations were premature.

When *S.1767* reached the House, Rep. John Rankin of Mississippi treated it like an infectious disease. Rankin eliminated the 52-20 measure. He saw a "tremendous inducement to certain elements to try to get unemployment compensation." It would encourage 50,000 black servicemen from Mississippi to "remain unemployed for at least a year," he claimed.

Rankin balked and the GI Bill stalled in committee. Prodded, he called the bill "explosive" and "half-baked," declaring that the committee was not going to be stampeded into getting it on the floor for a vote.

In response, a fresh media campaign was launched. The *Army Times* addressed Rankin's tirade against the 52-20 Club. "What kind of people do you think are waging this war? The GI Bill is not charity— it merely provides an opportunity for service men and women to navigate under their own power. They have been taken away from jobs, homes and futures to win a war. Certainly they deserve a little assistance in making their readjustments."

After further weeks of wrangling over the educational provision, the bill was finally ready to be reported out of the seven-man House committee. But only if the controversy over the unemployment section could be resolved. The vote was 3-to-3 by committee members. The seventh member, Rep. Frank Gibson of Georgia, had gone home. He left Rankin to cast his proxy ballot in favor of having veterans job placement overseen by a board headed by VA.

On June 8, the committee voted again, but Rankin refused to cast Gibson's proxy and the issue was deadlocked. If the vote scheduled for the following day remained unchanged, six months of unrelenting work would be for nothing. The GI Bill could be doomed. By this time, the invasion of Normandy was 48 hours old.

It was then that Bernard W. "Pat" Kearney stepped into the breach. The representative from New York's 32nd District, he had fought in France in 1918 and became VFW commander-in-chief in 1936. Since he also was a member of the American Legion, he saw things from both sides. Kearney knew the salvation of the GI Bill was in Gibson's hands. He had to get back to Washington by 10 a.m. the next morning. Frantic telephone calls to Douglas, Ga., went unanswered. Calls to Gibson's friends elicited the discouraging news that he was believed to be on the road to Valdosta and out of touch.

Calls went out to radio stations asking for on-air pleas to locate the traveling congressman. Georgia State Police cars streaked down the highways and byways. Night fell, the hunt continued. Gibson was nowhere to be found. The gloom in Washington deepened.

At 11 p.m., Gibson pulled into his driveway and heard the telephone ringing incessantly from inside the house. The voice at the other end briefed him about the situation and told him to get ready to return to Washington. A car soon had him on his way to Jacksonville, Fla., 200 miles away, where an

Rep. "Pat" Kearney of New York, VFW commander-in-chief from 1936-37, co-sponsored the GI Bill. He enlisted the aid of Capt. Eddie Rickenbacker and Eastern Airlines in getting Georgia Rep. John Gibson to Capitol Hill in time to cast the deciding vote in committee.

Eastern Airlines DC-3 was being held for his arrival.

Gibson never forgot that wild ride through the night in a pouring rainstorm, the sedan slipping and sliding over the crowned road, at times threatening to career into the ditches on either side, the speedometer sometimes hitting 90 mph. Fate rode with Gibson and his driver that night— they reached the tarmac at Jacksonville safely and Gibson hurried up the metal steps and strapped in.

The DC-3 landed at Washington National Airport at 6:37 a.m. At 10 a.m. Gibson entered the House conference room and said: "I'm here to lick anyone who tries to hold up the GI Bill of Rights. Americans are dying in Normandy — I'm going to expose anyone who doesn't vote for the GI Bill."

Rankin retreated, as did other opponents — the vote was unanimous and *S.1767* headed for the floor and lightning approval. On June 22, 1944, Franklin D. Roosevelt attached his flourishing signature and the GI Bill of Rights became the law of the land.

World War II ended little more than a year later when a peace treaty was signed with Japan on Sept. 2, 1945. A new America ultimately emerged, thanks in large part to the GI Bill. It paid tuition of up to $500 a year — enough to get veterans into Harvard — along with textbooks, pencils and a stipend of $50 a month; $65 for married vets.

Educators fears that veterans would be unruly, if not dangerous, on campus were quickly laid to rest. They had lost years out of their lives and settled to work with a vengeance. To his surprise, Harvard President James Conant discovered that "the mature student body that filled our colleges in 1946 and 1947 was a delight to all who were teaching undergraduates."

Non-veterans were dismayed at the fierceness with which veterans attacked their studies, resenting the rising grade point averages that left them behind. Scions of old Eastern families enrolled in

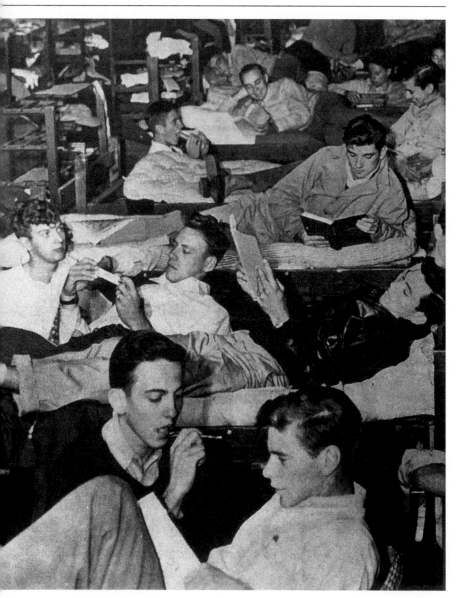

The GI Bill effected the core of American society by providing advanced education to every honorably discharged veteran who wanted to attend college. Universities were swamped in the late 1940s, but most of these University of Maryland students had seen barracks and ship's quarters just as crowded.

traditionally exclusive Ivy League universities learned to share classrooms with sons of coal miners from Appalachia and oil field roustabouts from Oklahoma.

Veterans had no time for beanies or traditional college hijinks. Upperclassmen quickly discovered that a man who had fought at Aachen or survived a torpedoing in the Pacific would tolerate no freshman hazing.

Nearly 8 million WWII veterans took advantage of the GI Bill. They were in colleges and vocational training most of them could have only dreamed about during the Depression. They took the opportunity seriously. That was reflected in the fact that 10 times more non-vets flunked out than did veterans.

It cost the government $1,858 for every veteran the GI Bill sent through school, but the financial and social dividends were enormous. The Department of Labor estimated that male college graduates would earn $250,000 more during their working lives than those with only high school diplomas. Federal income taxes repaid the initial expenditure many times over.

By the July 25, 1956, cutoff date, 2,232,000 WWII veterans had enrolled in college using the GI Bill. They had infused $14.5 billion in federal monies into American institutions of higher learning.

Social historians, if not the general public, have long understood the importance of the GI Bill. In *Post-Capitalist Society*, author Peter Drucker wrote: "The GI Bill of Rights — and the enthusiastic response to it on the part of America's veterans — signaled the shift to the knowledge society. Future historians may consider it the most important event of the 20th century."

Few Americans comprehend that the society they live in today was, at least in part, created by this monumental piece of legislation. It was not some form of "giveaway" program. In his *Days of Sadness, Years of Triumph*, Geoffrey Perrett noted the GI Bill's recipients had the "assertive, self-respecting attitudes of people whose claims are based on having earned, not simply deserved, what they received."

This was without "the sullen, self-destroying agonies of welfare clients...It was a very middle-class program, all the more effective for the disguise it wore...They and their children are the bedrock of America's modern middle class."

In later years, VFW leaders would look back on the passage of the GI Bill as a watershed in VFW history. Cooper T. Holt, long-time executive director of the Washington Office and past Chief, believes

Housing shortages on college campuses after WWII were severe. Education-hungry ex-GIs, however, were willing to live in tents to take advantage of the GI Bill in 1946.

VA counseling centers were set up on campuses such as this one on the University of Wisconsin at Madison in the late 1940s. Centers provided valuable GI Bill advice.

"It was a very middle-class program, all the more effective for the disguise it wore...They [WWII vets] and their children are the bedrock of America's modern middle class."

Geoffrey Perrett
Author, *Days of Sadness, Years of Triumph*

VFW's efforts in getting the GI Bill through Congress ranked among its greatest achievements. Howard E. Vander Clute, Jr., also a past Chief and former VFW adjutant general, agrees: "There are a great many people who are unaware of the role VFW played in getting the GI Bill passed."

VFW was in the forefront of the next major change in education assistance. In the fall of 1998, the organization called for a comprehensive package of benefits including full tuition at colleges for today's active duty recruits. So powerful was the societal impact of the WWII GI Bill that the idea of extending it to future armed forces volunteers was revived in early 1999 by the congressional Commission on Servicemembers and Veterans Transition Assistance, a 12-member panel convened to evaluate veterans benefits and programs.

Among the commission's suggestions were full scholarships, including tuition and other expenses, at any four-year college for four-year enlistees. This and some 100 other suggestions was the first general overview of veterans benefits in more than 40 years. VFW heartily endorsed some of the Commission's ideas.

Post 8935 in Sacramento, Calif., had the unique distinction of being the first VFW Post composed exclusively of Nisei— U.S. citizens born of immigrant Japanese parents and educated in America. Many of these veterans served in the famed 442nd Regimental Combat Team in Europe. Some 80 of them became charter members in 1947.

V.F.W. Organizes First All-Nisei Post

tion corps with which he was servi... backed up the 82nd and 80th Airborne Divisions.

Senior Vice Commander William Sakai was an original member of the famed 442nd Nisei Regiment, which saved the "lost battalion" of the 36... Infantry Regiment in the Vosges Mountains of Northern France at the cost of having one of its own battalions almost completely wiped... Sakai wears three battle stars... Purple Heart and a Presidential citation.

Other charter members of the...

FIRST all-Nisei unit in any veterans organization in this country is Post... of the Veterans of Foreign Wars... currently at Sacramento...

Heroes of the National Home

Children raised at VFW's National Home in Eaton Rapids, Mich., have always understood patriotism and learned responsibility to others. They knew of their father's service to the nation — and why some dads made the ultimate sacrifice. Not surprisingly, many of them served, too.

Since the National Home opened in 1925, more than 200 young residents have served in the nation's armed forces during wartime: World War II (114), Korean War (59), Vietnam (34) and Persian Gulf War (five).

Four lost their lives in combat:

Larry Sims survived the Japanese attack on Pearl Harbor on Dec. 7, 1941. That same day, he manned his radio operator's station aboard a Navy patrol bomber that went aloft to seek the Japanese fleet. The plane never returned.

In November 1944, Maurice Chadwick was killed fighting Germans in southern France with the U.S. Army. Three months later, Anthony Walker was killed by the Japanese during the bitter fighting on Luzon in the Philippines.

The fourth Home son to die in action was Pfc. Elgie Hanna. On March 20, 1968, Hanna was on patrol with Company B, 2nd Battalion, 5th Cavalry Regiment, 1st Cavalry Division, near Quang Tri in Vietnam when a sniper's round found its mark. Hanna had been in country only 33 days.

Clarence Powers discovered that life at the National Home prepared him for the rigors of military life. "From 1933 to 1940," he explained, " I was in the Citizens Military Training Corps. It was like basic training, so I was ready to serve when my draft call came." Powers fought with the 34th Infantry Division in North Africa and later during the battles for Salerno and Cassino in Italy.

When duty called in Korea, Robert Hovey credited the "regimentation" at the Home with enabling him to "take it while everyone else had trouble adjusting." A second lieutenant in the 24th Infantry Division, he said, "The National

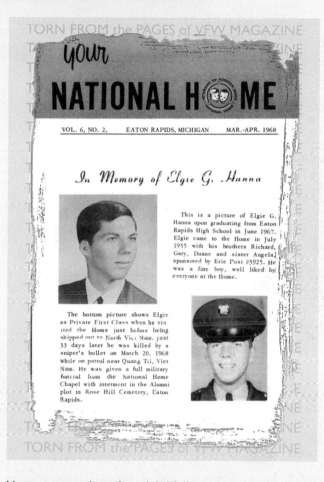

TORN FROM the PAGES of VFW MAGAZINE

your NATIONAL HOME

VOL. 6, NO. 2,   EATON RAPIDS, MICHIGAN   MAR.-APR. 1968

In Memory of Elgie G. Hanna

This is a picture of Elgie G. Hanna upon graduating from Eaton Rapids High School in June 1967. Elgie came to the Home in July 1955 with his brothers Richard, Gary, Duane and sister Angela, sponsored by Erie Post #3925. He was a fine boy, well liked by everyone at the Home.

The bottom picture shows Elgie as Private First Class when he visited the Home just before being shipped out to North Viet Nam, just 33 days later he was killed by a sniper's bullet on March 20, 1968 while on patrol near Quang Tri, Viet Nam. He was given a full military funeral from the National Home Chapel with interment in the Alumni plot in Rose Hill Cemetery, Eaton Rapids.

TORN FROM the PAGES of VFW MAGAZINE

Home prepared me for adult life."

To Jack Haley, it was a "natural progression to grow up and join the military. We had 250 brothers and sisters at the Home, and we leaned on each other and stuck up for each other. We were raised in an environment that instilled love of country. We knew we were there because our fathers fought and died in a war or were disabled because of it. We wanted to follow in their footsteps."

Haley served with the 5th Marine Regiment in Vietnam. His brother, George, was wounded at Khe Sanh with the 26th Marines in 1968.

As a young girl, Carol Rattigan remembered: "Vets were always coming by, a lot of them with war wounds. I came to appreciate what they had done for our country. Seeing so many people supporting us made us want to join the military and give something back." She enlisted in the Air Force, serving with the 3rd Combat Communications Group in Saudi Arabia during the Persian Gulf War in 1991.

Clarence Powers, WWII; Robert Hovey, Korean War; and Isabelle Miars, WWII.

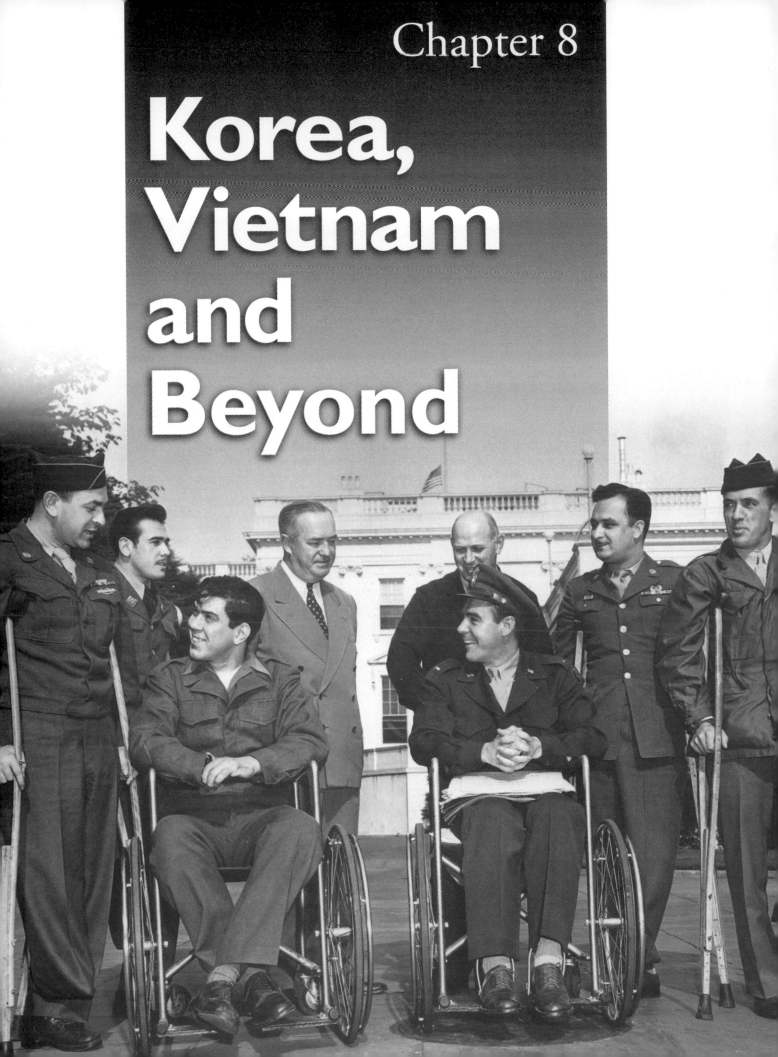

Korea, Vietnam and Beyond

Veterans from different wars return to varying homecomings. VFW is there in every case to fight for well-deserved benefits, such as the Korean and Vietnam War GI Bills.

World War II veterans, bolstered by the GI Bill, came home to a grateful nation. An ex-GI displaying a "ruptured duck" honorable discharge pin meant a hearty handshake, free beer or an invitation to dinner. It seemed that nothing was too good for the Americans who had liberated continents and laid Nazi Germany and Imperial Japan in the dust.

They mothballed their uniforms and seized the opportunities provided by the GI Bill. Unemployment was not the nightmare endured by their fathers. They were assured first crack at federal government jobs and those vacated by millions of women who were leaving factories. These plants were rapidly converting to production of such peacetime goods as automobiles, kitchen appliances and baby buggies. This time, there would be no shabbily dressed veterans peddling apples on street corners.

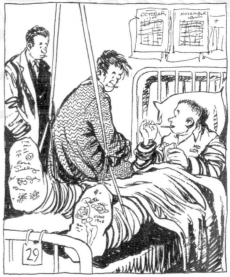

Copyright©1945 Bill Mauldin

"How's things outside, boys? Am I still a war hero or a drain on th' taxpayer?"

In October 1946, with membership at a record 1,555,444, VFW established a separate section in the Washington Office to brief veterans on employment procedures and to safeguard their rights. Vets soon discovered VFW had put teeth into the *Veterans Preference Act* when abuses were uncovered within the system. Legal representatives provided free counsel to veterans who took grievances before the Board of Appeals and Review. If layoffs loomed, veterans would be the last to go.

Returning disabled vets found VFW's expanded National Rehabilitation Service (NRS) helped ease their passage into civilian life. NRS was staffed with permanent members, which avoided changing officers after each encampment. Career service officers recruited from the ranks of the disabled were intensively trained in veterans affairs at schools located throughout the country. They were paid by VFW — no federal money was required.

Opposite page:
Disabled veterans from a New Jersey VA hospital with VFW representatives on the White House lawn. They had met with President Harry S Truman in June 1946 about hospital closures.
Standing, left to right: Tech. 5 Walter Bernstein, Pfc. Frank Baraccini, VFW's Tom Kehoe, Harry Rodensky (driver); Pfc. Wallace Daczkowski and Pfc. Donald Murray. Seated in wheelchairs: Cpl. Ernie Sardo (left) and 1st Lt. Austin Kelly.

By 1947, VFW was spending more than $2 million a year for veterans rehabilitation and welfare work. Half or more of all World War II veterans who needed help chose VFW to handle claims against the government. Powers-of-attorney granted to VFW almost equaled the combined assignments to all other agencies—including the American Legion, DAV and American Red Cross.

To meet postwar needs of returning veterans, VFW opened a training school for service officers in 1944. The graduates of this class were stationed throughout the country to supervise the work of VFW service officers in local communities. Their primary mission: to help veterans obtain their much-deserved VA benefits.

Rep. John F. Kennedy (D-Mass.) discusses the National Veterans Housing Conference with Gray S. Tilly, junior vice commander of the VFW Alaska Department. The two-day conference began Feb. 29, 1948. It attracted more than 2,000 delegates from seven major veterans organizations and 33 states.

Between 1945 and 1947, NRS won 560,970 awards with monetary recovery amounting to $383,019,820. The cash went directly to veterans—the VFW took no commission, charged no fees.

The GI Bill that Omar Ketchum helped knit together equipped veterans with the means to buy homes. Still, they faced the most critical housing shortage in the nation's history. America needed 5 million new houses, but most builders were busy with more lucrative industrial construction.

President Harry S Truman, who moved into the White House when Roosevelt died in April 1945, asked Congress for authority to channel half the country's building materials into low-cost housing for veterans. The powerful housing lobby blocked the proposal.

Meanwhile, veterans and their families lived with in-laws, in Quonset huts and in temporary wartime buildings turned over to them by the Senate. At one point, 14,000 veterans and their families crowded into abandoned Army barracks. A fellow veteran named William J. Levitt solved the problem. In so doing, he led the way for a host of other builders.

Levitt, son of Russian-Jewish immigrants, had been a Seabee in the Pacific

and knew how to build things fast. He leased 1,500 acres of open land on Long Island only 20 miles from midtown Manhattan. Then he started building houses the way ships had been turned out during the war—on assembly lines using pre-fabricated components. His sales office opened on March 7, 1949, and 1,400 contracts were signed that same day.

Veterans moved in with no down payment and paid $58 a month for the basic two-bedroom, one-bathroom $6,900 frame house. There were no basements. But as one veteran commented, "Living without a cellar beats one room in an attic where you freeze to death." Levitt built 17,441 houses in two years and then expanded into Pennsylvania.

With loans guaranteed by the federal government, a host of other builders got on the GI bandwagon and tract developments filled once barren landscapes all across the

Volunteering at VA Hospitals

Soon after the original World War I-era Veterans Bureau was created, VFW members were volunteering their time in its facilities. With the advent of WWII, VA's patient load ballooned, creating a demand for help. On May 15, 1946, the VA Voluntary Service (VAVS) was established to fill the need. VFW was a charter member of the network.

Nothing exemplifies the volunteer spirit of VFW better than VAVS. It grew to become the largest volunteer program in the federal government — 56 major civic and service organizations make up its National Service Committee supported by more than 350 local groups.

VAVS has had at least 271,738 volunteers on its rolls who have donated more than 440 million hours of service to veteran-patients. They account for the 27,267,295 letters written for patients unable to handle pen and paper.

In any given year, nearly 94,000 volunteers will give more than 14 million hours of their time at the VA's 172 medical centers. It is time worth $40 million to paid workers in the medical field.

Volunteers take on duties ranging from "search and rescue" missions to find elderly or confused patients who wander off hospital grounds to forming burial details at national cemeteries. Bill Jacques, VFW VAVS representative at the West Palm Beach, Fla., VAMC and member of Post 4143 in Riviera Beach, Fla., put skills he learned with the 1st Cavalry Division in Vietnam to good use. He developed a "search and rescue" team to locate wandering veterans on the VAMC's 60-acre site.

Ed Swartz, a WWII Navy vet of Post 4357 in Ann Arbor, Mich., explained why he is among the corps of volunteers:

"Something inside you says you've got to go. You do it because you see these guys suffering."

Jim W. Delgado, national VAVS director, said: "We're proud to say that VAVS continues to be a member of the health care system. Volunteers provide tremendous potential for advocacy and ambassadorship for VA health care. They promote a positive public image."

Dale Albee of Post 1442 in Portland, Ore., offers a hand of encouragement to a patient at the Portland VA Medical Center. Albee is part of the invaluable VA Voluntary Service whose members have played a significant role in cheering up patients throughout this decade and for 40 years before.

---

country. Money flowed into mortgage companies, contractors enjoyed a boom and veterans elevated their families from renters to owners. It was the beginning of American suburbia.

World War II vets had five years to settle in before the next war erupted. A showdown with communism had finally come. Those still in the Reserves would be ripped from peaceful suburbia and sent overseas once again. Many of their younger brothers who missed "the big one" would taste combat in Korea.

The general postwar euphoria evaporated on June 25, 1950, when Communist North Korea, backed by Red China, invaded South Korea. As usual, VFW was quick to defend soldiers in the field. Moral support, regardless of the politics of the situation, was forthcoming. As the war

A Golden Jubilee

In 1949, VFW marked its 50th anniversary with a week-long celebration. More than 140 million Americans were invited to the party.

Festivities opened on April 3 with a one-hour NBC radio special hosted by that GI favorite, Bob Hope. His travels to war zones around the globe entitled him to every U.S. campaign medal issued during World War II. He shared the microphone with Dinah Shore, known for appearances at dockside to welcome home Pacific veterans long after V-J Day. VFW was represented by Commander-in-Chief Lyall Beggs, an infantryman gassed by Germans in 1918, and by Janis Paige, that year's National Buddy Poppy Girl.

In place of anniversary cards, VFW mailed 300,000 booklets outlining veterans benefits to 850 radio stations and to more than 600 newspapers. The Ladies Auxiliary sponsored a poetry contest with a *Why-I-Love-America* theme and duly sent a check for $20,000 to a veteran from Utah who called himself simply "Pop" Warner.

The Golden Jubilee Encampment that followed in Miami that year drew President Harry S Truman to the podium. He told survivors of three wars, "I am proud to be a member of the nation's oldest active veterans organization."

Cheers greeted one of the founders, Jim Putnam. During the Boston Encampment two years earlier, he refused to be chauffeured along the two-mile hike down asphalt streets. Then 70, he waved aside the offer, declaring, "I'm going to walk with the boys and that's all there is to it." He told the Miami group: "It is given to few men to have a dream so richly realized as has been my early dream of a veterans organization that would not die with my generation."

Putnam turned the podium over to another founding father, James Romanis. The usually reticent Romanis rose to the occasion. "The war veteran," he said, "is an outstanding citizen. He typifies the real American. In spirit he is a rambling, gambling, adventuring explorer, always seeking to better the conditions for himself and his people. Undaunted by adverse circumstances, he pushes ever onward to his

President Harry S Truman salutes fellow VFW members at the 1949 Convention in Miami during the Golden Jubilee. At his left is Commander-in-Chief Charles C. Ralls. Truman, the only overseas WWI vet to become President, had long been active in VFW's affairs around his native Kansas City area. Truman said, "I am proud to be a member of the nation's oldest active veterans organization."

goal. Regardless of what parts of the world his quest may carry him, the war veteran is always willing to take a chance, ignoring the odds against him."

At 71, Romanis had lived to see the VFW grow from 13 members and a single Post to an organization of 1.5 million overseas vets and 10,000 Posts stretching coast-to-coast and across two oceans. Perhaps that was the best anniversary present of all. Romanis died five years later on Dec. 7, 1954 at age 76.

VFW celebrated its Golden Jubilee in 1949 in grand style. April 3-9 was designated "Golden Jubilee Week," which drew national attention via 637 radio broadcasts—including an hour-long NBC special featuring Bob Hope—and stories in 850 newspapers.

Veterans Day

America's allies — England and France — began the tradition that has become so much a part of this nation's heritage. Two years after World War I ended on Nov. 11, 1918, those two countries began recognizing the sacrifices made in the war by honoring its unknown victims. In 1926, Congress officially dubbed November 11 Armistice Day.

But it was not until 1938 that it became a legal national holiday. The 12-year battle to achieve this goal was hard fought. And the victory is owed much to the efforts of the VFW. VFW member Rep. Bertrand W. Gearhart led the crusade in the House of Representatives. The California congressman succeeded, and President Franklin Roosevelt approved the measure — which became *Public Law 510* — on May 13, 1938.

Gearhart was gracious in his praise: "I am free to admit that I do not believe that we could have attained the success we did had it not been for the intelligent and purposeful support of the Veterans of Foreign Wars and the strategy which you assisted me in devising."

In addition, VFW launched a campaign to have the states declare Veterans Day a legal holiday, as well as urging governors to proclaim November 11-18 as "Veterans Week." In 1938, the 20th anniversary of the Armistice, at least 20 states set aside that week for special observance.

World War II and the Korean War added a new generation of veterans deserving of national recognition. Consequently, Rep. Edwin K. Rees of Kansas spearheaded a move to make that special day all encompassing. His work paid off. On June 1, 1954, Congress changed Armistice Day to Veterans Day. VFW had helped score another win.

Raymond Weeks, a member of Post 668 in Birmingham, Ala., was largely responsible for Veterans Day. When President Ronald Reagan presented Weeks with the Presidential Citizens Medal for a lifetime of volunteerism in 1983, he said: "He [Weeks] was the driving force behind the congressional action which in 1954 established this special holiday [Veterans Day] as a day to honor all American veterans."

Later, the nation entered a new era complete with a domestically divisive war. Lawmakers voted to change the observance of Veterans Day to the fourth Monday in October to placate those who wanted additional long weekends. President Lyndon Johnson signed *P.L. 90-353* on June 28, 1968, mandating the change three years later.

Observance of this sacred day on the last Monday of October 1971, with complete disregard for the symbolism of November 11, galvanized veterans into action. As usual, VFW was in the forefront. Moving Veterans Day back to its traditional date became an all-consuming objective.

Grassroots action at the state level proved most effective. After six years of strong lobbying, 46 states had redesignated November 11 as Veterans Day by 1977. Only four states short of a clean sweep, Congress finally took notice and restored (with *P.L. 94-97*) the day to its rightful place on America's calendar of historical events, beginning in 1978.

Members of Company A, 353rd Infantry, 89th Division, celebrate Armistice Day, Nov. 11, 1918, on the steps of a church in Stenay, a ruined village north of Verdun, France.

dragged on with no end in sight, however, domestic politics overshadowed the fighting front.

VFW soon became embroiled in the so-called "Truman-MacArthur controversy" in 1950-51. Commander-in-Chief Clyde A. Lewis was asked to withhold Gen. Douglas MacArthur's statement about the Korean War to be made at VFW's upcoming national encampment. Lewis complied, but MacArthur's controversial views were by then already widely disseminated by the press.

On April 28, 1951, Commander-in-Chief Charles C. Ralls presented MacArthur with a VFW Gold Medal and a citation. Then the two veterans of the Pacific war — Ralls was a line officer with the V Marine Amphibious Corps — launched VFW's Loyalty Day parade down Fifth Avenue. MacArthur's parade attracted an estimated 7.5 million people lining a route from the tip of lower Manhattan to midtown and back again — nearly 20 miles.

The crowd "roared and shrilled itself into near-exhaustion," reported *The New York Times.* Tons of shredded paper cascaded from windows to fall on MacArthur's open car. But the famous general's reception was hardly typical.

On April 3, 1951, Gen. Douglas MacArthur was fired by President Truman as commander-in-chief of U.N. forces in Korea. On April 28, VFW Commander-in-Chief Charles C. Ralls (left) presents MacArthur with the VFW's prestigious Gold Medal and Citation. Afterward the two veterans launch the Loyalty Day parade down New York City's Fifth Avenue. MacArthur attracted an estimated 7.5 million people.

The Korean War lasted until July 27, 1953. By then the fighting had vanished from newspaper headlines. A policy of individual rotation sent 1.6 million vets of that war home mostly piecemeal. In many cases, they received a cold shoulder from their fellow Americans.

Both symbolically and materially, Korea vets were denied full credit. Yet they did receive some tangible benefits. VFW, of course, was there to fight for their rights. In 1950, for instance, the organization advocated an emergency measure granting medical benefits, which were provided on May 11, 1951.

As appropriate, the needs of wounded veterans were the top priority of postwar assistance planners. Disabled vets were taken care of under the *Vocational Rehabilitation Act* of 1950. An estimated 77,000 disabled vets of the era used its programs. It created a Vocational Rehabilitation and Education Advisory Committee, too.

Public Law 550 — Veterans Readjustment Assistance Act of 1952 — covered the needs of all the era's vets. An ex-GI would receive 1.5 times his service up to a maximum of 36 months for school. Schooling had to begin within two years of discharge. A single vet received $110 a month, from which he paid for his tuition, books, supplies and on-campus housing.

The Korean War GI Bill was less generous than its WWII counterpart. Korea vets had to pay their tuition out of a monthly stipend rather than having it paid separately and entirely. As a result, only half as many of them, on a per capita basis, were able to attend private colleges. Still, 43 percent of eligible Korean War-era vets used VA-sponsored educational benefits. Total cost of the Bill was $4.5 billion. When it expired on Feb. 1, 1965, nearly 2.4 million of that era's veterans had used the Bill's benefits.

VA also guaranteed 649,000 Korean War-era veteran home loans in 1955 alone and more than 1.5 million before eligibility expired in January 1965. The act provided other assistance, as well. Mustering-out pay of $100-$300 was given to each vet. Job placement and unemployment insurance were handled through the states. Unemployment compensation was set at $26 per week for 26 weeks.

Veterans preference in federal employment was well-entrenched. Congress passed a bill on July 14, 1952, extending preference to Korean War-era vets, regardless of whether they actually served in the war zone.

By July 1957, 17 states offered bonuses to Korean War veterans. In 1962, New York debated a bonus of $50 to $250 that would cost $100 million to be financed by an increase in the state's cigarette tax. But as *Newsweek* reported, Gov. Nelson A. Rockefeller "bucked the well-oiled, persistent veterans lobby." By then, remembrance of the war was fast fading.

Dr. Frank Lakin (left) became administrative assistant to the president of Colorado State College. He discusses administrative matters with Dr. Norman T. Oppelt, dean of students. Both men served with the 1st Marine Division in Korea. VFW took a leading role in assuring that Korean War veterans received equitable benefits.

Yet the crusade against communism at home was at its zenith before, during and after the Korean War. A series of sensational postwar trials pointed to the fact that communism was a deadly virus that had infiltrated America.

Eleven members of the national board of the Communist Party were put on trial in federal court in 1949, charged with conspiracy to teach and advocate the overthrow of the government by force. A former State Department official, Alger Hiss, was convicted of stealing government documents intended for Moscow. Two Americans were eventually electrocuted for passing along secrets of atomic weapons to their spy masters in the Soviet Union.

VFW took the stand that since citizens could not seek out and destroy this enemy — that was the job of the assault teams of the FBI, special congressional committees and the Justice Department — it would fight communism's spread at the grass-roots level. Instead of the weapons of war, the tools of education would be employed to win this war.

An effective anti-Communist campaign would have to be essentially a

Perhaps the youngest veteran ever to join VFW was Pvt. Frank Jedure. Before his true age was revealed to be 16, he served five months in Korea. Honorably discharged, Post 2290 in Manville, N.J. signed him up in 1951.

JOIN THE VFW & FIGHT COMMUNISM

The entire community knows that Post 2036, Fort Smith, Ark., is conducting a membership...

The Cold War drew attention to the threat of Russian domination of Europe and Communist subversion at home. In 1952, VFW Post 2036, Fort Smith, Ark., strung this 50-foot banner across the city's Main Street to remind veterans to counter Communist ideology.

promotion of patriotism. As *Foreign Service* magazine reminded its readers: "When we carry out the patriotic, fraternal, historical and educational ideals of our organization, we are fighting communism. Only through active, personal commitment is it possible to build the good society that is invulnerable to the lures of the enemy."

To reach the audience in America's largest metropolis, Commander-in-Chief Charles C. Ralls was invited to be the principal guest speaker at the Fourth Anti-Communist Convention at Carnegie Hall in New York City on Feb. 25, 1951. Ralls read a telegram from MacArthur who pointed out that "communism may no longer be discussed as an economic, political or social philosophy. It has become but a means to satisfy a lust for personal power. Freedom is its very antithesis. Let only those who would see freedom perish ignore the potentiality of communism's threat."

Chief Ralls declared, "We must sustain an intellectual enthusiasm against communism in all its hydra-headed aspects." He proposed a non-partisan government agency to establish information centers throughout the country. It would distribute anti-Communist facts and information to schools, colleges and civic groups.

VFW took the battle to even higher echelons. At the 1955 National Convention, *Resolution 184* put the organization squarely on record as opposing admission of Communist China to the United Nations. VFW agreed with Gen. George C. Marshall's contention that "no aggressor should be allowed to shoot its way into the United Nations."

Aid to the victims of Communist aggression was not overlooked either. A VFW presence was directly felt in Austria, where thousands of Hungarian refugees fled when driven from their homes by Russian forces during the

1956 uprising in Budapest. VFW cooperated with Care, Inc., and President Eisenhower's People-to-People program in raising money from Posts and Auxiliaries to buy food and clothing for destitute Hungarians. Chief Cooper T. Holt expressed pride in the fact that VFW was the first veterans organization to take positive action in the President's program.

In 1959, an even stronger anti-Communist resolution was passed—a call for severing diplomatic relations with the Soviet government because "the Russian embassy in the United States is directing espionage and propaganda activities designed to destroy this country."

Momentum for the anti-Communist crusade was added during the 1960 National Convention in Detroit when delegates were addressed by CIA Director Allen Dulles and presidential candidates Sen. John F. Kennedy of Massachusetts and Vice President Richard M. Nixon. Dulles called for a program of education in American schools to "acquaint our youth with the true aims and purposes of communism and the manner in which it destroys the freedom of human beings forced to live under Communist rule."

Kennedy told his fellow VFW members, "America's enemies daily grow more arrogant, more threatening and more powerful." He advocated an acceleration of the missile program and modernization of conventional armed forces "regardless of cost."

Post 5404 in Auburn, Ala., took Dulles' call to educate seriously, fighting communism using the old adage, "know your enemy." Members contributed funds to the University of Auburn library so it could add to its collection of books on Russian and Asian history and culture. "The average American," said past Post Commander Leon Gray, "knows little about Russia and even less about the trouble spots of Asia. We hope to encourage general education."

In 1957, Quartermaster General Robert B. Handy, Jr., presents a check for $3,880 to Jane Allvine, Midwest director of CARE, Inc., to aid Hungarian refugees in Austria. VFW was the first veterans group to become involved with Eisenhower's People-to-People program.

Education was only one arena in the war on communism. Politics was equally important. The fight to outlaw communism in the United States was a 26-year struggle for VFW. As far back as 1926, VFW became the first major organization to ask Congress to make the Communist Party illegal. In 1932, Texas Rep. Martin Dies got a bill passed by the House, but it died there.

Twenty-two years later, on Feb. 9, 1954, Dies introduced *H.R. 7814*, saying, "As long as the Communist movement has a legal status in the United States, no agency of the government can cope with it." That same year,

Congress enacted *Public Law 637,* the *Communist Control Act of 1954. P.L. 637* did not make it a criminal act to be a Communist, so the VFW pressed for a stronger bill and launched a petition drive. On Aug. 15, 1954, the Senate approved *H.R. 8912* by a vote of 85-0; the House a similar bill by 305-2. Six days later, the final measure outlawing the Communist Party in the U.S. was signed by the President.

Incoming Commander-in Chief Merton B. Tice called it a "glorious victory for the free world." He paid tribute to Past Chief Wayne E. Richards whose "valiant, aggressive championship of this cause mobilized public sentiment so effectively that Congress did not dare adjourn without adopting this vitally important new law."

"World government" was another thorny issue. When the United Nations was created in San Francisco in the spring and summer of 1945, VFW representatives were present. They worked as consultants on a charter that was adopted that October. Though an international organization dedicated to peace was certainly in keeping with VFW objectives, surrender of American sovereignty was out of the question.

Moves to create some sort of international governing body following WWII were met with stiff resistance from VFW. In May 1950, national headquarters created the American Sovereignty Campaign under the direction of Rear Adm. Harley Cope. He said the American people were being asked to "buy a pig in a poke when it comes to world government."

An information blitz was quickly organized and facts presented to the Senate Committee on Foreign Relations. That September, after lengthy hearings and thousands of words of testimony, the committee rejected every proposal submitted by world federalists. Cope called it a signal victory, saying VFW "stood head and shoulders" above other organizations in the sovereignty fight. Because of VFW efforts, 22 state legislatures rescinded resolutions that were pro-world government.

Public outreach was key to the fight against communism. Florida Sen. George A. Smathers proposed a North-South hemispheric cultural exchange center to

The notion of a "world government" surfaced not long after WWII. VFW took an immediate stand against relinquishing U.S. sovereignty over its own affairs.

An editorial cartoon in the August 1950 issue of *Foreign Service* summoned ghostly images of three notorious dictators—Adolf Hitler, Josef Stalin and Benito Mussolini— over the shoulders of a monolithic figure whose head swarms with nuclear imagery.

VFW's campaign was partly responsible for many of 22 states rescinding resolutions endorsing world federation.

Loyalty Day

Communists believed May 1 belonged to them in celebration of the 1917 Russian Revolution. VFW believed otherwise. As a counter to the Communist day of commemoration, VFW launched "Americanization Day" on April 27 — President U.S. Grant's birthday — in 1921.

A decade later, the organization was no longer willing to grant the Reds their special day. On May 1, 1930, 10,000 VFW members turned out in New York's Union Square to stage a massive rally to promote patriotism. Rallies were held every year thereafter across the nation. In 1949, a resolution was adopted calling for federal recognition of May 1 as Loyalty Day.

Observances in 1950 began on April 28 and climaxed on May 1 with parades across the nation by an estimated 5 million people. In New York City, 100,000 people marched down Fifth Avenue in a cold rain watched by cheering spectators. The reviewing stand included Commander-in-Chief Clyde A. Lewis, Mayor William O'Dwyer, Secretary of Labor Maurice J. Tobin and Broadway star Ethel ("Miss Loyalty") Merman.

The cover of the April 1959 VFW magazine.

It was truly an all-American parade: The line of march included civic and religious groups, foreign language units in national costumes, fraternal organizations, patriotic groups and labor representatives. Massed colors of Old Glory were carried by marchers ranging in age from tots to aged Spanish-American War veterans. Notable was Mrs. Oksana Kasenkina, a Russian school teacher who had made headlines by leaping to freedom from a window inside the Soviet consulate.

In 1955, Rep. Jimmy Van Zandt of Pennsylvania, three times VFW Chief, introduced a bill proclaiming May 1 as Loyalty Day. Congress passed it, but only for that year. Terrier-like, Van Zandt persisted. He wrote another bill.

Mississippi Sen. James Eastland, assisted by Wisconsin Sen. Alexander Wiley, authored a companion bill in the Senate.

In 1958, Congress enacted *Public Law 529* proclaiming Loyalty Day a permanent feature on the nation's calendar. President Dwight D. Eisenhower signed it July 18. That year, VFW sponsored 1,059 projects, including huge parades in 136 cities.

The popularity of Loyalty Day declined within a decade. "By the late 1960s, the political ramifications of the unpopular Vietnam War had seriously affected Loyalty Day parades," wrote Jane Hatch in *The American Book of Days*.

Loyalty Day parades, however, continue today in VFW realms, but on a far smaller scale than in the glory days of the 1950s.

VFW members parade through the streets of New York City on April 28, 1950, in honor of Loyalty Day, a counter to the Communist May Day demonstrations.

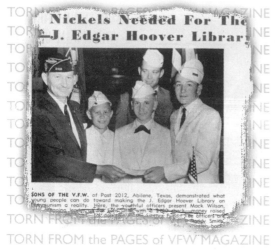

Nickels Needed For The J. Edgar Hoover Library

SONS OF THE V.F.W. of Post 2012, Abilene, Texas, demonstrated what young people can do toward making the J. Edgar Hoover Library on communism a reality. Here, the youthful officers present Mack Wilson...

be known as the University of the Americas. VFW immediately supported the concept of a place "where peoples of the Americas may pursue the search for truth."

In April 1961, Chief Ted C. Connell presented a check for $1,000 to Smathers, chairman of the Council of Inter-American Affairs of the People-to-People program. The VFW check was the first contribution made by any organization. Posts assisted in the combined national effort to prevent future Fidel Castros from rising to dictatorial power in the Western Hemisphere.

VFW's crusade against communism was on full throttle well into the early 1960s. In the summer of 1960, the organization adopted three resolutions calling for courses on communist ideology to be added to high school curriculums. In Kansas City that fall, VFW hosted the All-American Conference to Combat Communism. The keynote address was delivered by CIA Director Allen W. Dulles. The following year, VFW's national Americanism Committee approved a 10-point Code of Ethics for fighting communism.

Sons of VFW Post 2012, Abilene, Texas, demonstrate what youth can accomplish. They helped make the J. Edgar Hoover Library on Communism a reality. In May 1963, the kids give a $100 check to Mack Wilson, outgoing leader of the Sons unit, to donate to the library fund. The money was raised through popcorn sales.

The sons, left to right: Junior Vice Commander Jimmie Beyers, Senior Vice Commander Randy Smith and Commander Billy Ryan. The new unit leader, Paul Wheeler, stands in the background.

By 1962, *VFW* magazine was publishing a monthly column called "Along the Red Front." It preached the gospel for nearly two decades. And a major effort was undertaken in 1963 to raise $55,000 to fund the J. Edgar Hoover Library on Communism in the Freedom Center at the Freedoms Foundation in Valley Forge, Pa. Since that initial $55,000 donation, VFW has given $71,500 for maintaining the library.

Incidentally, Freedoms Foundation, based in Valley Forge, Pa., and founded in 1949, has bestowed numerous awards on the organization. Distinguished Service awards went to VFW for 10 consecutive years. Freedoms Foundation President Kenneth D. Wells, in 1957, called VFW "the nation's most honored institution." The relationship between the Foundation and VFW has remained close to this day. Says Executive Director Russell Schulz: "Veterans have a special place at Freedoms Foundation. They know firsthand the meaning of citizenship. And VFW members — among whom I am counted — have a never-ending role to play in instilling democratic ideals in young minds."

Freedoms Foundation Executive Vice President Russell K. Schulz, in September 1998, emphasizes VFW's contribution to the J. Edgar Hoover Library on Communism.

In 1963, VFW raised $55,000 for the library and later gave an additional $72,000 for maintenance. A VFW honor roll lists the donors.

While the battle against domestic radicalism was being waged, a simultaneous effort was under way overseas in support of Radio Free Europe (RFE), a non-profit corporation. It beamed uncensored news, religious programs, youth forums and contemporary drama banned by Moscow. Broadcasts reached nearly 80 million eastern European listeners. RFE had begun sending messages about freedom behind East Europe's Iron Curtain on July 4, 1950.

In 1952, VFW Posts and Auxiliaries took an active leadership role in the Crusade for Freedom, launched by the American Heritage Foundation which was headed by Henry Ford II. The crusade raised money for additional RFE transmitters. It also financed a barrage of helium-filled "Wings of Freedom" balloons to drift across the Iron Curtain bearing messages of hope. Within two years, more than 18,000 "Freedom Scrolls" were distributed through VFW and Auxiliary channels as part of the campaign. "Truth dollar" contributions paid for words on the scrolls. In 1955, "Phone for Freedom" also began to raise funds.

Commander-in-Chief Merton B. Tice toured RFE installations to assess their effectiveness. He found "the people know they are hearing the truth from the lips of their own citizens. Radio Free Europe is a powerful force for the rebirth of freedom."

By 1960, 28 transmitters and a million watts of power beamed programs in five East European languages. The Russians spent $100 million each year to jam RFE broadcasts because, as Senior Vice-Commander-in-Chief Byron G. Gentry noted, "The greatest Communist fear is the fear of truth."

Gentry and others in a fact-finding party traveled along the barbed-wire and watch-towered frontier that separated the two Germanys. "We were protected by an armed escort of jeeps," he reported, "each with mounted, loaded and manned machine guns." To Gentry, who had served with the Army in Europe during WWII, "the long hanging belts of cartridges brought back bitter memories, somber and forbidding, of my last visit to this troubled land."

Junior Vice Commander-in-Chief Richard W. Homan (right) speaks his mind about freedom on the near side of the infamous Berlin Wall in 1966. Homan was among 30 U.S. civic and business leaders who inspected Radio Free Europe's facilities in West Germany and Portugal.

On VFW's other major front, threats were equally obvious. A Commission on Organization of the Executive Branch of the Government, known as the Hoover Commission, began serious assaults on veterans health care in 1953.

The former President wanted no more VA hospitals built and to sell or shut down those judged to be poor economic performers. His commission intended to deny treatment to veterans with non-service-connected disabilities who had not shown need for medical care within three years of discharge. Those with the same disabilities were to be denied treatment unless they signed what amounted to a pauper's oath. Hoover's commission planned to reduce or halt

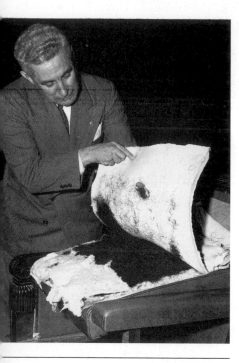

Van Zandt inspects a bullet hole in the chair occcpuied by Rep. Clifford Davis (D-Tenn.) when he was hit by a pistol round fired by Puerto Rican terrorists on March 1, 1954, in a shooting spree from the gallery. Van Zandt risked his life to disarm a would-be assassin. Three other lawmakers were wounded in the fusillade.

pensions and disability allowances after penetrating reviews of the cases on file. The American Medical Association (AMA) joined the attack.

VFW counterattacked with its own investigations. Members of the VFW Veterans Affairs Committee became increasingly familiar to the White House staff. The three-year struggle ended with an agreement by VFW that no new hospitals were needed—at least for the moment— but that those already under construction would be completed and older facilities would be re-equipped.

No public servant was more vehement in his objections to the sweep of the Hoover Commission than Rep. James E. Van Zandt, already a legendary VFW figure and three times re-elected as the representative from Pennsylvania's 23rd District.

Van Zandt had vacated his seat to rejoin the Navy on Sept. 23, 1943, and left for the Pacific to command LST Group 19, part of LST Flotilla 7. His CO, Capt. Richard M. Scruggs, wrote a commendation for the energetic commander: "You have made a record for D-Day participation and troops and cargo carried that in my opinion no other flotilla can equal. You have been bombed, shelled and torpedoed, but the fires were extinguished, the holes plugged, and not a ship has been lost."

Van Zandt returned to Congress in 1946 and was continually re-elected. He earned praise from his constituents and Americans in general after the events of March 1, 1954. At 2:32 p.m. a fusillade of pistol shots erupted from the House gallery. Slugs ripped through chairs and desks; ricochets sang through the chamber. A Puerto Rican flag sailed from the balcony.

The shots were fired by a group of handgun-wielding Puerto Rican nationalists. Van Zandt instinctively hit the floor when the first round was fired. He started a combat crawl to the cloakroom and then up the stairs leading to the gallery where he wrested the pistol clutched by one of the male terrorists.

When it was over, five representatives lay wounded on the floor and all four Puerto Rican gunmen and women — proponents of independence for the island — were in handcuffs. No one disputed that Jimmie Van Zandt deserved an additional oak leaf cluster to the Bronze Star he already had.

Inquisitions aimed at gutting veterans benefits continued. A second team known collectively as the Bradley Commission arose in 1956 during Dwight D. Eisenhower's first term as President. Van Zandt observed that this new body of ferrets "took up where the Hoover Commission left off."

Two VFW commanders-in-chief had to deal with this new threat. The first, Timothy J. Murphy, served as a line officer aboard a carrier in the Pacific. Murphy was one of 10 brothers who wore the uniform during WWII—three of whom were killed in action. The second Chief, Cooper T. Holt, also saw action in the Pacific, but as a rifleman with the 164th Infantry Regiment, American (23rd) Division.

Eisenhower inherited an $85 billion budget and was leery of excess expenditures and the growth of what he called the "military-industrial complex." But neither Murphy nor Holt believed that Eisenhower— once supreme commander of Allied Forces in Europe — would fail the veterans who had crushed Hitler and the Japanese warlords.

FIRING SQUAD — 1956 MODEL

Eisenhower was incensed when the Senate quashed 16 veterans bills, then voted itself a 50 percent pay raise. He was further angered when the Bradley Report characterized wartime service as "nothing special," merely another duty to be welcomed by citizens. Eisenhower replied that "war duty was indeed extraordinary service," then shelved the Bradley Report and let it gather dust.

An unofficial armistice between Congress and organized veterans began in 1957. Disability payments were increased by 24 percent to totally disabled veterans and a 10 percent increase went to those with disabilities of 50 percent or more. A new veterans housing bill raised the interest rate from 4 1/2 percent to 4 3/4 percent— but was compensated for by providing an additional $300 million for direct housing loans in rural areas and small towns.

In 1958, pensions were increased for the dwindling number of veterans and widows from the Indian wars, Mexican War (1846-1848), Civil War (1861-1865) and Spanish-American War (1898).

The following year, VFW came under criticism from ambassadors abroad, members of Congress and Vice President Richard M. Nixon. The new commander-in chief, Louis G. Feldmann, summed up the criticism: "While we called ourselves Veterans of Foreign Wars because we fought overseas, we had never sent a commander-in-chief overseas to observe, on behalf of our organization, those countries that had a radical change in government during or since Word War II."

Feldmann, a former Parris Island (Marine boot camp in South Carolina) drill instructor and veteran of the 9th Marines in the Pacific, worked out an ambitious tour sponsored by the U.S. Information Agency. Together with his aide, Vice Adm. Leland P. Lovette, Feldmann took off from New York on Feb. 23, 1960, to begin a 10-week, 21-nation odyssey.

In his briefcase was a telegram from a recent critic: "I want to congratulate you on undertaking this important mission. Your travels will enable you to gain a broader understanding of the thinking and aspirations of the countries you visit, and I wish you the greatest success. Your dedication is doing much

to serve our country." Dick Nixon

Feldmann experienced the homicidal tendencies of Japanese drivers on Tokyo's streets and wished for a tank. He was invited to exchange viewpoints with the director of the Japanese Veterans Association and found he had similar benefits' problems. His party was steered around violent Communist demonstrations and Feldmann observed: "The Communists are not great in number — but they are well-organized and have their fingers in newspapers, among teachers and most important, the labor unions. This should be emphasized to our people back in the States."

He gave a purposely provocative interview to *Stars and Stripes* in which he said: "The great belief of veterans that all they have to do is ask, and it will be granted is a fallacy. The truth is, unless veterans organizations are strong they will never get anything."

At each stop, Feldmann recorded 10-minute radio talks for later re-broadcast by the Voice of America. *This is Lou Feldmann talking from Kowloon…This is Lou Feldmann talking from Tehran….This is Lou Feldmann talking from Rome…This is Lou Feldmann talking from Beirut…*became familiar phrases in the Near East and Europe as he and Lovette made their way across continents.

They were treated like visiting royalty everywhere they went. He was a guest of Nehru and Indira Gandhi in India. He explained the operations of VFW to the crown prince of Thailand.

In Ankara, Turkey, Feldmann was made an honorary member of the Turkish Disabled Veterans and given a ceremonial tour of the impressive marble tomb of Ataturk, their great national hero. Turkish guards, a "pretty snappy looking outfit," presented arms. He later learned that only two other such ceremonial tours had ever been staged—one for Eisenhower and the other for a Russian field marshal.

In Beirut, Lebanon, they were welcomed by retired Marine Col. William A. Eddy, former ambassador to Saudi Arabia and one of the great Middle East experts. Eddy, a veteran of both world wars, was born in Lebanon of missionary parents and was fluent in Arabic and several other languages. A visit to an outlying Palestinian refugee camp made a strong impression on both Feldmann and Lovette. The scene was reminiscent of the outdoor hovels that littered the European landscape after World War II.

Feldmann learned that more than $24 million a year was gathered to feed these refugees — with the U.S. footing 70 percent of the bill — but that only 9 cents worth of food a day per person reached the hungry. There were then more than 1 million Palestinian refugees. To Feldmann, the refugee problem was a "tinder box that might erupt into flames at any moment."

VFW 's delegation returned to the States on April 30, after 66 days of what Feldmann called one of the most enriching — and occasionally sobering — experiences of his life. He cautioned Americans "not to forget that the new countries of the world want one thing most of all — complete

Commander-in-Chief Louis G. Feldmann (right) traveled extensively to feel the pulse of the nation. In 1960, he visits Bergstrom Air Force Base near Austin, Texas, during a fact-finding mission.

He is seen with Base Commander Col. Frank E. Marek under the nose of a B-52 capable of delivering nuclear payloads to the Soviet Union.

and unbinding sovereignty. They do not want to be the vassal of any state or any world power. If we help them in that direction we can make a substantial contribution to world peace."

Douglas MacArthur was among the first to greet the world traveler. He put his arm around Lou Feldmann for photographers and said, "I want to do this to show the American public that I appreciate the Veterans of Foreign Wars. It is the greatest organization in the world."

No sooner had Feldmann turned over VFW leadership to the new commander-in-chief than the cease-fire against veterans was broken. Ted C. Connell, a WWII artilleryman, found the guns turned in his direction.

Kiplinger's *Changing Times* magazine accused the government of "squandering tax funds on able-bodied and well-to-do veterans." It blamed groups like the VFW for the "boondoggle."

Taking a cue from Kiplinger, a writer named Fletcher Knebel used *Look* magazine as a gunnery platform to fire a broadside at the VA, calling it a "haven for evaders and chiselers." The insult did not form the basis for a libel suit, but it drew heavy return fire from Omar Ketchum and from VA Administrator J. S. Gleason, Jr. "Inferences of this nature," replied Gleason, "are a serious and totally unwarranted reflection on honest and dedicated VA employees and the disabled and deceased veterans on whose behalf they are privileged to serve."

Civil service workers at Wright-Patterson Air Force Base in Ohio joined the assault after a reduction-in-force cost them their jobs. Those affected hired lawyers to challenge the *Veterans Preference Act of 1944* as "unfair." After expensive litigation that paid off only for the attorneys, the suit failed in the Ohio Federal District Court and in the U.S. Court of Federal Appeals.

A court case of another sort emerged next — this one in the court of public opinion. The Internal Revenue Service targeted one of America's most respected heroes. Sgt. Alvin C. York was a backwoods Tennessee farmer who wrestled with a newly found

"I want to do this to show the American public that I appreciate the Veterans of Foreign Wars. It is the greatest organization in the world."

Gen. Douglas MacArthur

In March 1961, Commander-in-Chief Ted. C. Connell meets with Texas Rep. Olin "Tiger" Teague (at right) and Rep. William H. Ayres of Ohio, the ranking Republican member of the Committee on Veterans Affairs. Both congressmen were staunch VFW supporters.

On July 1, 1941, Sgt. Alvin C. York arrives in New York City for the premiere of his movie *Sergeant York*. At York's left is Hollywood producer Jesse Lasky.

The exploits of Sgt. York as a WWI infantryman who single-handedly captured 132 Germans in 1918 were recalled in this film. VFW Post 599 formed a guard of honor.

In 1960, the Internal Revenue Service went after the Medal of Honor recipient, demanding $25,000. VFW members sprang to his defense, donating cash and appearing on national television to explain his plight. York was a member of Post 5017 in Jamestown, Tenn.

Christian conscience before accepting the idea of being drafted to kill other Christians, that is, German soldiers in World War I.

In 1918, York single-handedly flanked a hill where German machine guns were slaughtering his buddies. Using deadly marksmanship honed while bagging wild turkeys for the dinner table, the Tennessean shot down enemy gunners as fast as he could work the bolt of his Springfield.

When the action ended, 25 dead Germans lay sprawled where York had "tetched them off." Some 132 others — with their hands in the air — came down the hill in front of the lanky American buck sergeant. Gen. John J. Pershing pinned the Medal of Honor to York's uniform. York returned to the hills a national hero to resume the simple life.

In 1941, Hollywood produced a film starring Gary Cooper based on York's life and his exploits in the Argonne — an honest portrayal that inspired other Americans who soon would face similar challenges. York was paid $160,000 for the rights — money York turned over to the local high school. He refused $1 million in movie and book offers because he believed it was wrong to profit from killing.

Nearly 20 years after the film and 42 years after York was awarded the nation's highest decoration, the IRS went after him with a vengeance. It demanded $25,000 in back taxes, interest and penalties — a sum York could barely imagine, much less pay.

The nation rallied to the defense of this aging veteran. Speaker of the House Sam Rayburn set up a fund for the beleaguered York. VFW's Ted Connell donated $1,000 to the York fund and appeared on the Ed Sullivan Show to explain York's plight to millions of television viewers. A national magazine, *Cavalier* — whose editor, Robert S. Curran, was a Purple Heart recipient of the 95th Infantry Division — published a piece called "The Desertion of Sergeant York." The article called attention to a bureaucracy that defamed an icon of battlefield courage and treated him like a tax evader.

York, then 73 and confined to a wheelchair, paid his taxes. He was a member of Post 5017 in Jamestown, Tenn. and had appeared at various VFW functions over the years, including the Los Angeles convention in 1940.

A new Administration took over in 1961. Commander-in-Chief Robert E. Hansen was readily admitted to the John F. Kennedy White House. Both men had served in the U.S. Navy — Kennedy as a PT boat commander and Hansen as an enlisted crewman aboard a transport plane in the Aleutians.

Kennedy put Hansen at ease during his first visit to the Oval Office. The President, seated in his trademark rocking chair, grinned and said, "Now, commander, you realize that I'm an old VFW Post commander — so don't try to give me any guff." Hansen, who knew very well that the President once led Post 5880 in Brockton, Mass., said he wouldn't dream of it. The promising relationship between VFW and Kennedy was cut short on Nov. 22, 1963, when he was assassinated.

His successor, Lyndon Johnson, came into office looking for places to cut the budget to pay for his sweeping social reforms. He turned automatically to the VA, calling for the closing of 32 hospitals. Reaction was immediate. VFW South Dakota State Commander Raymond Gallagher made a point that was not lost on Capitol Hill. "There is something wrong with our democracy if the President can execute with the stroke of a pen and Congress is powerless to stop it."

VFW Commander-in-Chief John A. "Buck" Jenkins, a former artillery officer, commented, "Evidently, the Great Society is not for veterans." Then he launched a counterattack. He created "Truth Squads" whose members spent weeks presenting facts to counter what Jenkins called "double talk" from VA administrators. VFW achieved a victory: Johnson backed off in a compromise that saved 15 VA hospitals threatened with closure in 1965.

An even greater threat loomed on the horizon that would require the beds in VA hospitals — a land war in Asia. During Johnson's campaign against Arizona Sen. Barry Goldwater in 1964, he told Oklahomans, "We don't want American boys to do the fighting for Asian boys." In Pittsburgh, Johnson reiterated his vow: "There can be, and will be, as long as I am President, peace for all Americans." The Vietnam War would last more than eight years.

Cooper T. Holt recalled a visit he and Commander-in-Chief Andy Borg had with Lyndon Johnson in 1966: "Andy knew LBJ through and through. Andy and I were invited by LBJ to the big map room where he pointed to a picture of an American tank sitting in a clearing. 'See that damn tank?' he asked. 'That [SOB] won't move until *I* tell it to.'" Holt remembered: "We walked out of that room convinced that it was purely a political war. VFW's attitude toward the *purpose* of the war changed at that moment."

Democratic Party presidential nominee Sen. John F. Kennedy flanked by Senior Vice Commander-in-Chief Robert E. Hansen at the 1960 VFW convention in Detroit. A former Post commander, Kennedy was co-chairman of VFW's 1946 Boston National Convention.

GIs of the 3rd Bn., 60th Inf., 9th Inf. Div., parade through Seattle on July 10, 1969. They were members of the first major unit (814 men) to be withdrawn from Vietnam.

VFW Posts provided moral support to troops in the field as well as fighting for their rights when they returned home.

President Lyndon Johnson signs the Vietnam War-era GI Bill of Rights on March 3, 1966. Commander-in-Chief Andy Borg (shaking hands with Johnson) and Washington Office Executive Director Cooper T. Holt were on hand for the ceremony.

Texas Rep. Olin E. Teague, HVAC chairman, said "Its [GI Bill] final enactment is due in no small part to the efforts of VFW."

Turmoil at home increased in proportion to U.S. involvement in a war that seemed to have no end with no clear goals.

Protesters trooped around the White House waving Vietcong flags. An anti-war parade down Fifth Avenue in New York attracted 14,000 marchers. University of Wisconsin students tried unsuccessfully to arrest the commander of Truax Air Force Base as a "war criminal." In Berkeley, Calif., protesters sprawled on the tracks in an effort to halt troop trains. These were just a few of the actions in '65.

Draft cards and U.S. flags were burned — always with prior notice to TV stations so the cameras would be rolling. Campus riots became a steady feature of the American way of life. Increasing numbers of draft-age youths fled to Canada to avoid conscription.

Many veterans who returned from Vietnam, either whole or maimed, were treated like pariahs. Peter Forgues wrote to the VFW: "We returned to civilian life and discovered the crackpots, the ignorant and the misguided. Few knew or cared about what we had been doing in Vietnam. I was told I had been involved in a dirty war. Bitterness was in me.

"True Americans stepped forward to aid the fighting men and veterans of Vietnam and their families ... The VFW did not 'coast out' this black period— the men of the VFW sought out us veterans, clasping our hands, welcoming us back and invited us to join them." (Chapter 11 details, in depth, specifically how VFW supported GIs during the Vietnam War.)

Shunned except by their own, Vietnam veterans sought camaraderie. More than 500,000 of them ultimately joined VFW. They wanted to be among those who had shared the hell of combat—men who knew what you were talking about when you spoke of Charlie, C-rats and Claymores. And of tree lines, Lurps, K-bars, corpsmen, Willie Peter and "The World."

Knowing full well their plight, VFW began the battle for benefits almost as soon as the first Marines waded ashore at DaNang in March 1965.

The *Veterans Readjustment Benefits Act of 1966* (Vietnam GI Bill) was reluctantly signed by President Lyndon Johnson on March 3, 1966. The fight for the bill on Capitol Hill was led by two men from Texas: Sen. Ralph Yarborough and Rep. Olin E. "Tiger" Teague. Yarborough, the principal author of the bill, said, "The VFW was a tower of strength in lending its support to a comprehensive bill rather than a limited measure." Teague commented that final enactment "was due in no small part to the efforts of the Veterans of Foreign Wars. In the final weeks, VFW national officers were working daily to assist in its enactment."

Johnson favored a so-called "hot spot" bill that would have restricted benefits to war zone veterans only, unlike the all-encompassing Korea and WWII-era bills. Congress prevailed, though, and the act covered anyone on active duty during the Vietnam era. To get the equivalent of a full, four-year college education, a vet had to serve 36 months. Later, 1.5 months of college eligibility would be given for each month of service. A vet was entitled to GI Bill benefits for eight years after discharge, later extended to 10 years.

But unlike WWII when veterans were paid separately for subsistence and tuition, Vietnam and Korea vets received a single monthly payment to cover all expenses. This effectively ruled out attending a prestigious private university. In 1947, 59 percent of students at Harvard were veterans; only 1.5 percent were in 1972. The discrepancy in opportunity was glaring.

SHOW HIM WHERE YOU STAND
KEEP YOUR V.F.W. MOVING
By Leslie M. Fry
Commander-in-Chief, V.F.W.

Battles had to be waged to secure increases to keep pace with inflation so more vets could take advantage of the Bill. By October 1969, for instance, only 25 percent of eligibles were using its benefits. In April 1970, President Richard Nixon signed an amendment boosting stipends by more than one-third. The amendment also provided extra money for tutoring and created an outreach program to better inform potential participants.

Two years later, the *Vietnam Era Veterans Readjustment Assistance Act* raised the monthly college stipend for a single vet to $220. Colleges were encouraged to establish special veterans programs through the Veterans Cost-of-Instruction program. Another monthly increase of 22.7 percent was passed over President Gerald Ford's veto on Dec. 3, 1974. Education benefits, after a 10-year extension, came to an end for Vietnam-era veterans in December 1989.

States also provided financial rewards to resident vets. Ten states — Connecticut, Delaware, Illinois, Louisiana, Massachusetts, North Dakota, Pennsylvania, South Dakota, Vermont and Washington — gave one-time cash bonuses ranging from $100-$750.

The real fight would be for two forms of assistance unique to the Vietnam War — Agent Orange and Post-Traumatic Stress Disorder (PTSD) compensation. But before such compensation was awarded, a far more fundamental struggle had to be fought— one that has never been fully won and again, is peculiar to this war. As the authors of *The Vietnam Veteran* found: "To win the battle to gain benefits, they would first have to lose the battle for pride against persistent stereotypes."

Perhaps those unjustified stereotypes were part of a societal problem. Newspaper columnist James Reston wrote: "There has been a sharp decline in respect for authority in the United States — a decline in respect not only for

In early 1967, when draft dodgers were teaching a course called "How to Dodge the Draft," when fighting men returning from Vietnam were pariahs, when patriotism was considered naive, VFW Commander-in-Chief Leslie M. Fry addressed members through *VFW* magazine.

He asked: "Who speaks for the veteran who has given the best years of his life for his country? *You do.*"

civil authority of government, but also for the moral authority of schools, universities, the press, the church and even the family. Something has happened to American life...something not yet understood, something different, important, and probably enduring."

Issues specific to Vietnam were not the only ones on the veterans affairs front during the 1970s. VFW actions included creating and protecting the Senate Veterans Affairs Committee and fighting for age-old rights such as veterans preference.

Texas Rep. Ray Roberts praised VFW in 1978. "Once again, congratulations are in order for your fine organization and its leadership at every level. In spite of all the pressure the Carter Administration brought to bear on Congress, veterans preference in federal employment has been preserved."

Taking on the VA was part of the decade's trials, too. Relations between VFW and the head of the VA, Donald Johnson, had never been good. When Johnson denied Vietnam vets dental care, relations reached flash point. Commander-in-Chief Raymond A. Gallagher, a WWII Navy veteran, called on President Richard Nixon. He left the White House with a promise to release $15.9 million held in bureaucratic limbo by the Office of Management and Budget (OMB).

Afterward, Gallagher and Johnson appeared on Ed Newman's NBC talk show to celebrate the VA's 40th anniversary. Gallagher gritted his teeth while Johnson sang the praises of his administration—it had never been in better shape, or so he said. Enraged, Gallagher took the microphone and said VA facilities were "rat-infested, short of staff and critically underfunded."

Nixon then told VA's Johnson and the OMB to take another look at the problems within their own agencies. Texas' Rep. Olin E. "Tiger" Teague and Sen. Alan Cranston of California reached for clichés to express their indignation. "Like putting a fox in charge of the hen house," said Teague. Cranston added, "Like putting Dracula in charge of the blood bank." The Disabled American Veterans, Paralyzed Veterans of America and Veterans of World War I added their voices to the call for Johnson's ouster. But Nixon stuck by Johnson while trying to force an end to the war.

Still, the campaign to force Donald Johnson out of office finally succeeded in June 1974 when he resigned under fire. He was replaced by a man to veterans liking, Richard L. Roudebush, an Army veteran with five battle stars on his ETO ribbon. From Indiana, Roudebush had been VFW Chief in 1957-58 and served in the House of Representatives from 1961-1970.

On Aug. 9, 1974, Nixon himself resigned. He was replaced by Gerald R. Ford. One of Ford's first acts angered Roudebush and vets who had been in

This oil painting of Past Commander-in-Chief Richard L. Roudebush (1957-58) was donated by the VFW to the Indianapolis VA Medical Center upon the renaming of the center in Roudebush's honor in 1982.

Roudebush served as a representative in Congress for 10 years (1961-70) and as VA administrator, 1974-76.

Vietnam: He granted conditional clemency to draft dodgers and deserters. Ford said some could earn a special "clemency discharge" provided they worked in VA hospitals. Many deserters during the war did not fit the stereotype: They went AWOL *after* their Vietnam tour of duty for reasons unrelated to politics.

Ford's successor, Jimmy Carter, was largely an unknown. He was an Annapolis graduate and nuclear submarine commander. Yet unlike Ford, Carter granted unconditional amnesty to those who had refused to serve. The new VFW Chief, R.D. "Bulldog" Smith, called the move an "insult to every man who has fought and died for his country and to all the men who have served honorably in the armed forces."

Smith, who had been an aviation engineer with the 20th Air Force during WWII, also took on Illinois Sen. Adlai Stevenson III, who wanted to dismantle the Senate Veterans Committee. That committee had become a reality only in 1971, after a 25-year struggle by VFW — now, six years later, Stevenson wanted it abolished.

In response, Smith summoned a spectrum of VFW resources. The Ladies Auxiliary made thousands of telephone calls to Capitol Hill. Letters from Departments around the country flooded in. Encouraged by South Carolina's Sen. Strom Thurmond, VFW mustered 3,000 members who gathered in a winter blizzard to protest. "Grass-roots politics at its best," said Smith.

The debate before the Rules and Administration Committee drew support from a host of senators — some vets, some not. Here is how it went:

Sen. Robert Dole (Kansas): "To maintain the trust of our veterans we should retain the committee as it is."

Sen. Gary Hart (Colorado): "It is important that the Senate continue the commitment, especially regarding the problems of our younger veterans."

Sen. Hubert H. Humphrey (Minnesota): "Why did we get a veterans committee? They are special, they are different, they served their country, they have special needs."

Sen. John Tower (Texas): "It is essential that we in Congress retain a committee structure that recognizes the singular

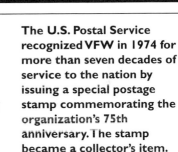

The U.S. Postal Service recognized VFW in 1974 for more than seven decades of service to the nation by issuing a special postage stamp commemorating the organization's 75th anniversary. The stamp became a collector's item.

When President Jimmy Carter assumed office in January 1977, one of his first acts was to grant unconditional amnesty to those who evaded service during the Vietnam War.

Commander-in-Chief R.D. "Bulldog" Smith called the move an "insult to every man who has fought and died for his country."

> **"I wish to commend the Veterans of Foreign Wars for its leadership. Without the formidable efforts of this great veterans organization, the committee [Senate Veterans Affairs] would have been lost and the interests of veterans and dependents would have been subordinated to the endless demands of the social welfare system."**
> Sen. Strom Thurmond
> South Carolina

importance of the debt the American people owe to their veterans."

VFW was victorious. Thurmond told the Senate: "I wish to commend the Veterans of Foreign Wars for its leadership. Without the formidable efforts of this great veterans organization, the committee would have been lost and the interests of veterans and dependents would have been subordinated to the endless demands of the social welfare system."

Veterans affairs were not VFW's only concern in the '70s. Defense and foreign policy have always been high priorities with the organization. So proposed ratification of the treaties to turn over the Panama Canal to the Panamanians prompted one of VFW's most memorable battles. "Saving the Canal" was the emphasis of the organization's programs in 1977-78. A hard-hitting editorial in *VFW* magazine launched the campaign in July 1977. Resolutions, petitions, letters and bumper stickers followed. "Truth Squads" led by VFW National Security Director F. Phelps Jones explained that the Canal was vital to defense.

All these efforts culminated in a March 7, 1978, rally on the steps of the Capitol Building. Some 3,000 members demonstrated. Besides the Senate Veterans Affairs Committee protest, this was the first VFW-sponsored national rally since the days of the Depression-era bonus fight. Jimmy Van Zandt called the Canal "the greatest issue of the day." *VFW* magazine's November 1977 cover boasted — "The Canal: It's Ours; Let's Keep It!" But it was all for naught. The Carter Administration prevailed.

Though disappointed over the final outcome, VFW Chief John Wasylik said: "We are satisfied that this organization and others concerned about the future of this great country did force the government to make some very necessary amendments it tried to avoid."

Conflicts with the Carter Administration continued. When Howard E. Vander Clute, Jr., assumed office as VFW commander-in chief in 1979, he launched a broadside. "Today," he said, "we see the Administration laughing at Congress and doing as it pleases. We see the director of the VA — who should be the champion of veterans programs — applauding each cut and backing each piece of negative legislation, instead of fighting for adequate care for veterans and veterans programs."

Vander Clute addressed the Senate and House Veterans Affairs committees, lambasting VA head Max Cleland (a paraplegic Vietnam vet) for failure to restore 3,100 beds to VA hospitals ordered by Congress. He pointed to the fact that between 1962 and 1979, the veterans population increased by 8 million, while VA hospital beds were cut by 34,800.

Carter's intransigence on the VA hospital system and the Panama Canal issue forced a decision VFW had avoided for years — formation of a Political Action Committee (PAC). The issue was resolved during the 1979 national convention in New Orleans. The televised debate ended with a majority of "yea" votes cast by delegates. VFW-PAC would endorse and funnel voluntary contributions only to those presidential and congressional candidates who advocated a strong national defense and the preservation of veterans benefits.

Cooper T. Holt, past Chief and executive director of VFW's Washington office, was appointed PAC's first director. Holt had his hands full with Carter. Interest rates soared to 16 percent under Carter, but he insisted on what he called "straight line budgets" for VA hospitals. Congress approved the purchase of nine CAT scanners — Carter released funds for two. Carter vetoed the *VA Health Care Personnel Act* designed to restore previous cuts in hospital beds and staff. The House and Senate overrode his veto 401-5 and 85-0, respectively, to hand Carter the worst defeat of a presidential veto ever.

In January 1981, Carter was replaced by Ronald Reagan, many of whose defense policies were in line with those of VFW. He took a strong anti-Communist stand overseas and increased defense spending. Reagan — the first President endorsed by the VFW PAC — was immensely popular among many veterans, even though he had served stateside during World War II.

As a candidate for President in 1980, he horrified remnants of the anti-war movement when he told delegates to the August national convention that the Vietnam War "was, in truth, a noble cause...They [Vietnam veterans] fought as well and as bravely as any Americans have ever fought in any war. They deserve our gratitude, our respect and our continuing concern."

Eight years later, well into his second term, President Reagan would tell those gathered at the 1988 Washington Conference: "I'd travel halfway around the world to meet with the VFW."

Commander-in-Chief (1982-83) James R. Currieo — former Army sergeant major, Korean War vet and later executive director of VFW's

More than 3,000 determined VFW members rally on the Capitol Building steps to protest President Carter's plans to relinquish U.S. control of the Panama Canal.

Despite its best efforts, this major VFW campaign failed. On March 7, 1978, the Senate ratified Carter's treaty, handing over the Canal to the Panamanians in the year 2000.

Past Commander-in-Chief Cooper T. Holt, executive director of the Washington Office, hugs Jamie Weaver, 1975 National Poster Child for the March of Dimes.

More than 20 years earlier, MD's president said "members of your organization have shown boundless ingenuity, imagination and devotion to the cause."

In 1983, President Ronald Reagan signs a bill widening job opportunities for Vietnam and Korean War veterans.

Standing behind the President, left to right: Commander-in-Chief James Currieo, Quartermaster General J.A. Cheatham, VA Administrator Harry N. Walters, Washington Office Executive Director Cooper T. Holt and Senior Vice Commander-in-Chief Clifford G. Olson, Jr.

VFW conducted an open hearing on Agent Orange held by the VFW Rockland County (N.Y.) Council in 1980. Maxine Hartley (second from left), of Orange and Rockland Utilities Co., is honored for helping make the forum a success.

With her are the chairmen: Council Junior Vice Commander Joseph Cardone, Council Commander Arthur Mikayelian and Post 2973 Junior Vice Commander Glenn Taylor, the co-chairman.

At last year's first open forum on Agent Orange held by the Rockland County, N.Y., Council...

Washington office —visited Reagan in the White House to stir action on an issue still festering from the Vietnam War. That issue would emerge as one the most controversial in the history of the veterans movement.

Agent Orange compensation had recently risen to the top of the agenda. Vietnam veterans who suffered from the effects of the chemical defoliant that had withered entire forests in Vietnam found relief nowhere.

So, VFW prodded VA and Congress to resolve the controversy. News stories in the *Washington Action Reporter* and *VFW* magazine heightened awareness among members, politicians and the concerned public. VFW representatives appeared before the House Veterans Affairs Committee and documented the debilitating effects of the infamous herbicide.

As early as 1978, VFW's Department service officers (stationed at VA centers) urged veterans to file claims for exposure to Agent Orange. VFW reports were issued in October 1980 and June 1981 indicating that VA had failed to pursue Agent Orange claims.

Two years went by; the VA took no action. It wasn't until 1984 that Congress passed the *Dioxin and Radiation Exposure Compensation Standards Act*. President Reagan signed *S.1651,* acknowledging government responsibility for treatment of and eventual compensation to exposed Vietnam veterans.

In the '90s, disability compensation was provided to Vietnam veterans for nine ailments related to exposure. Included on the list in September 1993 was lung cancer. "Including lung cancer on the list was a big step forward," said Fred Juarbe, director of VFW's National Veterans Service. "It was one of the more contentious ailments attributed to the chemical defoliant."

The list of diseases grew again on May 28, 1996. Vietnam veterans afflicted with prostate cancer and acute and subacute peripheral neuropathy were also entitled to disability payments based on their exposure to Agent Orange.

These decisions were preceded by a review of a report issued in March 1996 by the National Academy of Sciences on the long-term health effects of exposure to Agent Orange. Another finding in the report was a possible link between Agent Orange exposure and veterans children with spina bifida.

Congress enacted the *Agent Orange Benefits Act of 1996* in response. Based on three levels, it provides monetary, health and vocational assistance to Vietnam veterans' children with spina bifida. This was the first time children of American servicemen ever received compensation for health problems related to war. "VFW took a leading role in this legislation," said Wayne Thompson, VFW's Department of Colorado judge advocate and an activist on this issue.

VFW's National Veterans Service took the lead in securing first-ever benefits for the children of veterans afflicted with an Agent Orange-related ailment in 1998.

Vietnam vet Jim Hudson and son Jeremy now receive compensation for spina bifida, a possible consequence of Jim's exposure to Agent Orange.

Internally, VFW also was busy during the post-Vietnam War years. It launched an intensive recruiting drive. Because the organization loses about 7 percent of its members a year, that meant 180,000 new members would have to be added to the rolls. At the 1984 National Convention, delegates cheered when they learned that the 2-million member mark had been reached and even exceeded by an additional 149 members. Howard Vander Clute ranked reaching that membership milestone among the VFW's greatest achievements.

Much of the groundwork for that achievement was laid years before by two men who left indelible marks on VFW. Julian Dickenson served as adjutant general for some 30 years (1950-81). When he died soon after retirement in 1981, *VFW* magazine offered the highest praise: "More than any other man in the post-WWII history of the VFW, Mr. Dickenson molded and shaped the organization into the vigorous and aggressive association of overseas veterans that it is today." Few would disagree with that assessment.

Al Cheatham was among the giants who served on VFW's staff. Taking over as quartermaster general in 1962, he had $5 million in assets to work with. When he retired in 1985, those assets had ballooned to $100 million. All told, he had registered 40 years of unflagging service to VFW. Cheatham, who now resides in Springfield, Mo., set a sterling record of financial integrity.

Membership Growth Chart

1899	>100
1910	1,000
1915	5,000
1920	15,000
1921	60,000
1928	69,976
1936	199,999
1942	240,952
1945	741,310
1946	1,544,444
1983	1,960,000
1984	2,000,149
1990	2,103,564
1992	2,167,788

Federal finances were another matter. Budget battles were destined to plague veterans programs. A fresh imbroglio erupted in the early 1980s over a long-time nemesis, the Office of Management and Budget. Director David Stockman said professional soldiers were more interested in pensions than in national defense. Benefits accrued to retired military personnel, he said, were a "sacred cow" beyond the reach of budget cutters. *VFW* magazine called for Stockman's ouster — he resigned before Reagan could fire him.

But matters were not always rocky during the decade. By 1987, there were 29 million veterans in the country; the time had come to elevate the Veterans Administration to Cabinet status—a move VFW had long advocated. In the House, New York Rep. Gerald Solomon, among others, fought long and hard for it. Sen. Strom Thurmond introduced the bill creating the Department of Veterans Affairs. It was signed by President Reagan on Oct. 25, 1988. Edward J. Derwinski, a life member of Post 2791 in Tinley Park, Ill., became the first secretary of veterans affairs on March 15, 1989.

Rep. G. P. "Sonny" Montgomery, chairman of the Committee on Veterans Affairs and a champion of veterans rights, wrote a letter of congratulations to his fellow VFW members: "Dear Comrades: I want to take this means to thank the Veterans of Foreign Wars for your initiative, input, support and encouragement. ... Our success has been directly related to the deep concern and involvement of the VFW on behalf of not only your members, but for all veterans ...

"The VFW should take great pride in its instrumental role in the formation and passage of legislation that has refined probably every program administered by the Veterans Administration during my eight years as chairman. ... Veterans are fortunate to have the VFW looking out for their best interests.

"I am proud to be a life member of the VFW, and I look forward to many more years of seeing those VFW caps up and down the halls of Congress." Montgomery retired from his Mississippi seat in the House in late 1995

A VFW campaign is won on Oct. 25, 1988, when President Ronald Reagan signs the bill elevating the VA to Cabinet-level rank to be known as the Department of Veterans Affairs. Rep. Gerald Solomon of New York, ranking HVAC minority member and prime House sponsor, stands at right.

Soon after the first VA secretary took his place in the Cabinet, the Administration of George Bush (1989-93) was immersed in the Middle East. The lightning campaign that drove Saddam Hussein's army out of oil-rich Kuwait in January and February 1991 required the services of 541,425 American troops in the Persian Gulf. This was the first time in a generation that a new and large pool of wartime overseas veterans had been created.

When they returned home, a number of Persian Gulf vets were afflicted, for no known reason, with severe headaches, fever, insomnia, fatigue, loss of memory, skin rashes, diarrhea, muscle spasms and general irritability. Even spouses complained of the same symptoms. Birth defects were reported where no genetic traits existed. Family doctors were helpless to diagnose the problem.

Thousands of sick vets turned to VA hospitals, where physicians were equally in the dark. As the cases grew in number, the mysterious illness was

"The VFW should take great pride in its instrumental role in the formation and passage of legislation that has refined probably every program administered by the Veterans Administration during my eight years as chairman....Veterans are fortunate to have the VFW looking out for their best interests."
Rep. "Sonny" Montgomery
Chairman, House Veterans Affairs Committee

Rep. G.V. "Sonny" Montgomery (D-Miss.), then chairman of HVAC, wrote: "I am proud to be a life member of the VFW, and I look forward to many more years of seeing those VFW caps up and down the halls of Congress."

Indiana VFW Assistant District Service Officer Bill Hays interviews *Desert Storm* veteran Diane Pettit in 1992. VFW remains in the forefront of the effort to solve the continuing mysteries of Gulf War Syndrome (GWS).

labeled Gulf War Syndrome (GWS)—but cause and cure remained elusive.

Some blamed Iraqi nerve gas, others cited anti-nerve gas pills handed out, as well as anthrax injections administered before the battle. Theories ranged from exposure to depleted uranium used in American anti-tank rounds to hypersensitivity to chemicals given in combination. It was all guesswork.

VFW began a campaign in October 1993 to resolve the mystery with a comprehensive report containing facts known at the time. On Nov. 16, VFW representatives testified during simultaneous hearings conducted by the House and Senate. VFW was the only veterans service organization (VSO) to sponsor a witness at both hearings. It was at the House hearing that VFW asserted that the Defense Department might be "stonewalling" efforts to gather data.

On April 28, 1994, VFW representatives testified before the National Institutes of Health (NIH) Technology Assessment Workshop. A week later, VFW member and Gulf vet Barry Walker testified at a hearing before the Senate Veterans Affairs Committee. The possibility that precautionary inoculations given Gulf War veterans could be the cause of GWS was explored.

Furthermore, VFW initiated its Persian Gulf Registry Survey—the first in a series documenting the illness. The survey was conducted primarily to provide a non-government source of data, as well as to allow VFW to have an unfiltered source of information. It was conducted through *VFW* magazine.(By early 1999, the registry had enrolled 1,500 Gulf War veterans.)

Then on Dec. 6, 1995, VFW provided the White House with the names of several individuals on its Gulf War Registry. One of the respondents, Tom Cross, was selected to serve on the Presidential Advisory Committee on Gulf War Veterans Illnesses. Cross was both a VFW and Action Corps member. A review of the committee's draft interim report on Jan. 24, 1996, prompted VFW to address the problem of "lost" and "misplaced" medical files to ensure that similar instances would not crop up in the future.

A review of the *Presidential Advisory Committee's Final Report* elicited VFW recommendations that the committee be granted an indefinite extension; creation of an independent entity to oversee the Pentagon's internal investigation; and creation of some type of case-definition for what was commonly called "Gulf War Syndrome." VFW

was the only VSO to publicly make such a request.

Moreover, on Oct. 3, 1996, VFW sent a communiqué to then-VA Secretary Jesse Brown calling for establishment of an open-ended presumptive period. VFW believed "that in light of available scientific and medical data, in conjunction with experiences reported by Gulf War veterans themselves, it is far too early to establish a time limit when exposure symptoms will manifest."

With diagnosis beyond reach, VFW added its weight to passage of *Public Law 103-446*, which authorized compensation from the VA for undiagnosed illnesses. While doing so, VFW won an extension to 10 years for the presumptive period to compensate ailing Persian Gulf veterans. "If that's not long enough," said National Veterans Service Director Fred Juarbe, "we will be there to continue the fight."

By the end of 1998, VA had admitted 75,500 vets for Gulf War Syndrome exams, but findings remained inconclusive. Research by VA medical staffs and by the National Academy of Health Sciences continued — but so did the headaches, nausea and wracking pain. VFW's battle on behalf of the nation's latest generation of war veterans continued as well.

Remains of an Iraqi SCUD missile, shot down near the 11th Air Defense Brigade at Riyadh, Saudi Arabia, in early February 1991.

Since the war's end, some veterans of the Persian Gulf War have experienced an affliction termed Gulf War Syndrome (GWS). VFW staffers have worked diligently for treatment of and compensation to those vets who have suffered a variety of ailments.

The VFW-sponsored Gulf War Syndrome Forum held in Washington, D.C., from Feb. 8-11, 1997, addressed the problems of veterans with baffling maladies. Testimony was constant and, at times, intense.

John R. Mucklebauer, then VFW's point man on GWS, stressed that "an open exchange of ideas is essential in addressing an issue as complicated as this one."

Veteran Gilbert Swenberg is helped along by hospital employee Ronni Miller outside the VA medical center in Fargo, N.D., in 1992.

In early 1992, VA Secretary Edward J. Derwinski, a life member of Post 2791 in Tinley Park, Ill., proposed what he called the "Rural Health Care Initiative."

It was a pilot program that would admit non-veterans to under-utilized VA hospitals in Alabama and Virginia.

VFW torpedoed Derwinski's plan: It sank when the Senate voted against it 91-3.

Ailing Persian Gulf vets, like their predecessors, also were concerned with the overall integrity of VA's health care system. This massive medical network consists of 172 hospitals, 128 nursing homes and 37 domiciles. With 268,000 employees, VA runs the largest health care system in the U.S. It is a system that came under increasing fire during the Bush Administration.

In 1992, *Washington Monthly* criticized VA for "clinging to a bureaucratic arrangement that's about as up-to-date as leech therapy—the VA is not just wasting money, it's hurting the very constituency it's supposed to help. We need an entirely new approach."

VA Secretary Derwinski tried a new approach during his third year in office, but ran afoul of veterans organizations as well as the President.

Derwinski joined forces with the Department of Health and Human Services in a pilot program allowing non-vets admittance to vacancy-heavy VA hospitals. Those targeted were located in rural Alabama and Virginia—states where VA hospitals are widely separated and few in number. Derwinski's plan was known as the Rural Health Care Initiative (RHCI).

The test program was blown apart. Veterans groups were in an uproar. Mario Ramondi, a VFW member from New York, told the press: "This proposal is a tragic error and a shameful display of unconcern for American veterans and their continued need for medical assistance." Yet the hospitals in question were almost empty, with occupancy running about 20 percent. But RHCI was not the solution most veterans had in mind, believed Commander-in-Chief Bob Wallace.

It was an election year, and Derwinski's canvass of the Senate was not encouraging. "Privately, everyone was saying, a great idea, but I can't vote for it," the secretary pointed out. "Everybody is for the veterans—there is no opposition to the VA lobby. I decided, Hell, I have a chance of getting rolled over or getting off the road."

The Senate crushed the RHCI proposal with a vote of 91-3. Derwinski was rolled over by President Bush who fired him on the eve of the 1992 election. The press credited or blamed, depending on one's perspective, VFW.

VFW advocated new plans to make the VA hospital system more accessible and more efficient without sacrificing the quality of medical care. Eligibility reform became the rallying cry of the 1990s. But planners faced formidable obstacles, both legislative and practical.

In any given year, only 10 percent of the nation's veterans used VA health care services. But that amounted to nearly 3 million individuals seeking help from a system that became a perennial target in attempts to balance the budget.

WWII vets — 6.3 million in 1998 — were at least in their mid-70s, a time when medical attention reaches its peak. VA estimated that 600,000 of them will be struck with Alzheimer's and other severely disabling conditions by the year 2000. In short, while the numbers of veterans would inevitably decrease, more of them would require long-term care.

Budget bills fixed until the year 2002, however, made no provision for inflation or cuts in Medicare and Medicaid. Then-VA Secretary Jesse Brown told *Time* magazine: "If you lock us into 1995 spending levels for the next seven years, you make assumptions that there's nobody out there to treat. A lot of people are behaving as though our veterans are already dead."

A move in the right direction was made with passage of *P.L. 104-262*, the *Veterans Health Care Eligibility Reform Act of 1996*. Signed into law Oct. 6, 1996, it took effect Oct. 1, 1998. VFW was involved in nearly 10 years of debates and drafting of provisions to make this landmark reform.

The greatest change was the way VA altered delivery of health care. Ailment- or site-specific care would be changed to comprehensive care. Once accepted into the system, veterans would become eligible for comprehensive care, which might be given at some place other than a VA-only facility.

The new act emphasizes preventive medicine and focuses on out-patient treatment when appropriate, which saves money to be used to treat more veterans. Enrollment was streamlined with a new database, the VA Patient Enrollment System. Instead of waiting for a brief annual enrollment period, veterans could register at any time. One-time processing, valid throughout the VA system, was simply updated on the enrollment anniversary date.

Dr. Kenneth W. Kizer, VA's undersecretary for health, explained to *VFW* magazine the concept of subvention as one solution to the VA-Medicare dilemma. Subvention is direct payment to the VA from Medicare and would allow veterans to use Medicare benefits at VA hospitals.

Kizer, a former Navy doctor, said: "The only people who can't use their Medicare benefits wherever they want to are veterans. If we can provide the care more cheaply and of equal or better quality, then patients ought to have

VA Secretary Jesse Brown, wearing his Americanism Award at the VFW's 1995 National Convention, addresses delegates about the need to remain vigilant. A VFW life member, the Marine Vietnam vet was the head of VA from 1993 to mid-1997.

VFW's Tactical Assessment Center (TAC), established in 1997, assists veterans secure their VA benefits.

National Veterans Service Assistant Director Jim Jewell reviews the TAC operations map. The map shows every VA medical center, community-based outpatient clinic and VA regional office in the U.S.

Looking on are (from left) Fred Burns, George Estry, George Hawley and Bill Dozier, all TAC representatives.

the right to choose." But Medicare reimbursement would be a goal delayed.

Despite great strides in eligibility reform, mandatory nursing home care is not available. With one-third of all veterans 65 or older and the percentage of vets 75 doubling by 2010, this is a critical issue. Only by investing the necessary resources into the VA system will aging veterans be properly cared for, in VFW's view.

On the plus side, 1998 ended with two legislative landmarks on the books. The *Veterans Employment Opportunities Act (S. 1021)* streamlined and strengthened the case for a redress system for veterans preference during federal layoffs. The *Veterans Programs Enhancement Act* comprised 11 sections covering everything from veterans funerals to health care for Gulf vets. Many of the latter provisions — including extending VA health care to Persian Gulf returnees through the end of 2001 — were advocated by VFW.

VA's community-based outpatient clinics are destined to play a prominent part in any medical network. Some 600 medical way stations of all types are already in operation, with 143 community-based clinics scheduled to open before the turn of the century. What the future holds in store for VA health care will preoccupy VFW well into the 21st century. Only modern medicine and the course of international events will tell.

Women Win the Right to Join

Admission of women as bona fide VFW members was a sore subject for decades. Although admitted after WWI, they were denied membership during WWII. More than 30 years passed before change occured.

In 1977, Commander-in-Chief John Wasylik's motion that women be given full membership status was voted down. Wasylik, who had seen Army nurses under combat conditions while a machine gunner in Korea, persisted.

During the 1978 convention, he told delegates: "It is only right that everyone with a campaign ribbon be eligible for membership. We are not endorsing the Equal Rights Amendment or women in combat — let's keep the question where it belongs."

Following a two-hour debate, the measure was put to a vote. It went in favor of women by 9,745 to 4,011. The men-only rule was jettisoned after too many years of stubborn resistance.

Today, women veterans — particularly as a result of the Persian Gulf War — have assumed more prominent roles in the organization. For the first time in American military history, large numbers of female veterans have become eligible by virtue of overseas campaign service.

In fact, Post 11555 in Topeka, Kan., is the first predominantly female Post in VFW history. Instituted March 12, 1995, the Post has 45 charter members, 85 percent of whom are veterans of the Persian Gulf War. That 85 percent,

Precilla Landry Wilkewitz, Louisiana's adjutant-quartermaster, became the first woman to hold that position. A Vietnam veteran, she joined Post 4224 in Baker, La., in 1980 and later became Post commander.

or 38 members, are from units — 190th Air Refueling, 410th MEDEVAC and the 129th Transportation Squadron — all based at Forbes Field in Topeka.

But simply admitting women to membership is not enough. VFW has always supported memorial efforts honoring women vets. Life member Diane Carlson Evans of Post 4393 in Northfield, Minn., led the Vietnam Women's Memorial Project from start to finish. VFW endorsed the project in 1985, and continued to raise funds ($76,000) even after the memorial's dedication in 1994.

On Oct. 18, 1997, the Women in Military Service for America Memorial in Arlington National Cemetery was dedicated. A contingent of women VFW members, state VFW officer Precilla Wilkewitz among them, was on hand. Once again, VFW contributed generously — $118,000.

A landmark for women in VFW occurred when Patricia Potter became the surgeon general for 1994-95. Potter, a Vietnam War Navy nurse who served aboard the USS Repose, is the woman who has held the highest national VFW office.

In the early '90s, VFW hired the first female veteran staff member at national headquarters. Robbie Fazen Marchant was employed as assistant director of marketing. She was later promoted to director of the VFW Foundation prior to moving on.

Women have a vital role in VFW's future, according to Department of Louisiana Adjutant-Quartermaster Precilla Wilkewitz. "I feel there is a real need for women veterans to join the organization for the sake of prosperity," she said.

Wilkewitz, who served in Vietnam from 1968-69, encourages all veterans to join VFW. "If we [veterans] weren't there in times of conflict, we wouldn't be the society we are today. We've always served this country, and we always will."

On March 12, 1995, the first all-women VFW Post was inaugurated in Topeka, Kan. With hand placed above flag, VFW Post 11555 is instituted by Past Department of Kansas Commander Lewie B. Cooper.

Chapter 9

Quest for a Full Accounting

On July 29, 1996, the remains believed to be those of an American soldier killed during the Korean War are received in Panmunjom. A United Nations honor guard stands at attention while a U.S. Army chaplain leads a prayer service.

Resolving the fate of Americans held as prisoners of war or missing in action is a mission without end.

Issues of the future — for the 21st century — will center on those who serve during, as well as after, war. VFW's long-standing tradition of concern for POWs and the missing in action dates back to 1929 when VFW completed its mission of repatriating the bodies of 86 Americans killed in North Russia (1918-19), as chronicled in Chapter 5. That same commitment was in evidence in WWII's aftermath. The organization moved quickly to secure justice for GIs captured by Japan and the Axis powers.

VFW's *H.R. 1000,* introduced Jan. 14, 1946, called for creation of a POW claims commission. Meanwhile, throughout 1947-48, Posts participated in repatriation ceremonies for servicemen being brought back home for burial. An office of national graves registration was set up in Chicago to help Posts offer honor guards for funerals.

A War Claims Commission (under *P.L. 896*) was created by Congress in 1948. However, no money was appropriated to

Members of VFW Post 577 in Tulsa, Okla., bear Seaman Louie E. Mouser to his final resting place in Tulsa Memorial Park on Jan. 8, 1948. VFW Posts across the country participated in ceremonies for America's returning WWII dead during 1947-48.

operate it until more than a year later. Shortly thereafter, VFW processed 2,000 POW claims. Another law, *P.L. 303,* set the deadline for filing claims at April 9, 1953. By then, America was nearing the end of the Korean War and a brand-new POW experience.

American POWs captured by North Koreans endured the agonies of disease-ridden camps where brutal guards, sub-zero temperatures and inadequate rations were the norm. These GIs of the 2nd Infantry Division are being held in March 1951.

Johnny Cash receives a POW/MIA flag from VFW New Jersey District 6 Commander Mel Grossman. At Grossman's right: Past Department Commander of New Jersey Ed Kwik and Past District 6 Commander Joe Scott.

Cash, who served in the Air Force in Germany during the Korean War, was an activist for the cause. The famed country singer began playing the guitar while in the military.

Many American POWs in Korea never made it to internment camps. On Aug. 17, 1950, advancing units of the 5th Cavalry Regiment, 1st Cavalry Division, encountered a bloodied American crawling toward them down a hill near Waegwan. He was Pvt. Roy Manring of Chicago, and he told a sobering tale.

Manring's outnumbered platoon surrendered to more than 300 North Koreans who stripped the Americans of their shoes, watches and wallets. They then forced them to carry water and ammo boxes up a ridge. Next, the GIs were herded into a gully flanked by Communists with raised Russian burp guns.

Manring recalled: "The Reds walked up and down the line of prisoners, firing. I was hit in the leg. I reached down and got some blood and smeared it on my head and lay down under a dead man. When they came back along the line I got shot in the arm, but didn't yell. When they left, I started crawling."

A 5th Cavalry trooper went into the gully and found 26 dead Americans. "The boys lay packed tightly, shoulder to shoulder, lying on their sides, curled like babies sleeping in the sun," he recalled. "Their feet, bloodied and bare from walking on the rocks, stuck out stiffly. Their hands were tied behind their backs, some with cord, others with regular Army communications wire."

Nor did captured Americans who reached camps inside North Korea have a guarantee of life. Some 700 POWs of the 34th Regiment, 24th Infantry Division, were pulled out of one camp and put on the road for another along the Yalu River. Behind them straggled a group of 87 civilians, including Catholic nuns, British consuls and Methodist missionaries, some of them in their 70s. (At VFW's 1998 Washington Conference, Larry Zeller — held by the Communists when he was a missionary — enthralled attendees with personal accounts of his harrowing experiences in similar situations during the war.)

The march overland to Chungganagji was made over cruel terrain in freezing rain. It began to snow. Exhausted POWs and civilians lurched from the column and collapsed by the side of the trail. They were shot one by one, along with an aged Catholic mother superior. The death march lasted 13 days, leaving almost 100 frozen corpses strung out along more than 100 miles of desolate countryside in unmarked graves.

A few American POWs escaped. Sgt. 1st Class Charles E. Ashton, now a

VFW member, was one of them. A highly decorated WWII vet, he broke free near Pyongyang after 42 days of captivity, made his way to allied lines, then carried out a rescue plan releasing 159 other Americans. When interviewed by *VFW* magazine correspondent Carl Miller in Tokyo, Ashton said he had put in a request for combat duty in Korea because "our nation's fighting men should be given assignments wherever they are best fitted to serve."

When the war ended in July 1953, 3,746 American POWs were released and sent home. Two years later, 944 POWs known to have been in North Korean hands were still unaccounted for. Graves Registration teams scoured battlefields inside South Korea's 38,000 square miles and uncovered 555 of the missing—but 389 POWs remained permanently unaccounted for. Most of the war's 8,000 missing GIs died in the North and fell into the "body not recovered" category.

VFW was among the first to welcome home POWs from Korea. Posts across the country held special ceremonies in their honor. In November 1953, the Department of Illinois even joined with news commentator Paul Harvey to broadcast special appeals on ABC news stations to the families of 23 brainwashed GIs who had refused repatriation.

In 1954, the North Koreans turned over 1,869 sets of remains to the U.S. 8th Army. The bones, they said, belonged to Americans—but 900 sets were not identified as such. Some 36 years passed before any new developments occurred. Piecemeal remains delivery was resumed. Between May 1990 and May 1992, North Korea returned 46 sets of remains to U.S. honor guards on the DMZ.

On Nov. 10, 1992, the Senate Select Committee on POW/MIA Affairs renewed the quest. New Hampshire Sen. Robert H. Smith — a member of Post 2616 in Swanzey — made two trips to North Korea, the last that December. He was allowed inside the once-forbidden North Korean war museum to look at documents and photographs reflecting the Communist side. But he was denied access to a nearby military language school, rumored to house former U.S. POWs teaching English.

To maintain the momentum, VFW Commander-in-Chief Jack Carney followed Smith's visit with one of his own to the 8th Army along the DMZ. He also went to New York and sat down with North Korean ambassador to the U.N., Kim Jong Su. The meeting was amicable, but Carney came away certain that only continued economic and diplomatic pressure would force the diehard Communists to fully cooperate.

In the interim, intensive negotiations persuaded the North to grant access to former battlefields by joint search teams. In July 1996, a U.S.

Commander Charles R. Lewis (left), Brooklyn County Council, passes out the first of 10 cartons of cigarettes presented by the Council to each of eight Brooklyn servicemen who were prisoners of war in Korea. Accepting a carton from Commander Lewis is Sgt. Manson Johnson, who was punished by the Reds for refusing to use the pages of a Bible to roll cigarettes. To right: PVT. Theo. Thompson, Jr., ..., Pedro Pereira, Cpl. Frank ...

When POWs returned home from North Korea, VFW members were on hand to provide support as in the case of the Brooklyn County Council in New York in 1953.

Paul Harvey, famed radio announcer, was enlisted to assist VFW in Chicago in 1953. Commander-in-Chief Wayne E. Richards presents a VFW Certificate of Merit for Harvey's efforts.

Commander-in-Chief Wayne E. Richards (left) presents a V.F.W. Certificate of Merit to Paul Harvey, noted radio and television commentator, in appreciation of his "effective campaign against communism." The presentation took place at the Dept. of Illinois membership kick-off dinner, held recently in Chicago. More than 1,200 attended the affair.

Pat Duncan (left), of the Korea/ Cold War Families Association, and Ken Steadman, executive director of VFW's Washington Office, examine artifacts at the site of an MIA remains recovery operation in Unsan, North Korea in October 1997.

Search teams painstakingly probe a hillside burial site in South Korea in the 1990s to uncover remains and personal effects of a missing American. When remains are found, bones and fragments are taken to the Central Identification Laboratory, Hawaii (CILHI) for high-tech detective work.

team of nine servicemen and one State Department official was allowed inside North Korea. It was guided to a spot 90 miles north of the capital city of Pyongyang, where excavation uncovered what was left of an American killed 46 years before.

About a year later, in October 1997—after seven years of persistent effort—VFW accomplished a major objective. Washington Office Executive Director Ken Steadman and others spent eight days on old battlefields deep inside what was once enemy territory.

The visit was timed to coincide with a joint U.S.-North Korea remains recovery operation at Hill 615, near Unsan, a five-hour road journey from Pyongyang. Steadman walked the site of a fierce engagement between the U.S. 8th Cavalry Regiment, 1st Cavalry Division, and Chinese Communist forces on Nov. 1, 1950. Several U.S. units were overrun, and 297 Americans were listed as MIA when the fighting ended.

Steadman recalled: "We first visited a ridge line that had been defended by the 2nd Battalion. Depressions in the ground, old fighting positions, had already been excavated. Some .30-caliber ammunition belts, grenade pins and C-ration items were scattered near excavations. In a hollow between two fingers of the ridge was the grave site of five soldiers, possibly Americans, whose remains were recovered the previous August."

Steadman said the former enemy still didn't trust Americans. He recalled the North Korean colonel in charge of the operation who admitted that he suspected the U.S. team of spying. Then he complained that his men had to ride in the rain in open trucks while U.S. troops were in covered vehicles.

Steadman pressed North Korean Ambassador Kim Byong Hong on the subject of live POW reports. He wanted to question four U.S. defectors who remained in North Korea after the war. The ambassador said it was impossible — the turncoats were now North Korean citizens and could not be forced to meet with Americans. VFW's representative and others in the group drafted questions to be given to the four renegades. The North Koreans said the submitted questions *might* be passed on to the defectors.

When the field trip was over, Steadman reported: "The North Koreans

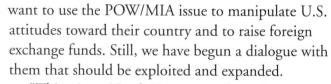

want to use the POW/MIA issue to manipulate U.S. attitudes toward their country and to raise foreign exchange funds. Still, we have begun a dialogue with them that should be exploited and expanded.

"This trip to North Korea was a historic opportunity to carry VFW's views directly to North Korea's leadership. Ambassador Kim indicated North Koreans were developing a plan for three one-month long operations per year over the next five to six years. Future visits by veterans groups and VFW national officers are possible."

By the end of 1998, 29 sets of remains had been recovered since search operations began three years earlier. But only one set was positively American. During 1999, six joint searches were scheduled between April and November.

The quest also has turned to China. It wasn't until 1996 that the U.S. Army's assistant chief of staff for intelligence finally declassified reports dealing with Red China's complicity in hiding American POWs. The reports, once stamped *secret*, revealed that as early as Dec. 15, 1951, Army intelligence was reporting that a "careful assessment" led to the conclusion that about 2,500 POWs were imprisoned in Manchuria, with another 1,500 behind barbed wire elsewhere north of the Yalu River.

"Specifically selected groups," said the report, "are sent to China in small numbers to undergo political indoctrination. Of those POWs processed in Manchuria, the ones not going to China are apparently being sent to mines and labor camps in Manchuria itself."

On June 20, 1952, a second report said that more than 1,000 American POWs were held in a former military prison outside Nanking "with a Russian colonel named Nokelov in charge." Intelligence indicated that "all POWs [are] 20-25 years old, brought here from Peking in December 1951 for re-indoctrination in Communist thought."

Another report dated Aug. 20, 1952, said: "POWs were grouped according to perceived political leanings. Those judged by the Chinese to be promising for anti-Western propaganda were kept in what the Army described as 'peace camps.' Because of obvious diplomatic complications, it follows that the Communists would neither wish to return these men to U.S. control nor admit to their existence."

What happened to Americans in Chinese captivity, how many died from disease, malnutrition or at hard labor, remains a mystery. The bamboo curtain that separated China from the United States began to part with

An American begins the long journey home. North Korean cooperation in returning remains was slow in coming, but visits by VFW representatives have added momentum. In July 1996, North Korea began working jointly with U.S. search teams across the demilitarized zone (DMZ).

Richard Nixon's visit in 1972—but the fate of U.S. POWs there has remained as murky as ever.

In January 1998, Defense Secretary William Cohen visited Beijing and asked that the archives of the People's Liberation Army be opened for inspection. President Jiang Zemin listened, but Cohen came away with no promises. Another delegation visited China a year later, but came up empty handed. As Steadman told *USA Today*, "There are a large number of questions to be answered, and the Chinese may have the only answers."

War in Vietnam produced a whole other set of obstacles to resolving the fate of America's unaccounted for. Organized VFW efforts to force the hand of the North Vietnamese over the POW-MIA question in Southeast Asia date from 1969. Fighting was still in full fury when VFW began *Operation Speak Out* under Commander-in-Chief Richard W. Homan. The project was backed by Ross Perot, a Texas multi-millionaire. With VFW's help, 200,000 message cards were sent throughout the nation calling the public's attention to the plight of U.S. POWs.

Meanwhile, VFW had been working closely with the wives of Americans held captive in Hanoi. Four wives were honored at the 1969 national convention. In a letter to VFW delegates, they expressed "heart-filled gratitude for your efforts in our behalf, especially your resolutions." That August, VFW launched its campaign for the humane treatment and early release of U.S. POWs in Hanoi.

In May 1970, *VFW* magazine Editor James K. Anderson focused attention on the sadistic treatment of POWs by their North Vietnamese captors. Anderson quoted Navy Lt. Robert F. Frishman: "I don't think solitary confinement, forced statements, living in a cage for three years, being put in straps, not being allowed to sleep or eat, removal of fingernails, being hung from a ceiling, having an infected arm—which was almost lost—not receiving medical care, being dragged along the ground with a broken leg, or not allowing exchange of mail to prisoners can be considered humane."

Shot down over North Vietnam, Air Force Lt. Col. James L. Hughes is prodded along the streets of Hanoi by North Vietnamese guards in 1967. Hughes was released in March 1973 during *Operation Homecoming*.

The war in Vietnam left more than 2,400 Americans unaccounted for. For years, the Communists attempted to barter American remains for diplomatic recognition and economic aid.

Rescue Raid on Son Tay, 1970

Americans who fell into the hands of the enemy in Vietnam endured years of brutal captivity with no hope of repatriation until the end of the war. Most were tortured; many perished. Condemnation and appeals based on the Geneva Convention were futile. Adhering to the old Roman motto, *deedum non verbum*—deeds, not words—America took direct action later in the war.

In May 1970, the Interagency Prisoner of War Intelligence Committee proposed a daring plan to Gen. Earle Wheeler, chairman of the Joint Chiefs of Staff. Airborne raiders would alight from helicopters and free 70 or more POWs from Son Tay, a camp 23 miles from Hanoi, deep in enemy territory.

Wheeler gave it the green light and six months of planning followed. Overflights by SR-71 Blackbirds provided high resolution recon photographs of the camp's layout. They revealed the proximity of about 12,000 NVA troops garrisoned nearby along with a cluster of anti-aircraft artillery installations. A North Vietnamese fighter base was about four minutes away by MiG-21 jet.

The mission got under way on the night of Nov. 21, 1970, from Udorn, Thailand, under the command of Col. Arthur "Bull" Simons. The force was made up of C-130Es and a gaggle of HH-53 "Jolly Greens." They reached Son Tay undetected and the raiders debarked— even the ones aboard one of the HH-53s that slammed into a tree 150 feet high. Another mistakenly landed a quarter of a mile away in a barracks compound filled with enemy soldiers. A fierce firefight followed that left an estimated 100 enemy dead.

Inside the Son Tay compound, there were no replies to the bullhorn announcement that rescue was at hand. Startled NVA guards rushed outside and were cut down by automatic weapons fire. By now, the neighborhood was fully aroused and an NVA reaction force was probably on the way. The crippled HH-53 was destroyed and the raiders headed home after 27 minutes on the ground. One raider returned with a broken ankle, the only casualty of the mission.

Two days before the raid, Adm. Thomas W. Moorer, the new chairman of the Joint Chiefs, was told that the American POWs had been moved to Dong Hoi, 15 miles to the east of Son Tay. In fact, Son Tay had been evacuated the previous July when an adjacent river threatened to overflow its banks. Moorer decided to let the Son Tay mission proceed, fearing that a sudden switch in plans might cause "catastrophic results."

Special Forces Sgt. Terry Buckler, today a VFW member, recalled: "What really stood out in my mind was the dedication the guys had. I was the youngest person on the raid, so I felt my life was unimportant. But the others had family. And they could have gotten off the mission at any time. That impressed me. These guys were willing to lay down their lives for their comrades."

A 14-man assault team code-named "Blueboy" aboard a C-130 prepares for the forthcoming raid on Son Tay in November 1970 to liberate American POWs in North Vietnam. Though the daring raid failed to rescue any Americans — they had been moved to another camp — POWs later said the rumored attempt bolstered their morale.

A shipment of petitions demanding humane treatment and immediate release of American POWs held by Communists in Southeast Asia is prepared by Pat Robertson (L) and Helen M.

At national headquarters, employees Pat Robertson (left) and Helen McWhinney prepare 1,200 pounds of petitions for shipment to Paris, France. The petitions demanded humane treatment and early release of American POWs held by Hanoi. They bore the signatures of more than 2 million Americans.

In 1970, Commander-in-Chief H.R. Rainwater and Mary Cottone, president of the Ladies Auxiliary, attempted to deliver the petitions to the residence of the North Vietnamese chief delegate. They were turned away. Rainwater told the world, "My crusade has just begun."

VFW was only getting started. "My crusade has just begun," declared Commander-in-Chief Herbert R. Rainwater in 1970.

Operation POW obtained 2 million signatures on petitions demanding release or humane treatment of Americans held captive. Rainwater took the bulky petition package to Paris and tried to deliver it to the North Vietnamese embassy. The petitions, weighing 1,200 pounds, were sent to Paris in 11 cases. Signatures were collected by VFW members in less than four weeks. VFW also raised funds to send wives of five POWs to Paris to meet with Hanoi's officials.

At a critical juncture in the POW saga, Patrick E. Carr of Louisiana became commander-in-chief. A POW himself for 8 1/2 months in Stalag Luft IV, a compound for airmen near the Baltic Sea, he experienced malnutrition and near-starvation firsthand. Taking office in the fall of 1972, he was firmly committed to "working as diligently and as effectively as I can" on the POW issue.

As Carr put it: "If we don't get those prisoners out, we will not survive as a free nation. The moral fiber of our country, the willingness of our people to defend it, will disintegrate." In early 1973, *Operation Homecoming* began bringing home American POWs from Hanoi.

War's end hardly finished the job of accounting. Hanoi's stonewalling prevented any cooperation for five years. In January 1978, past VFW Chief Richard Homan had numerous meetings with Rep. G.P. "Sonny" Montgomery, who chaired the House MIA Committee. He met with State and Defense Department officials to press VFW's call for redoubled efforts. Homan stayed in touch with next-of-kin to let them know how VFW felt and where it stood.

He told the VFW's National Council of Administration: "At every level of the VFW, our long-term mandate on the POW-MIA issue has been, is and will be vigorously carried out."

That was especially the case during the 1980s. "We are particularly pleased with the VFW's support of our petition campaign," wrote Ann Mills Griffiths, executive director of the National League of Families in 1981. "With the VFW's support, we will soon achieve our goals." VFW formed a POW/MIA

Subcommittee shortly after to place renewed emphasis on a full accounting.

VFW's original stance on attaining this goal demanded that "maximum U.S. and diplomatic pressure be sustained, for as long as it takes, to the end that those nations and movements that are hindering the search for the MIAs desist from this cruel practice and assist in the search effort as called for not only in the Paris Accords of 1973, but also in the interest of common humanity."

Gen. John A. Vessey, Jr., appointed special presidential emissary to Hanoi, soon made headway. Vessey knew the Vietnamese and the country. As a result of his negotiations, remains were delivered to recovery teams on 10 separate occasions between August 1987 and June 1989.

VFW's role was essential, too. "It was through the efforts of the VFW that we have been able to keep this a priority," said New York Rep. Gerald Solomon in 1987. "We have been able to keep the pressure on Vietnam, and we have made great progress."

Opposition to formal relations with the Communists continued. VFW POW/MIA Committee Chairman Billy Ray Cameron told his colleagues: "The American people — especially veterans — would not stand for diplomatic recognition of Hanoi considering its abysmal human rights record. Recognition would reward 16 years of Communist intransigence, manipulation and duplicity and would dishonor those who died in Vietnam. Perhaps more importantly, recognition would be a disincentive to the satisfactory resolution of the fate of American MIAs in Vietnam."

In 1991, VFW Commander-in-Chief Bob Wallace went to Vietnam as part of a seven-member delegation. Its first stop was Thailand, where Wallace got the impression that the Thais "wanted to see Americans accounted for to relieve the sufferings of their families." In Hanoi, the French ambassador told the veterans delegation that the Vietnamese "have always underestimated how emotionally attached the American people are to the POW/MIA issue."

MAY • 1971

V ★ F ★ W

VETERANS OF FOREIGN WARS MAGAZINE

© 1971 St. Louis Globe-Democrat

"I Hope Those Withdrawal Plans Include Us"

When President Richard Nixon announced plans in 1971 to begin withdrawal of U.S. forces from Vietnam, the fate of American POWs was unresolved. This editorial cartoon from the St. Louis *Globe-Democrat* expressed VFW's concern for Americans imprisoned in such hellholes as the infamous "Hanoi Hilton."

VFW Post 6063 in Toms River, N.J., erected a sign expressing the feelings of many VFW members across the country toward pro-Hanoi activist Jane Fonda.

In 1988, Fonda offered an apology for what many considered treasonous conduct.

Her open support of the North Vietnamese enemy during the war outraged veterans and families of those under fire in Southeast Asia.

Douglas "Pete" Peterson became the first post-war U.S. ambassador to Vietnam on April 10, 1997. Peterson, an Air Force pilot, was shot down over the North and spent six years as a POW. He said one of his objectives was to "bridge a river of pain between the two countries."

When asked why more remains had not been located, the Vietnamese pointed to terrain that made discovery difficult and the fact that heat and humidity are not conducive to preservation of human remains. Peasants, seeking small rewards, turned over a lot of bones to Vietnamese officials. But in most cases, they proved to be remains of long-dead animals.

Veterans visited a crash site north of Hanoi, one of 14 such sites that had been excavated since the searches began. Twenty years earlier, a fighter-bomber had plunged out of the sky to disintegrate in a fiery explosion. Now the site was a serene landscape of paddies and dikes shimmering with water. What remained of the twisted metal and the men inside had been taken away long ago.

Findings of VFW executive officers generally corroborated the Senate's earlier 585-page POW/MIA report. That report, based on a 15-month investigation that cost $2 million, concluded Pentagon efforts were sometimes flawed, but there was neither conspiracy nor cover-up. Many POW activists, of course, have for years maintained otherwise.

By 1994, the Clinton Administration ended the 19-year trade embargo on Vietnam. On July 11, 1995, full U.S. diplomatic recognition of Hanoi was granted. Two years later, on April 10, 1997, Douglas "Pete" Peterson, a former Vietnam POW, was confirmed as the first post-war U.S. ambassador to Vietnam. He took up his post that May, fully supported by VFW.

With new doors opened through diplomatic channels, the way was paved for the expansion of the search and recovery effort on the ground. This task, little-appreciated by the American public, has gone on for most of the 1990s. Teams of dedicated young Americans labor in the jungles of Indochina sifting through soil for the slightest clues that might lead to a serviceman's remains.

Joint Task Force-Full Accounting (JTF-FA) headquarters on Oahu, Hawaii, supervises field research by detachments based in Southeast Asia. Joint Field Activity searches require teams to spend as much as 30 days in the bush at a cost of $400,000 per mission.

More than 4,000 U.S. fixed- and rotary-wing aircraft were shot down during the Vietnam War. The wreckage provides sure markers for the remains of those who failed to eject. Searches are always arduous, often disappointing, but sometimes rewarding. Recovery follows classic archaeological procedures: site coordinates, careful excavation, photography of unearthed items, tagging of finds, bagging the clues. Local villagers are asked to probe their memories of a crash for leads on burial sites and traces of wreckage.

Searches also extend to water. An ancient Vietnamese fisherman said he had watched a U.S. warplane plunge into the sea. A preliminary scuba dive found the wreckage 30 feet underwater and marked it for eventual recovery.

Crash sites in Vietnam and Laos were pinpointed — each given the same thorough examination characteristic of Joint Field Activity teams. Log books and contemporary flight plans of thousands of wartime missions are used in concert with tail numbers, aircraft serial numbers and engine placards to tie in with megabytes of other data.

When remains are found, they are taken to the U.S. Army Central Identification Laboratory, Hawaii (CILHI) for high-tech detective work. From skeletal remains, forensic scientists can deduce age, sex and even the race of the MIA. Teeth are the most valuable, as no two sets are alike, and can be compared with dental records held on a computer data base by the casualty data team. Some excavations turn up dog tags, wallets and weapons

An American excavation team, assisted by contracted Vietnamese workers, excavates a hillside crash site above the village of Mai Chau in 1995.

Joint Task Force-Full Accounting (JTF-FA) headquarters in Hawaii oversees field operations by detachments based in Thailand, Vietnam and Laos. Search missions often last 30 days.

whose serial numbers can be matched against issue records. But artifacts that arrive with packaged bones are never used for final identification. In fact, lab technicians don't want to know names deduced by other team members—their research is done "blind," based on pure forensic science.

One of the tools at their disposal is mitochondrial DNA, which is passed along maternal lines through the generations. A five-gram bone sample is enough for analysis, with the results adding another piece to the jigsaw puzzle that is forensic identification.

Fitting the pieces together can take months, cross-checking each painstaking step along the way. When identification is made to the satisfaction of CILHI, findings are forwarded to the Armed Services Identification Review Board for final determination. When all concur, the MIA's branch of service is notified and years of uncertainty for the next-of-kin is over.

Dr. Pete Miler, at the Central Identification Laboratory in Honolulu in 1995, uses video superimposition equipment to compare a recovered skull with a photograph of a serviceman listed for years as MIA.

Forensic scientists can deduce age, sex and even race from skeletal remains. Identification is a painstaking process that can eventually end years of uncertainty for families.

VFW enthusiastically backed the work of both CILHI and JTF-FA from the very start. *VFW* magazine sent its editor to cover their operations in Vietnam and Laos in 1995, resulting in a four-part series of articles describing the arduous work performed by these teams.

But VFW's support is far more than simply symbolic. It also is tangible for the teams. In 1998, VFW's Washington office worked with Arizona Sen. John McCain in securing permanent hardship duty pay for task force members. In introducing an amendment to the *1999 Defense Authorization Bill*, McCain remarked: "I commend my friends of the VFW for bringing this to my attention. Their concern for the state of the military and those who serve is unsurpassed."

Lt. Col. Roger King, spokesman for JTF-FA, praised VFW's efforts over the years: "The contributions of the VFW and other veterans groups have been significant, especially in their initiatives to gather information on MIAs and in informing the public of the continuing mission.

"Organizations like the VFW get the word out to the American people about efforts to locate, identify and repatriate the remains of U.S. war dead. Without this valuable exposure, few in America would know what we do, that the nation cares about the ultimate sacrifices made by those in uniform and the feelings of the loved ones at home."

As Washington Office Executive Director Ken Steadman declared: "Our MIA search must remain a top priority for as long as it takes. By 1999, we were receiving the closest possible cooperation from the Vietnamese."

Some of that cooperation can be linked to the assistance being provided by U.S. veterans in accounting for 300,000 Vietnamese MIAs. The *VFW MIA Initiative* has sought help from its members to aid the Vietnamese. In the mid-'90s, the word went down to the Post level to contribute any information and war souvenirs members brought home from the war.

VFW's initiative sought information about battle sites, dates, Vietnamese grave sites, maps, photographs, diaries, field notes—anything to help the former enemy locate its own MIAs.

"Organizations like the VFW get the word out to the American people about efforts to locate, identify and repatriate the remains of U.S. war dead. Without this valuable exposure, few in America would know what we do, that the nation cares about the ultimate sacrifices made by those in uniform and the feelings of the loved ones at home."

Lt. Col. Roger King, JTF-FA

As part of VFW's MIA Initiative, *VFW* magazine published a full-page announcement in January 1996 calling attention to the need for a free exchange of information. Vietnam veterans were urged to contribute details and artifacts to help their former enemy account for its own 300,000 MIAs.

An MIA/POW flag goes up in front of Cubic Corporation's headquarters in San Diego in 1993. The flag was donated by VFW Post 11044, Mission Bay, Calif. Left to right: Post Commander Ralph McClain, Harry Jenkins—held captive by the North Vietnamese as a POW for seven years—and Jim McKeon.

Hanoi lost the equivalent of 15 U.S. infantry divisions, and their soldiers are no easier to find and unearth than are Americans. Members have responded — one notable contribution consisted of grid coordinates for the remains of 818 NVA and VC buried during the war.

This spirit of cooperation has paid dividends. By the end of 1998, the quest for a full accounting of America's missing in Indochina had consumed 25 years. Though the full fate of 2,076 Americans still remains unknown, 507 servicemen have been accounted for. They were repatriated and given full military honors over a marked resting place, where those who loved them have a link with a past filled with irreplaceable memories. VFW can take pride in being part of the effort that made this all possible.

As a fitting symbolic gesture in honor of all POWs, Post 6442 in Macon County, Ga., dedicated a *Parade of Flags* from Montezuma through Oglethorpe in April 1998. The line of flags stretches nine miles along SR 49 to the gates of the new National Prisoner of War Museum at Andersonville National Historic Site.

Fostering public awareness of the POW/MIA issue is a never-ending VFW resolution. For the last three decades of the 20th century, VFW both nationally and locally promoted remembrance activities such as those sponsored on National POW Day (April 9) and National POW/MIA Day, which is honored in September each year. While these two days trace their origins to World War II and Vietnam, respectively, VFW's concerns embrace the unaccounted for of all wars.

The remains of 78,000 Americans were never recovered after WWII. Searches continue, though, to this day. Teams comb the most remote corners of the world, ranging from Brazil to China and New Guinea. And the brave aviators of the Cold War, shot down during covert missions, cannot be neglected either. That's precisely why VFW strongly supports retaining the U.S.-Russia Joint Commission on POWs, as well as full congressional funding for the Pentagon's Office on POW/MIA Affairs.

Tomb of the Unknowns: America's Shrine

One of VFW's purposes as defined in its congressional charter is "to perpetuate the memory and history" of America's war dead. So it's no surprise that the Tomb of the Unknowns at Arlington National Cemetery holds a special place in the hearts of all the organization's members.

In fact, VFW members were present at the original interment ceremony on Veterans (then Armistice) Day, 1921. The man responsible for selecting the remains that would represent the first Unknown Soldier was WWI Medal of Honor recipient Edward F. Younger. He later became a VFW member of Post 2202 in Chicago. Younger, who died in 1942 and is buried at Arlington himself, chose the remains from among four identical caskets.

VFW also has other connections to that historic day. Commander-in-Chief Robert G. Woodside presented a "VFW National Aide-de-Camp, Medal of Honor class, special medal" and officiated the traditional VFW ritual services.

Another WWI veteran and future member of Post 797 in Port Arthur, Texas, was even more involved in the ceremony. Frank C. Puddy, who was then an 18-year-old seaman first class serving aboard the USS North Dakota, was chosen to be a member of the military escort.

Puddy later recalled the huge crowd that filed through

Sgt. Edward F. Younger places a wreath of white roses on the Tomb of the Unknown Soldier of WWI on Nov. 11, 1930. Nine years earlier, on Oct. 24, 1921, Sgt. Younger was chosen to place a similar wreath on one of four caskets containing the remains of four unknown American dead taken from French battlefields. The casket Younger chose was taken across the Atlantic aboard the USS Olympia and met by Gen. John J. Pershing and a guard of honor. More than 100,000 people gathered to pay their respects while the body lay in state.

the Capitol Rotunda that day: "This chain of fellow countrymen was proof that America was truly grateful to her sons who had not died in vain."

Two wars and 37 years later, on Memorial Day 1958, America buried unknown soldiers from World War II and the Korean War in the Tomb. The selection process was similar to that in 1921, with a Medal of Honor recipient choosing the remains to be buried.

This time, however, VFW Commander-in-Chief Richard L. Roudebush was on hand to witness the selection process, which was held aboard the USS Canberra: "It was hard to realize what I had just seen. Everyone aboard seemed to have the same reaction because the ship was wrapped in a silent quietness, broken only momentarily by whispered bits of conversation." Roudebush attended ceremonies in the Capitol Rotunda and at Arlington, as well.

Perhaps the highlight of the ceremony was the participation of VFW honor guards from Post 3460 in Media, Pa., and Post 8757 in Mountville, Pa. They joined the VFW National Honor Guard in the five-mile procession of the remains of the two unknowns. (On the 25th anniversary of that event in May 1983, in what the Washington Post called a "Pilgrimage to Arlington," some of the original guards re-enacted the procession.)

On March 28, 1982, VFW's Distinguished Service Medal was presented to the museum adjacent to the Tomb for permanent display. That same year, a resolution calling for placement of an unknown from the Vietnam War in the Tomb was passed.

A grand interment ceremony was held in 1984 with Commander-in-Chief Cliff Olson representing VFW. However, those remains were identified through DNA testing in 1998 as belonging to Air Force 1st Lt. Michael Blassie, whose A-37 was shot down near Saigon on May 11, 1972.

Although VFW regards the sanctity of the Tomb as paramount, it supported the Pentagon's decision to reopen the Tomb. VFW believes the family of any veteran missing in action has the right to know the fate of its loved one.

With current identification techniques, no American may ever again be laid to rest in the Tomb as an Unknown. Perhaps that is most fitting. As Chief Roudebush said in 1958, VFW hopes to "never let us experience another ceremony such as this today."

A Historical Footnote: *The first unknown soldiers in America lie under the Martyrs Monument in Trinity Churchyard in New York City. They were unidentified Revolutionary War patriots who died in British prisons, according to a 1957* New York Times *story.*

Chapter 10

Woven Into the Nation's Fabric

Joseph R. Romero of Post 3242 in Las Cruces, N.M., chats with his grandson, Sonny, about the meaning of the flag. On Memorial Day 1982, Romero said: "My flag means truth. It means freedom and equality for everyone. The flag shows the glory of everyone who lives in the shadow of its wave."

Constructive community service is a founding VFW tenet, which includes natural disaster relief, sponsoring youth activities, providing college scholarships and voluntary civic projects.

To most Americans, VFW's attachment to issues such as accounting for a war's missing in action is natural. That fits the organization's profile. But mention what VFW members do in their local communities and you are most likely to encounter a blank stare. That's probably VFW's own fault, since its members carry out their good deeds without the intent of earning public praise.

Yet those deeds are obvious to some. "Everywhere I go," observed now retired Gen. Colin Powell, "I find that veterans are in the vanguard of voluntary service to America — in hospitals, schools, and in communities all across the country. You veterans are at the forefront of those wonderful citizens who devote their time and energy to helping others."

In 1996, Commander-in-Chief James E. Nier reinforced Powell's message: "Shaping VFW's future place in American society is paramount. To remain a broader civic organization capable of bringing critical issues to the fore — to the public arena — we must be *relevant*. That means boosting our public profile in the community. Selflessness — not selfishness — has to symbolize the VFW. Keeping in step with society is as vital as serving veterans needs. It is in the wide areas of civic life that the VFW can make some of its greatest contributions."

"Everywhere I go, I find that veterans are in the vanguard of voluntary service to America—in hospitals, schools, and in communities all across the country. You veterans are at the forefront of those wonderful citizens who devote their time and energy to helping others."
Gen. Colin Powell
Former Chairman, Joint Chiefs of Staff

Indeed, constructive service to the community is one of the four cornerstones of the VFW foundation. This has been so since the very beginning when members took an active interest in community affairs in the 1900s. As Commander-in-Chief Leslie M. Fry put it some 60 years later: "The morale of any organization is based on its achievements. Without worthwhile programs, we have no reason to exist."

VFW programs have taken every shape and form over the years. National headquarters began appointing civic-related directors as early as the 1920s, but it was not until 1965 that a full-fledged programs department was upgraded to the assistant adjutant general level. By then, so many VFW community activities were in force that a new position had to be created to coordinate them all.

The first assistant adjutant general for programs, WWII vet Curt Jewell, saw in the job a dual purpose. The focus of VFW programs would be changed to reflect the problems of the times. Jewell rightly believed that "community betterment programs translate into positive publicity."

VFW Posts, without direction from the top, have always demonstrated the concept of volunteerism. In every aspect of community life, their presence is felt. Assistance to the needy, sponsorship of youth sports, promotion of public safety, advancement of education and concern for a clean environment head the list. You name the problem, and Post members somewhere have probably been part of the solution. Let's take a sampling.

One of the more visible problems is litter strewn across the nation's highways — tons of paper plates, Styrofoam cups, beer cans and disposable diapers; the leavings of a throwaway society. VFW joined in the attack on this visual pollution by enlisting in the Adopt-A-Highway program that originated in Texas and has since spread throughout the country.

California, with 15,000 miles of highways and more cars than any other state, presents the greatest challenge. In one year alone, volunteers picked up nearly 300,000 tons of litter along its roadways. The California Department of Transportation issues to VFW Posts safety gear, including white helmets, orange vests, safety glasses and orange plastic trash bags.

Posts "adopt" stretches of highway anywhere from two to 10 miles. Volunteers sweep their particular stretch at least four times a year. The only items not picked up by volunteers are dead animals, used hypodermic needles and anything else that looks hazardous.

An average haul includes 40 bags of trash and six bags filled with aluminum cans and glass bottles. Trash is hauled away to landfills — but cans and bottles are recycled, the cash put into Post funds. In one time period, volunteers saved

As part of VFW's nationwide concern for community beautification during the 1990s, Post 4987 in Bethpage, N.Y., participates in the national Adopt-A-Highway project.

Top row: Bill Fortgang, Allen Beck, Odell Burfeind, Bob Totone, Bert Carlson and Bud Roach. Middle row: Bob Archer, John Lawrence, Bill Flanagan, Phil Madeo, Chaplain Gaspar Barresi and Al Cheosky.

Front row: Post Commander Charlie Reidlinger, Councilman Douglas Hines, Lindy Laterza, John Azzara and Vito DeFanis.

California $17 million in labor. Signs posted alongside highways alert motorists when the upcoming stretch has been adopted by VFW.

Once trash is picked up, some of it has to be recycled. Members of Post 8687 in Ft. Myers, Fla., tackled this growing environmental problem by working with Goodwill Industries.

When the county landfill had absorbed almost all the garbage it could handle, the Post started its own recycling program. It established curbside pick up — curbside, because Florida has the highest retirement population in the country. And senior citizens are less apt to drive to a central collection point. It worked, but VFW volunteers had to wade through the accumulated material to make separate piles of newspapers, aluminum, plastics and glass.

They found a partner in Goodwill Industries — a non-profit organization that hires the physically and mentally handicapped — which agreed to take on VFW contributions en masse. Goodwill had once sent plastic to Pennsylvania for recycling, but it built its own processing plant next to the sorting center and manufactured its own goods.

Goodwill does not pay by the pound for recyclable materials. So it was VFW's reasoning that by making materials freely available to Goodwill for conversion and resale, disabled workers who otherwise might not have jobs remained part of a productive work force. Over time, Post 8687 brought in more than 4 million pounds of materials once destined for the furnace.

Cleaning up the environment takes more than one form. When Mother Nature releases her destructive energy, the toll is often tragic in terms of destroyed lives and property. Among the more dramatic VFW community contributions have been those made on the heels of natural disasters. VFW has been responding to them since at least 1927 when $10,000 — a tidy sum then — was donated to victims of the Mississippi River Valley floods.

In 1936, Posts nationwide quickly mobilized all available resources when the Ohio River went on a rampage. In Ohio, Indiana, Illinois, West Virginia, Kentucky, Tennessee, Arkansas, Missouri and nearby states, VFW Department officers took charge of organizing local rescue and relief actions.

Nationally, Commander-in-Chief Bernard W. Kearney authorized an

Members of VFW Post 8687 in Ft. Myers, Fla., in 1992, pitch in to bag recyclables at a senior citizens center. From left: Sam Jessen, Richard Wilson, Ciel Lucas, Jim Lucas and Don Maclean. Recycling is part of the Keep America Beautiful Campaign.

VFW Commander-in-Chief Eugene P. Carver (left) presents a check for $500 to Judge John Barton Payne, chairman of the American Red Cross. The money was used for relief work in Florida and Puerto Rico, which sustained heavy damage and loss of life during a 1929 tropical hurricane.

This accolade from hospitalized vets and communities at large has been echoing ever since the Ladies Auxiliary was formed in 1914.

Today, it numbers 727,921 members in 6,595 Auxiliaries (including Guam and Germany). If there is one word to describe the Ladies Auxiliary, it is compassion. Members are familiar and welcome at VA hospitals.

The Ladies take on a multitude of civic responsibilities. For example, they donate money to the upkeep of the Statue of Liberty. Preservation and beautification of "Lady Liberty" has been a special project of the Ladies Auxiliary since her golden anniversary in 1936. The Ladies then played a role in the rededication ceremonies and sponsored a nationwide essay contest for high school students. While the essay contest ended in 1964, the birthday party has been celebrated by the Auxiliary each year ever since.

For the restoration of the Statue during the 100th anniversary in 1986, members donated $221,000. Many of the improvements — a portable stage, redwood benches, a public address system, wheelchairs, drinking fountains and American flags — there today are courtesy of the Auxiliary. Every Oct. 28, approximately 1,500 members and Junior Girls honor one of America's most revered landmarks by holding a patriotic ceremony and presenting a gift.

The Ladies Auxiliary sponsors 191 Junior Girl Units (ages 6-16), and awards cash prizes to winners of the National Young American Creative Patriotic Art Competition. Members contributed more than $200,000 to remodel the National Home's Health & Education Building and Nursery in Michigan.

They are without peers in promoting Buddy Poppies — more than 6 million are distributed each year by these energetic women. Much good work is done with contributions to the "relief funds." Funds garnered from Poppy drives are in turn creatively used to promote public awareness of the needs of others.

These women contribute an average of 20 million hours of volunteer service every year. This includes projects of their own and to VFW programs that have been in force for nearly a century.

Donations go to a wide variety of worthy causes, especially cancer research (see sidebar on p. 173). In 1998 alone, a dozen institutions benefited from the Auxiliary's generosity, ranging from the Ronald McDonald House to the Smithsonian Institution.

Ladies Auxiliaries also work with their "Connect America" partners during *Make a Difference Day*, a national day of helping others at the local level. Activities are sponsored by *USA Weekend* magazine and The Points of Light Foundation.

An Auxiliary call to arms urged: "Join us. Take one day and make life better for the homeless or clean up a local park. The VFW and its Ladies Auxiliary challenge you to join the hundreds of thousands who will make a difference across the nation on this special day."

Making life better for those in need could easily serve as the motto of the Ladies Auxiliary.

In 1997, the Auxiliary launched an initiative to increase opportunities for Junior Girls to participate in its scholarship program. Lowering the age range to 13 will enable more Unit members to qualify.

Ladies Auxiliary members are familiar figures at children's hospitals across America. Ladies of Auxiliary 367 in Joliet, Ill., donate stuffed animals for the pediatrics ward of Silver Cross Hospital in Joliet in 1990.

> "At this time, there can be no difference between veterans and their dependents and other citizens who are in distress as a result of the greatest catastrophe that has ever overtaken our country. Contributions to the Red Cross fund will allow each veteran and his dependents indirectly through the efforts of the Red Cross to aid all sufferers."
>
> **Bernard W. Kearney**
> **Commander-in-Chief (1936-37)**

appropriation of $10,000 from regular funds to meet the emergency. He recognized the disaster was bringing death, misery and destitution to thousands of VFW members and their families. So he allowed Posts to make contributions from their Buddy Poppy relief funds direct to local Red Cross chapters.

"At this time," he said, "there can be no difference between veterans and their dependents and other citizens who are in distress as a result of the greatest catastrophe that has ever overtaken our country. Contributions to the Red Cross fund will allow each veteran and his dependents indirectly through the efforts of the Red Cross to aid all sufferers."

In Kansas City, national headquarters put a temporary hold on routine work to concentrate on the coordination of relief efforts. Gerald C. Mathias, a member of the National Council of Administration, managed to secure a private aircraft and flew from his hometown of LaGrange, Ind., to Louisville, Ky., to deliver a VFW check for $1,500 to Mayor Neville Miller.

"I spent four days in Louisville," Mathias reported, "and was on hand when Post 1084 was feeding as many as 700 flood victims twice a day. Post 1834 was operating three relief stations. And Posts 3204 and 2921 maintained relief stations in their sections of the city."

Kentucky VFW Department Commander Clarence Stricker — himself dispossessed by flood waters — said: "I believe 90 percent of the membership in northern Kentucky had to move one way or another. And the other 10 percent was occupied with providing shelter for refugees."

Parkersburg, W. Va., was entirely cut off from the rest of the world with the exception of one narrow dirt road, impassable to ordinary traffic. A VFW relief squad from Post 573 in nearby Clarksburg borrowed a tractor from the state highway commission. It towed loaded trucks up the muddy trail and delivered several tons of food, water and bedding to the stranded flood victims.

It was the same story of heroic efforts throughout other flood-stricken regions. In Elmwood Place, Ohio, the mayor called on VFW to take complete charge of flood relief aid. The Ladies Auxiliary maintained a food kitchen in city hall, feeding victims around the clock. In Cairo, Ill., 50 VFW members sent their families to safety, staying behind as special volunteers for police and levee work.

A special sacrifice was made by WWI vet D.R. Danenberg of Grand Rapids, Mich. He gave his $50 Bonus bond — for which he had waited so long — to Red Cross flood headquarters. Danenberg said, "I put this aside for a rainy day.

Researching Cancer and Aiding Patients

For the past 10 years, the Ladies Auxiliary has raised $3 million every year for the war on cancer. That $30 million has done an immense job of relieving anguish and fostering hope for a cure someday. This most generous undertaking began quite inauspiciously more than 50 years ago.

In 1947, Auxiliary national President Dorothy Mann conceived a fund to support cancer research. Valuable research of this killer disease was being conducted at Jackson Research Laboratory in Bar Harbor, Maine. Unfortunately, the laboratory was destroyed by a forest fire just as Mann's project was getting under way. She and national Secretary-Treasurer Grace Davis immediately appealed for funds from Auxiliary members. An initial grant of $63,000 was given to begin rebuilding the research facility.

Some $12,000 was given to families of children with cancer between 1949-50. By 1952, the program was called Cancer Aid and Research and had expanded to include grants to Auxiliary members stricken with the disease.

In 1957, the first research grant (later called fellowship) was presented to Dr. Philip O'Bryan at Southwest Medical Foundation in Dallas to further his work with the "flying spot microscope." It was an instrument able to photograph living cancer cells. Since then, the Auxiliary has presented grants to major cancer centers throughout the U.S.

Annually, the Auxiliary funds three $25,000 post-doctoral fellowships to scientists researching cancer.

Today, the program combines three approaches to conquering cancer: education (Auxiliary members donate countless hours raising public awareness of the risk factors and warning signs of cancer), research (by sponsoring $150,000 in projects each year) and assistance (to members who have the disease).

In 1981, Ladies Auxiliary National President Marion Watson presents a donation to Danny Thomas. The funds are for cancer research at St. Jude's Children's Hospital in Memphis, Tenn., which Thomas founded. The Auxiliary began contributing to the hospital in 1972.

I guess it rained all right. Credit $5 each to me, my wife and eight kids."

VFW's efforts did not go unrecognized. On Feb. 10, 1937, Adjutant General Robert B. Handy, Jr., received a letter from the American Red Cross Chairman Gary T. Grayson: "The cooperation that has been given to us by the Veterans of Foreign Wars, together with the generous contribution to our Flood Relief Fund, has been splendid. It is most encouraging to us here at national headquarters to know that in time of great national emergency we can count upon such fine and loyal support from your organization."

Nature's fury continued to take its toll in intervening years. VFW felt compelled to do something of lasting value. So in 1951, Commander-in-Chief Charles C. Ralls set aside a permanent natural disaster relief fund. "VFW," he wrote, "must be instantly prepared to act swiftly when tragedies strike in the future. I call upon all VFW and Auxiliary members to contribute to the creation of a new fund...which may be a blessing to any VFW member in the future if disaster should strike any section of the United States — either in the form of floods, fires, explosions, hurricanes and perhaps enemy bomb attacks."

Ralls' wisdom was especially evident 13 years later. In 1964, a major earthquake ripped through Anchorage, Alaska, killing 131 people. VFW and its Ladies Auxiliary contributed nearly $100,000 toward relief efforts — half of that amount arrived within just 10 days.

VFW Posts also rose to the occasion when disaster struck the Sunshine Mine in Kellogg, Idaho, in the early '70s. Post 1675 took immediate action to organize relief efforts, which involved 35 persons working 24 hours a day during the two-week crisis. But only two of 93 miners survived the cave in — 10 of the lost men were Post members and 43 of the others also were veterans.

The Post gathered more than 12 tons of food for the men's families and made over 170 deliveries. Several thousand gallons of coffee and soft drinks were provided to rescue workers and family members who maintained a vigil at the mine entrance. Post 1675 saw rescue efforts through to the tragic end.

"This is a service that could not have been duplicated by any other organization except the VFW and its Auxiliary working as a team," said John Price of the VFW's National Public Relations Committee.

No decade has been spared the wrath of nature, but the 1990s seem to have been particularly hard hit by disasters. In August 1992, a series of catastrophic hurricanes struck Louisiana, Florida and Hawaii. Bulletins were immediately sent to all VFW Departments. Donations amounting to nearly $500,000 were raised for relief, including $196,832 in matching grants from national headquarters.

More than cash finds it way to the scenes of disasters — the human element counts above all. Precilla Wilkewitz, adjutant-quartermaster for the Department of Louisiana, watched trucks rolling in filled with food, water, clothes, baby supplies and even appliances after the hurricane hit.

"I saw two Vietnam vets — one with an artificial leg, another with two artificial legs

In 1952, the Donald D. Dunn family of Yakima, Wash., receives a certificate entitling them to a $50,000 farm located in the Columbia Basin. Dunn was selected as the outstanding farm veteran among 82 Post winners in the Department of Washington.

He was then judged "Most Worthy" of 48 state entries. Dunn shares the joy with his wife and two daughters, Sally Ann and Deanna.

— working around the clock. We had hundreds of volunteers. I was often moved to tears. There were so many little miracles, I can't remember them all." They included shelter and hot meals provided by Posts and Auxiliaries.

VFW volunteers were called out again in 1993. Floods bring out the worst in nature — the Mississippi and Missouri rivers in particular — but the best in human beings. That year, both rivers surged over their banks and converted much of the Midwest into a spreading lake that engulfed homes and ground floors of hundreds of buildings.

The quartermaster of Post 1308 in Alton, Ill., Willard Livingston, asked the Salvation Army, "What do you need most?" When told of the urgent need for a fully equipped boat to rescue residents stranded on roofs, the Post quickly raised $5,000 and turned a johnboat over to the saviors of the Salvation Army.

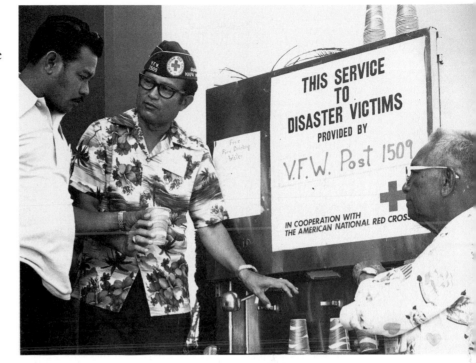

Commander Ben Alpuerto of Post 1509 in Sinajana, Guam, hands a glass of drinkable water to Fred Toves. Looking on is Vincent Valencia. Alpuerto served as VFW Red Cross coordinator following a typhoon in 1976 that disrupted the island's water supply.

VFW established five assistance centers on the island to aid its citizens.

In St. Charles, Mo., VFW and Auxiliary members teamed up with the Charitable Children's Fund of Maine. Together, they distributed 625,000 pounds of clothing and staples for suddenly homeless families.

Money for relief work at the Post level was raised by benefits and bingo. Funds were collected in one state for distribution in another. From Barrington, Ill., went $5,600 to the VA medical center in Des Moines, Iowa. In Midvale, Ohio, Auxiliary member Cheryl Snyder established 65 pick-up points throughout the town. An 18-wheeler provided by a local trucking company made the rounds. It then headed for Jefferson City, Mo., loaded with food, clothes and other survival necessities. A thousand turkeys also were distributed on Thanksgiving Day.

Disaster of another kind struck April 19, 1995 — a type, ironically, that Chief Ralls had foreseen 44 years earlier. A federal building in Oklahoma City went up in a titanic explosion triggered by a lunatic. When the last body was recovered from the jumble of concrete and iron, 168 people were counted dead, including nine children. It was the worst act of domestic terrorism in U.S. history.

"I felt a terrible loss," recalled Connie Lynch, a member of the Ladies Auxiliary of Post 7462 in Piermont, N.Y. "I wanted to do something that would let the whole world know that we are united here, that what happens in Oklahoma concerns us all."

She gathered baskets and collection cans decorated with purple ribbons to be placed in shops, stores and bars in Piermont and in surrounding towns. She designed posters reminding others that although Oklahoma was half way across the country, the "heartland is our land."

Posts from all over the country pitched in to help the survivors. Nearly $40,000 was given to Norman Lamb, secretary of the Oklahoma Department of Veterans Affairs, who in turn gave the money to the Governor's Disaster Relief Fund. The donation was earmarked for veterans and their families, including scholarship funds for children of veterans killed or injured when the building was destroyed.

Only when the rubble was cleared in Oklahoma City were the purple ribbons of mourning attached to trees and telephone poles in Piermont taken down. "It was like a burial," said Connie Lynch.

Exactly two years after the Oklahoma City blast — on April 19, 1997 — the Red River dividing Grand Forks, N.D., and East Grand Forks, Minn., over flowed, wiping out more than 1,000 homes. Lynn Stauss of VFW Post 3817, who was also mayor of East Grand Forks, got his family to safety aboard a National Guard truck. Stauss recalled, "Every able-bodied member was out sandbagging even while their own homes were taking on water."

Subsiding flood water left wreckage in its wake. Deep water engulfed and "blew out the roof" of the East Grand Forks Campbell Public Library. The new VFW-American Legion collection of 500 military history books and video tapes was reduced to a soggy mess.

April seems a particularly bad month, for on the night of April 8, 1998, winds topping 260 mph tore through Alabama, creating a 21-mile swath of destruction that left 33 people dead. It was the seventh deadliest tornado in the nation since 1950.

VFW swung into action across the nation. Post 6739 in Camp Verde, Ariz., dispatched a truckload of clothes, furniture and other household necessities to Post 3707 in Ensley, Ala. The items came from the Post's thrift shop, open since 1991. Shop manager

Members of the Ladies Auxiliary of Post 7462 in Piermont, N.Y., decorate collection cans to be distributed throughout Rockland County, N.Y. The funds were donated to the victims of the Oklahoma City bombing, which occurred on April 19, 1995.

Wayne Pouliot, a WWII vet, said, "Our Post is small, but we enjoy doing as much as possible to help people in need."

Post 4850 in Jasper, Ala., was only 35 miles from the scene of heavy destruction. Post Commander Allen Quinn, said, "We waited to find out specific needs — then we really went into action. We loaded up clothing, blankets, bottled water and case after case of non-perishable food and got it to a distribution center in Birmingham. We also donated a $1,000 check. I'm proud of the way our members moved."

That June, wild fires scorched Florida, resulting in sudden evacuations of entire counties. VFW Posts were ready to assist. Post 8696 in Palm Coast turned its Post home into a sanctuary. It served 1,000 meals in the first 24 hours and gave firefighters a place to rest. At Post 2380 in DeLand, members kept firefighters fueled with soda, Gatorade and water during the inferno. Others bulldozed large chunks of land, making it more accessible to those battling the blazes. Once again, VFW members had displayed the volunteer spirit.

Members of Post 4850 in Jasper, Ala., collect clothing and non-perishable items to be sent to victims of a deadly tornado that struck Jefferson County, Ala., in April 1998. Left to right: Lamar Pike, Dale Garner, Charles Kimbrell and Post Commander Allen Quinn.

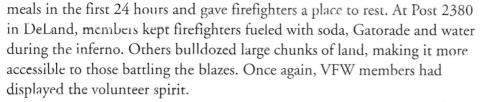

Public safety extends to every facet of daily life. It is not always as dramatic as confronting the consequences of nature run amuck. Usually, it is a lot closer to home and family. Every 10 minutes, two Americans are killed in accidents and another 370 suffer disabling injuries. Many of these accidents happen during normal activities — and almost all of them are avoidable.

VFW was determined to do something about personal safety. In 1966, it founded a safety program. And reducing auto accidents was first on the list.

Posts began sponsoring drivers' education courses available from the National Safety Council and later the American Association of Retired Persons' *55 Alive/Mature Driving* program. With 52 million drivers over age 50 (30% of all drivers), this course serves an essential need in the lives of senior citizens.

Bicycle safety was another priority. As far back as 1938, VFW began forming bicycle safety clubs. With more than 500,000 kids injured in bicycle accidents per year — many while pedaling at night on neighborhood streets — VFW started the Lite-a-Bike program in 1962. St. Paul, Minn.-based 3-M Company provided $300,000 worth of "Scotchlite" reflector tape. Some

VFW distributes thousands of attention-getting bumper stickers as part of its defensive driving effort. As a service to its members and the general public, the organization has long promoted safety on the nation's highways.

50,000 VFW members from 4,500 Posts nationwide took part that first year. Today, bicycle-related deaths have declined dramatically, but Lite-a-Bike continues.

Decline, unfortunately, does not characterize the use of drugs in this country. Drugs afflict every facet of society and the VFW intervened early on to combat their devastating effects. In 1923, when the head of the Society for the Suppression of the Narcotic Drug Evil — alarmed at the post-WWI tripling of drug use — approached the editors of *Foreign Service,* the response was swift.

The lady in charge wanted the magazine to print a resolution calling for President Warren G. Harding to declare a *National Anti-Dope Week* and to set up an international conference to deal with the problem.

She reminded VFW: "I have often heard that a soldier's discharge from the Army is not his discharge from the service of his country. The discharge was more in the nature of a diploma, charging the holder with the duty of guarding his country against dangers from within as well as from without." Her resolution was printed and VFW Posts took action.

Years later, in 1951, VFW's National Council of Administration pledged support for a narcotics control program. And two decades later, VFW cooperated with the federal Special Action Office for Drug Abuse Prevention. Despite all the effort, the problem still plagues the nation. When a new anti-drug movement was launched in the early 1990s, VFW enlisted.

A VFW member of Post 4043 in Liberty, Mo., affixes a reflective strip to the front of a kid's bike. Within the first two years of VFW's Lite-a-Bike program — launched in 1962 — more than 16 million kids' bikes were marked with reflective tape donated by the 3-M Company of St. Paul, Minn.

"No one is more prepared to lead the war on drugs than America's veterans," declared Air Force Medal of Honor recipient Leo K. Thorsness. A Vietnam POW and member of Post 1263 in Renton, Wash., he went on: "Importation of illegal drugs is an invasion of our shores as sure as if an enemy had landed. I am asking all veterans to fight one more war." VFW agreed wholeheartedly.

VFW stays active in this continuing war through its Drug Awareness program, which reaches inside grade schools and into the workplace. Posts throughout the country sponsor seminars, hand out *Just Say No* buttons and T-shirts and steer those who want to quit drugs to counselors.

A prime example of a Post's close ties with local law enforcement is the working relationship between the Sheriff's Department of Tuscarawas County and the Post in the town of Philadelphia, Ohio.

In the struggle to keep kids straight, the county adopted an expanded program in 1991 called CADET— Crime and Drug Education Training. As Deputy Sheriff Shawnee LeMasters observed: "We're dealing with a whole new generation. Attitudes are different, especially toward authority figures. It's sad to observe our youth today. Parents don't always make the best role models — they're often abusers of drugs and alcohol themselves. Kids end up living what they learn by example. It's scary."

Post 1445 donated more than $25,000 toward drug and crime awareness

Minnesota VFW Funds Cancer Research Center

On Sept. 20, 1959, the Department of Minnesota put the finishing touches on the largest project ever undertaken by a state unit. That day, the VFW Cancer Research Center at the University of Minnesota was dedicated.

Located in Minneapolis, the center was the culmination of a six-year effort by VFW and its Ladies Auxiliary. Together, they raised over $500,000 for the center. Adopted in June 1953, the project was unique because it was solely financed by donations of VFW Posts, Auxiliaries and individual members. No outside fund-raising was sought. Expenses were kept below 1.5 percent of the donations, a noteworthy accomplishment in itself.

The three-story structure is connected to the Masonic hospital, located directly behind the university hospital and medical school. At one time, virtually all cancer research in

the state was conducted in the VFW-financed facility.

The Department sought yet another project related to cancer research at the 1976 state convention. Called *Cancel Cancer*, it had a $100,000 goal to aid in cancer research. However, university regents, objecting to VFW support for the Vietnam War, forbade researchers like Dr. Charles McKhann, director of the VFW Cancer Research Center, to seek further funds from VFW. Fortunately, he did so anyway. Other *Cancel Cancer* campaigns followed until the '80s.

Today, the center still bears the VFW name. Minnesota VFW members continue to make regular contributions to the center. By 1999, they had given $1,015,738, according to Bill Sullivan, executive vice president at the Institute for Basic and Applied Research in Surgery.

VFW Cancer Research Center at the University of Minnesota was the largest project ever undertaken by a VFW Department. Today, VFW's emblem is still prominently displayed on the side of the center. The Department of Minnesota and its Ladies Auxiliary have contributed over $1 million to the center.

179

VFW wages war against substance abuse during a 1980s drug awareness program. Then-Community Activities Director Ray Price pins a "Just Say No" button to a school child's shirt.

programs, reaching kindergarten through 8th-grade kids. Uniformed officers — some of them "moms" themselves — establish easy relationships with schoolchildren. They generate a sense of caring by grown-ups who want to help not to arrest and intimidate. Children are taught that giving in to peer pressure is for jerks, that saying "no" is a mark of the strong.

Recognizing those who guarantee public safety is a capstone of VFW's safety program. Citations are awarded to law enforcement officers, firefighters and emergency medical technicians (EMTs) who perform extraordinary service in the field. VFW publicly recognizes individual heroism — those who pull people from burning houses or the passerby who dives into a torrent of water to rescue a child. At each national convention, selected public service officers are presented with special awards.

Volunteering, for many VFW members, means time spent with patients in hospitals. This can be through the VA Voluntary Service (VAVS), discussed in an earlier chapter, or independently. Post 280 in Boone County, Mo., for instance, raised $33,275 in 1975 to provide 110 bedside-controlled color TVs in the private rooms of the Harry S Truman VA Hospital in Columbia, Mo.

VA's National Veterans Golden Age Games is another outlet for volunteers. Competition is open to all veterans age 55 or over and who receive medical care from the VA medical network. In 1998, some 400 vets participated in five age groups in a variety of sports. Begun in 1994, VFW has co-sponsored the games every year with a $50,000 donation raised from Posts and auxiliaries. Various sites are selected each year, with local VFW members helping participants.

Back in 1990, Post 6626 in Poughkeepsie, N.Y., and the Eastern Paralyzed Veterans Association provided the means to break the wall of isolation in VA facilities. The brainchild of VFW member

Robert A. Jones, Illinois public relations chairman, Commander Frank Jellinek of Post 1596 in West Chicago and Commander Ken Richardt of Post 6791, West Chicago, join in honoring James Partridge for heroism in 1986.

Partridge, a legless Vietnam veteran, rolled his wheelchair 80 yards and crawled another 20 yards to revive a 1-year-old girl who had fallen into a swimming pool. Partridge was made a life member of Post 6791.

Frank Dosio, these two groups set up the PT (Patient) Phone Home program and installed 250 bedside telephones in the Castle Point VA Medical Center with the help of New York Telephone, the Communications Workers of America and VA.

Columnist James Slater of the *Poughkeepsie Journal* — himself a disabled vet — pointed out that "95 percent of marriages are effectively ended when a spinal cord injury is involved — the problem often amplified by inability to keep in contact with the spouse." To Slater, the PT Phone Home program was "large in compassion and consequence."

Before long, 40,000 phones were installed in 90 VA medical centers and volunteers had assisted with 23,000 others. In 1998, the program was moving into high technology, installing computers and modems in VA hospitals.

PT Phone's success proves the value of working with outside groups to solve society's ills. Homelessness is a case in point. In 1994, VFW formed the National Homeless Veterans Committee to coordinate efforts to help homeless veterans get back on their feet.

Mike Gormalley, VFW's director of Community Service, explained: "The VFW has always been involved with the homeless through state organizations and Posts. But this committee will now coordinate our efforts and enable us to help more homeless and their families."

So-called "Stand Downs" are the primary means for dispensing assistance. A stand down, as most field veterans know, means pulling an outfit out of the line for rest and recuperation. Kansas City hosted the "Heart of America" Stand Down in the summer of 1993. Haircuts and beard trims were provided, medical and dental checkups from civilians or medics in cammies made available and clerks with laptop computers retrieved VA records.

"The purpose of stand downs," said coordinator Steve Van Buskirk, "is to reintegrate these individuals back into the system designed to take care of them. Due to their problems, they are alienated from the very system they need. Many are eligible for benefits, but don't ask for them. Stand downs provide a way for social service groups to go to where these veterans are and consequently, have a tremendous impact."

Gormalley agrees: "By breaking down the red tape, stand downs can give these veterans the help they need in a caring atmosphere."

As the program continued to grow, Gormalley emphasized: "Assisting homeless veterans is a natural VFW obligation. But it can best be accomplished at the local level by Posts working with community agencies."

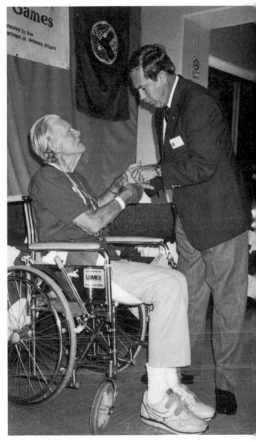

VA's Golden Age Games participant James Fenn, representing the VA medical center in Livermore, Calif., is congratulated by VFW Commander-in-Chief George Cramer for an outstanding finish in the 1993 Games in Mountain Home, Tenn. VFW contributes $50,000 annually to the sports event.

A homeless vet receives an inoculation from Air Force Staff Sgt. Jill Blake of the 442nd Medical Squadron at a VFW Stand Down in 1993 in Kansas City. Such "stand downs" provide on-site help to veterans who need medical care, job counseling and a square meal.

On Jan. 13, 1951, members of Post 1318 in Madison, Wis., are briefed on distribution of March of Dimes (MOD) coin containers. *Operation Iron Lung* was a part of a MOD Birth Defects Foundation project.

Alliances with other non-profit community groups is a long-standing VFW tradition. VFW has taken a keen interest in the March of Dimes and its predecessors since 1938. Basil O'Connor, president of the National Foundation for Infantile Paralysis, 46 years ago, said: "The 1952 March of Dimes was the most successful in the 15-year history of National Foundation of Infantile Paralysis campaigns. Members of the Veterans of Foreign Wars, through nearly every one of their Posts and Auxiliaries, were in the forefront of the vast army of volunteers who made this record possible."

Jump four decades and those words still ring true. VFW consistently ranks high in contributions to *Walk America.* On average, VFW raises $100,000 each year for the March of Dimes. Contributions come from Posts: top ones are recognized at national conventions. And always among them are Posts from Maryland and Phoenix City, Ala.

Through *Walk America,* donors pledge so much per mile for every mile an individual walks. "All monies collected go directly to the March of Dimes to maintain programs," said Pat Lynch, national director of Volunteer and Chapter Support for March of Dimes. "Many VFW Posts across the nation volunteer their color guards to start the walks."

Adds Lynch: "We have a partnership with VFW and Federal Express. Fed Ex ships clothing and supplies into the area and local VFW Posts let us use their halls as distribution points where people can come and pick up these essential items." (Lynch is a member of Post 453 in Union City, N.J.)

Mike Gormalley observes: "It's not just the walk teams. It's things like a

Post hosting a volunteer recognition party. It's getting involved that's important. Some people are unable to walk, but there are a lot of different opportunities. In some cases, it's just sponsoring a walk team, or registering walkers. VFW participation in March of Dimes highlights what veterans are all about."

Some of VFW's earliest ties to the community involve youth groups. Few are stronger — and none longer lasting — than the close relationship between VFW and the Boy Scouts of America (BSA). Locally, that partnership dates back to 1915 when Post 2100 teamed up with the Order of Elks to establish Troop 1 in Everett, Wash. BSA was founded in 1910 — only five years earlier.

Members of VFW's national headquarters staff get ready for the March of Dimes WalkAmerica through the streets of Kansas City, Mo., in April 1990.

In 1929, VFW established an annual $300 Scholarship Award for Eagle Scouts who showed "marked patriotism and love of country, outstanding scholarship, and consistent application in daily life of the ideals and principles of the Boy Scouts." The first recipient of the award, in 1930, was Perry E. Piper, 17, of Sumner, Ill. He dove 16 feet down in a raging torrent of water and pulled drowning Elmer Corrie to safety. Then he resuscitated the youth using life-saving techniques learned in the Scouts. The national award was presented to a deserving Scout at least through 1960. By then, it had increased to $1,000.

A plan of cooperation was adopted in 1936 formalizing ties between VFW and BSA. *Section 20* of the plan included information on how VFW could contribute to the Cub Scout program: "There may be community houses and social centers in sub-standard residence areas that need strong leaders. Veterans who are parents can take an active part in organizing Cub Packs and Dens. Veterans can render a real service in helping organize Packs and Dens to provide recreational programs for boys from age 9 to 12 in these neglected areas."

Not long after the Cubbing program was launched, Dr. Ray O. Wyland, then BSA's director of education, said: "Schools are telling us, 'Give us more Cub-trained youngsters. They simplify our work and give it new angles of incentive.' We commend Cubbing to every member of the Veterans of Foreign Wars as a new signboard on the trail

"Members of the Veterans of Foreign Wars, through nearly every one of their Posts and Auxiliaries, were in the forefront of the vast army of volunteers who made this record possible."
Basil O'Conner
President, March of Dimes (1952)

toward real American citizenship."

Not all merit badges are won in the great outdoors; not all Scouts sleep in pup tents in the woods. Since 1912, Sea Scouts — now called Sea Explorers — have been learning nautical skills at sea off America's great stretches of shoreline and while navigating waters across deep lakes.

The town of Penn Yan in upstate New York offers proximity to the Finger Lakes region — prompting Post 745 to sponsor Sea Explorer Ship 745. In 1989, as a chartered BSA organization, old salts of VFW began passing along their nautical knowledge to boys and girls from 15 to 20 years of age.

They learned to use scuba equipment in a swimming pool and became certified open-water divers. Serving aboard Navy and Coast Guard ships on training cruises — one lasting eight days from the Philadelphia Naval Yard to Oswego, N.Y. — Sea Explorers learned to box a compass, shoot the sun with a sextant and stand a nighttime bridge watch. Skills aside, Sea Explorers absorb, said one, "honor, responsibility and respect for naval and military traditions. ... an extraordinary experience."

In 1951, Commander-in-Chief Charles C. Ralls pins a VFW gold medal on Explorer Scout George Zimpfer of Buffalo, N.Y., winner of the annual $500 scholarship award for Scouts (established 1929) who show "marked patriotism and love of country, outstanding scholarship, consistent application in daily life of the ideals and principles of the Boy Scouts."

Close VFW association guarantees community service from the program. When the local soil conservation society needed a 1,000-foot stretch of stream cleared of years of accumulated trash and debris, the Sea Explorers volunteered. Harassed by insects, they waded through muck and weeds, getting the job done.

They also took part in a flag dedication ceremony at Penn Yan's county historical society. One Sea Explorer hoisted "Old Glory" while a uniformed VFW color guard stood at attention. "It was," said 18-year-old Michael Fordon, "a moving experience. Interacting with the veterans was a piece of living history."

By 1998, VFW Posts were sponsoring 1,203 BSA units with nearly 32,775 members in troops, Cub Scout packs and Explorer posts. VFW's continuing relationship with the nation's second largest youth group pays dividends for all concerned — boys, parents, VFW members and most of all, America.

Involvement with groups like the Scouts serves a dual purpose: It connects veterans with young people and provides an opportunity to instill traditional

184

values. Patriotism is part of VFW's philosophical core. The Americanism Department, established in 1921, based its credo on Daniel Webster's 18th century definition. "Americanism," he wrote, is "devotion or loyalty to the United States, to its traditions, customs and institutions." Though now known as Citizenship Education, the department's goal is still the same.

VFW's promotion of civic responsibility takes many forms. Squads of volunteers from Posts and Ladies Auxiliaries unfurl the flag before school children and adults to show how the Stars and Stripes should be properly handled. How it's folded so that only the blue field is visible, how it is displayed among other banners and how to dispose of flags tattered with use also is covered.

Jack Janik, president of the National Flag Day Foundation, observed: "We're getting it into schools using VFW members. They not only teach the basics of patriotism — they tell about those who sacrificed their lives so that we can live the way we do."

While a constitutional amendment to protect the flag is fully backed by VFW, education remains the mainstay of the organization's efforts to instill respect for the national symbol in the young.

Educating youth in classrooms includes other endeavors, too. In recent years, veterans have

Members of VFW Post 4409 of Harrisonville, Mo., in 1993 are among many who sponsor Boy Scout troops, including Sea Explorers.

VFW color guard of Post 5253 explains the intricacies of drill team procedures to the Cub Scouts of Pack 201 at Center Street Middle School in Mineola, N.Y., in 1995.

The 1936 Plan of Cooperation between VFW and BSA encourages veterans to help organize Packs and Dens.

increasingly accepted invitations of teachers to make history "living." There is nothing like actual war veterans relating their personal experiences for livening up a group of sleepy students. And today they have their choice — veterans from WWII, Korea and Vietnam are readily available. In 1986, the Vietnam Veterans of Westmoreland County, Pa., decided to break more than a decade of silence. Two men came forward: Dennis Baughman, a Navy corpsman with the 5th Marines, and Paul N. Yeckel, Jr., a mortarman of the 21st Infantry, 196th Light Infantry Brigade — both of VFW Post 33 in Greensburg, Pa. They formed the School Speaker Service, a volunteer corps of men who would share their experiences. They faced the first open meeting

The cover of *VFW* magazine for January 1957 draws attention to VFW's many youth programs aimed at fostering positive attitudes, healthy outdoor activities and love of country.

Kiyo Sato-Viacrucis of Post 8985 in Sacramento, Calif., speaks about patriotism in 1990 at a school. She was a captain in the Air Force Nurse Corps during the Korean War.

Topics include the famed Nisei 442nd Regimental Combat Team in Europe during WWII, internment of Japanese-Americans during the war and the history of the Constitution.

in Yeckel's old high school with some uneasiness, but found a respectful and eager audience. The program quickly expanded.

Curious students handle the tools of combat — rifles, bayonets, dummy grenades, helmets, packs, jungle boots, maps, Vietnamese money and propaganda leaflets. The middle aged men in business suits with briefcases look like their fathers — in some cases, they *are* their fathers. Seeing in these visits a valuable contribution to the community, organizations such as The Prudential Foundation donates funds to keep it going.

Firsthand reminiscences by men who were there leave lasting impressions. One student was awed by the revelation that Americans could be killed by children and that "one minute you could be talking to a friend — and the next minute he would be dead."

Baughman reflects: "People of *our* generation did not care what happened to us. It gives me a feeling of worth and satisfaction to know that young people actually care how we feel, that we are finally getting respect for the sacrifices we made."

Considering the success of such programs, it's no wonder that VFW's Citizenship Education Department is eagerly working with educators. The latest effort revolves around arranging interviews with veterans via the Internet, then inviting them to address students. This is just another example of adapting technology to the needs of the future.

On a more formal basis, that VFW department is now linked with the Vietnam Veterans Memorial Fund's *Young American Vietnam War Era Studies Project,* launched in 1998. VFW is the only veterans group with an advisor on the project's 15-member Advisory Board. *VFW* magazine's widely circulated *America's War in Vietnam: A GI's Combat Chronology* will be used as a primary teaching tool in courses.

Teaching kids in the classroom and ensuring good sportsmanship on the playing field are mutually compatible goals. VFW sponsorship of sports teams dates back to 1922, when hundreds of Posts began helping baseball, football and ice hockey teams. With the onset of the Depression, paying close attention to the problems of youth became especially critical.

In June 1934, *Foreign Service* magazine called attention to the problem: "On all sides, we see young Americans without a job or constructive leadership. Youth with no one interested in advising or leading. Thousands are homeless or friendless and drifting into crime for the very good reason that there is nothing else for them to do that will give them food and shelter."

VFW created a national youth program in 1937 to help to fill the void. Victor E. Devereaux, director of the Americanism Department, called it "the

VFW Trains Ice Hockey's Olympic Champs

Minnesota — the North Star State — is VFW's hockey home. Since 1956, the Department has offered ice hockey as a youth activity. That program has left a legacy few others can match. Look at the unexpected and emotional U.S. victory over the Soviets in the 1980 Winter Olympics at Lake Placid, N.Y. Twelve of those players and their coach, Herb Brooks, got their start in VFW hockey.

Four years later, in the 1984 Winter Olympics at Sarajevo, Yugoslavia, nine of the players on the USA hockey team came from the Minnesota VFW hockey program. That same year, 14 of the 20 Minnesotans in the National Hockey League were former VFW youth players.

Through the years, VFW's program grew from a league for "midget-age" players (ages 16-17) to a state-wide, 10-team tournament for "bantam" players (13-15) by 1966. Teams represent each of VFW's nine districts. The host city also enters a team representing its local Post. Approximately 75-100 Posts sponsor at least one team each season. Post 3915 in Brooklyn Park, has three A VFW state hockey chairman coordinates the league. He was Stan Ostby, a member of Post 8663 in Roseau, and never missed a tourney from 1956 on, until he died in June 1998.

America's Olympic victory in 1980 — an athletic triumph over an arch Cold War rival — also was in many respects a win for the Minnesota VFW hockey program.

In 1998, these VFW-sponsored players skated to victory as Minnesota state champions. VFW in Minnesota has promoted ice hockey in a youth league since 1956. By 1984, 14 of the 20 Minnesotans in the National Hockey League began on VFW teams.

Competitive shooting and hunter safety have long been VFW programs. As early as 1920, VFW became affiliated with the National Rifle Association (NRA) through the League of Associated Rifle Clubs to promote marksmanship. VFW's Junior Rifle Clubs were especially popular during the 1940s. By the early '60s, VFW Posts were sponsoring more than 300 such clubs with 7,000 participating kids.

A firearms safety essay contest sponsored jointly by *VFW* magazine and Browning Arms Co. in 1960 netted more than 500 entries explaining "Why Young Americans Should Be Trained in the Proper Use of Firearms." Posts such as Post 10273 in Stratford, Conn., continue to promote safety.

Americans
FOR AMERICA!

Young America
Wants to Know
"What's Going to
Happen to Us?"

In 1941, a few months before the Japanese bombed Pearl Harbor, VFW appointed Gene Tunney as national director of Youth Activities. Tunney, 1926 heavyweight boxing champion and WWI Marine veteran, said: "I am convinced that the sons and daughters of the veterans of our country's wars are best fitted to serve as crusaders in the battles against the enemies of America's democracy."

Three 1959 winners of the VFW-sponsored marble tournament at Eaton Rapids, Mich., proudly pose with their trophies. VFW's national marble tournaments were perhaps the most popular youth activities sponsored by the organization during the early postwar years. *Life* magazine even provided coverage of the 1950 tournament at the National Home.

most important mission the VFW has undertaken since the memorable days of the World War. It has answered the call to the colors that rings as clearly today as it did in 1918."

To provide a directed outlet for youthful energy, VFW took over Junior Softball from the Amateur Softball Association. The program was designed to be self-supporting: Each boys' and girls' team paid an entry fee of $3, of which $2 was returned to Junior Softball, and used to defray the expenses of sending state champions to the annual world championship tournament.

During the program's first year, 15 junior teams were sent to the championship playoffs in Buffalo, N.Y. The St. Rita's Community Center team of Detroit defeated the Ripley School team of Topeka, Kan., 7-6. Commander-in-Chief Bernard W. Kearney presented the trophy.

In writing up the game, *Foreign Service* observed: "Since this is a community activity in which every boy and girl in the United States is eligible to take part, it will bring in contact with the organization those who have never before been familiar with it. And in the course of another season or two, will put the VFW on every playground and sports page in America."

In 1941, a few months before the Japanese bombed Pearl Harbor, VFW appointed Gene Tunney as national director of Youth Activities. One of American's best-known and respected sports figures, Tunney retired as heavyweight boxing champion of the world in 1928. He was a Marine in France during World War I, and was a lieutenant commander in the Naval Reserve.

Tunney said: "I have accepted the appointment because I am convinced that the sons and daughters of the veterans of our country's wars are best fitted to serve as crusaders in the battles against the enemies of America's democracy. They, as well as other youngsters in every VFW community, must be trained and inspired as guardians of our American inheritance. They are ready to accept any task they are assigned — we need only to give these youngsters a chance to absorb the true significance of Americanism."

Tunney's ideas were part and parcel of the Sons of the VFW, a youth program that has had its ups-and-downs since it was founded in 1934. Sons, stepsons and adopted sons of VFW members were eligible if they were between the ages of 8 and 18. By 1939, there were 25,000 members on the rolls. Emphasis was placed on patriotism and community service.

Even into the late 1970s, the Sons was again going strong. Edward L. Burnham, a long-time VFW employee and then Youth Activities director, could report: "From only 150 or so scattered units of some 3,000 boys just 10

Protecting Old Glory

Flag-burning was not a serious problem until the Vietnam War. In 1968, when the practice was at its peak, Indiana Rep. Richard L. Roudebush introduced a bill in Congress to halt the desecration. A past VFW Chief, he castigated "malcontents who had given nothing to what the flag represents." He called for fines of $1,000 or a year in jail for anyone who "publicly mutilated, defaced, defiled or trampled" America's symbol. The law held for 21 years.

Then, on June 11, 1989, the Supreme Court overturned the Flag Act by a vote of 5-4 in a decision that shocked most Americans. It occasioned a salvo from Commander-in-Chief Larry W. Rivers in *VFW* magazine. Rivers had fought for the flag as a Marine in Vietnam.

"We find it offensive, knowing that, in our 200-year history Americans have fought, died and were carried to their graves under that flag," he wrote. "It is incomprehensible to us that there are those who would choose to desecrate the symbol that protects and guarantees their freedom of speech. As a political statement, flag-burning is shocking and offensive."

VFW steadfastly continued its campaign to reverse the Supreme Court decision through a constitutional amendment. Meanwhile, the flag remains a perennial issue in the

FOREIGN SERVICE February, 1926

Major Noel Gaines
Organizer of The American Flag Movement

MAJOR NOEL GAINES

In 1926, Commander Noel Gaines of VFW Post 1404 in Frankfort, Ky., organizes the "American Flag Movement." Gaines wanted a flag in every American home. He also launches the "Uniform Street Decoration" program, encouraging business districts to install permanent flag fixtures on major streets.

political arena. Each election year it is revived, but the necessary votes fall short.

VFW has long proved to be a strong advocate of flag protection through education. In fact, former commander of Post 1404 in Frankfurt, Ky., Maj. Noel Gaines, organized the *American Flag Movement* in 1926. It aimed to put the flag in every home across America. Gaines led the campaign from coast to coast.

VFW also was instrumental in the first official observance of Flag Day in Waubeka, Wis., the birthplace of Flag Day, which dates back to June 14, 1885. But it wasn't until 1946 that Waubeka observed Flag Day with ceremonies and a parade. In its charter year, VFW Post 7037 organized the festivities. More than 50 years have passed since the first observance and the parade still draws crowds of more than 15,000 spectators each year.

VFW continues to protect the flag's integrity. Post members help instill respect with VFW's citizenship education booklet. As a ready resource, they present a variety of flag education programs in classrooms. "VFW supports a constitutional amendment along with educating the public about respecting the flag," stresses VFW Director of Citizenship Education Mike Gormalley.

When the Visual Arts Center in Anchorage, Alaska, in 1992, spread the Stars and Stripes on the floor — inviting patrons to trample it — members of Post 9785 take action. George Pikus and Dick Brogan retrieve the flag and fold it prior to taking it for safekeeping

V.F.W. good citizenship award for Jackie Robinson, Brooklyn Dodger star. The presentation was made by Dept. of Illinois Senior Vice Commander Roy Frazier (right) and Commander T. M. Mann, Post 2024, Chicago.

TORN FROM the PAGES of VFW MAGAZINE

Jackie Robinson, Brooklyn Dodgers baseball star, is presented with VFW's good citizenship award. The award was made in September 1950 by Department of Illinois Senior Vice Commander Roy Frazier (right) and Commander T. M. Mann, Post 2024 in Chicago.

Robinson is best known for breaking the color barrier in major league baseball in 1947: He also earned the "Rookie of the Year" award.

years ago, the Sons of the VFW has soared ahead to over 800 units under the sponsorship of Posts in all 53 Departments made up of 16,000 to 20,000 sons and grandsons."

One of VFW's most popular youth activities was easily the National Marble Tournament, first held in the summer of 1947 at Boys Town, Neb. Hosted at the VFW's National Home in 1950, the tournament attracted even *Life* magazine coverage. Its June 26 issue devoted a two-page pictorial spread to the event. Because marble competition was such a well-liked VFW event, it earned the cover of *VFW* magazine on two occasions (in 1955 and 1961). By the mid-'50s, approximately 150,000 boys were participating in VFW's annual competition. Sadly, though, as the boys of the 1940s and 1950s matured, one of the nation's best-liked youth pastimes faded from popularity.

Of course, America's favorite pastime was baseball. As late as 1950, 21 teams from 11 states were still participating in VFW's national junior softball tournament. But it was soon eclipsed. The following year, VFW adopted Teen-er Baseball as a national youth sport. It had originated in Pennsylvania in 1950.

In 1952, the VFW National Teen-er Baseball Tournament was played in Pennsylvania's 1,000-acre Hershey Park. For boys 13-15, this was a wonderful opportunity. By the '61 season, 14,000 boys organized into 189 leagues from 22 states were playing courtesy of VFW. Coordination on a national level continued at least through the end of the decade. Today, states such as Pennsylvania maintain the Teen-er tradition.

VFW Post 1544 in Milford, Mass., takes pride in its 1961 Teen-er Baseball team that won 17 out of 21 games.

At left is Assistant Manager John Pilla. At right is Manager Gus Pavento.

While learning sportsmanship is essential, broadening intellectual horizons is of greater importance. Combining the competitive spirit with a thirst for knowledge produced VFW's premier program. Realizing that a democratic society needs continuous nurturing, the National Association of Broadcasters created the Voice of Democracy (VOD) not long after World War II. High school students were invited to compete for college scholarships by writing and narrating five-minute scripts dealing with the principles of democracy. The concept was so fundamentally American that the first judges included VA Administrator Gen. Omar Bradley, Adm. Chester W. Nimitz and Father Edward J. Flanagan, founder and director of Boys Town in Omaha, Neb.

In 1958, VFW was asked to fill the void left by withdrawal of the Junior Chamber of Commerce as a VOD sponsor. In 1961, VFW assumed sole sponsorship, joined not long afterwards by the Ladies Auxiliary. By 1974, more than 500,000 students were competing each year for generous scholarships.

Gordon R. Thorson, director of the program, explains: "Voice of Democracy provides the opportunity for high school students to become more articulate in expressing themselves not only in regards to democratic ideas, but also to polish their overall communication skills. These skills are critical in whatever endeavors they may choose to pursue later in life."

Entries are judged at Post and District echelons, then at the state level. Winners' expenses are paid to Washington, D.C., for a five-day tour of capital landmarks before final judging. These young men and women are guests at VFW's annual Congressional Banquet where the national VOD winner presents his or her speech before a host of dignitaries from VFW, the armed forces, the federal government and Congress.

From 1972 through 1998, Voice of Democracy winners attended the American Academy of Achievement's "Salute to Excellence" seminars held in a different city each year. VOD winners are among 500 outstanding high school students and 25 American men and women who have made significant contributions in their chosen fields.

Many VOD winners have gone on to excel in the professional world: medicine, government, engineering, economics, law and network television. A 1948-49 winner, Charles Kuralt's positive reporting on the human condition and the marvels of nature is considered beyond emulation. In 1997, VFW designated its second-place $15,000 award

Janice M. Woelfle is surrounded by well-wishers after receiving the first-place scholarship award in the 1961-62 Voice of Democracy (VOD) contest. That year marked VFW's first as primary sponsor of the competition.

Since then, VOD has become the organization's premier youth program, raising $2.6 million annually through the Departments and national headquarters.

Perhaps the best-known VOD winner is Charles Kuralt. His observations about everyday life in America on CBS TV's *On the Road With Charles Kuralt* endeared him to the nation. In 1997, VFW designated the second-place $15,000 prize the Charles Kuralt Memorial Scholarship in honor of the late journalist.

Ladies Auxiliary National President Jane Bingham, top VOD winner Heidi Holley and VFW Commander-in-Chief Tom Pouliot proudly display the $20,000 scholarship award check for the 1998-99 competition.

the Charles Kuralt Memorial Scholarship in his honor.

VOD participants share a common feeling. "I will always remember the thrill and excitement of competing," recalled Alan Whitney. "The Voice of Democracy program helped me form a better idea of what freedom is all about." Dale Rieger, a high school dean of students and 1967 winner, wrote: "In the long run, the program honors not only country and students, but the VFW as well."

Sally Anne Wellman was not on hand to receive the state VOD award from her native Idaho. As a volunteer Red Cross worker, she was knee-deep in flood waters meeting rescue helicopters when the ceremony took place. When reached by telephone, Wellman said, "I'm staying here to perform my responsibilities as a citizen." She was living the theme she had written about.

Eric Main went to Post 1643 in his home town of Redmond, Ore., to receive his award for *Why I am Proud of America*. Once among the vets, Main observed: "Your contest provides a valuable service to kids by asking them pertinent questions that they forget to ask themselves. War brought these people together in defense of basic values and ideas. I look at the VOD contest and realize that defense of core values and ideas still requires sacrifice."

In 1999, the contest attracted more than 100,000 participants. Top prize is the $20,000 T.C. Selman Memorial Scholarship. From there, amounts range from $15,000 to $1,000 for most of the Departments. Some 56 scholarships are available. A total of $132,000 in national scholarships were awarded to winners. Include all levels of the organization, and the amount soars to $2.6 million for scholarships and related VOD expenses.

A parallel program to VOD — VFW Youth Essay Contest — began in 1995. Good citizenship is literally spelled out by 7th-and 8th-grade students in 300- to 400-word essays. Middle-schoolers write for designated themes that force youthful minds to examine their nation's history and their own experiences in modern society. In 1997-98, 58,300 students from all 54 Departments participated in the contest. Some $447,500 in savings bonds and other contributions were awarded to the students.

You name it — college scholarships, conservation, natural disaster relief, public safety, services for the needy and ill, citizenship education and youth sports — and VFW has provided it. Looking to the future of VFW's commitment to the volunteer spirit, Assistant Adjutant General (Programs) Benny Bachand echoes the sentiments of VFW's early leaders: "Civic service has and always will be a foundation stone of the Veterans of Foreign Wars."

VFW Sponsors Amputees' Hunt in Montana

Some may call them heroes, but these men would point to others. Some may say they've sacrificed, but they'd counter that they're happy with their lives. Some may even ask if they're proud of their service, and they'd look the questioner in the eyes and say, "Absolutely."

Who are these men? Quite simply, they are patriots whose love for their country forever changed their lives. They also are veterans — the kind that VFW is proud to call members of the organization.

They are disabled veterans wounded in combat in the Vietnam War. Some carry emotional scars not visible on the surface; many are missing multiple limbs; all have endured a magnitude of pain that is unfathomable to the average American.

The importance and depth of disabled Vietnam veterans' sacrifices are not lost on VFW or Russ Greenwood, proprietor of Doonan Gulch Outfitters in Broadus, Mont. Since 1984, Greenwood and VFW have provided a disabled Vietnam veteran with transportation to Greenwood's hunting lodge — as well as a chance to bring home a trophy-sized antelope. Beginning with the 1997 hunt, VFW increased that number to four vets.

The reason for the hunting trips is best summed up by Greenwood. It is a sentiment shared by many VFW members. "When I saw what type of reception Vietnam veterans got when they returned to the States, I was infuriated," Greenwood recalled. "It still gets my dander up to hear people say why we shouldn't have been there. These men have given a lot to the country."

VFW pays the airfare for all four veterans. In addition, it picks up the tab for three of the vets lodging, their meals, hunting licenses and the accompanying hunting-guide services. Greenwood chips in for the other vet.

Greenwood and his twin brother, Roger, who served as a helicopter pilot in Vietnam, started the hunting program in 1982 with the help of VFW's Department of Wisconsin. When Russ Greenwood moved to Montana and established his own outfitting service, the program moved with him.

The trip is offered only to Vietnam War veteran amputees who suffered their wounds in combat. Finalists are chosen at random.

For many of the lucky winners, it's a once-in-a-lifetime opportunity to hunt antelope. Due to high trip costs, Greenwood normally caters to doctors, lawyers and other

Four vets who left legs and hands behind in Vietnam smile in front of pronghorn antelope trophies they bagged in Montana in 1997. VFW helps sponsor the hunting trip, an annual outing that began for one disabled vet in 1983. From left to right: Jim Sursely, John Devine, Raul "Rudy" Saucedo and Pat Schmitt.

professionals with large incomes. But the vets experience much more than average hunters on the annual VFW trip.

It gives them a chance to hunt with men who know intimately what they've endured. They also reminisce about their time in the service, recall their ups and downs during recovery and talk about their plans for the future.

Remarkably, they are all upbeat about life. For many of them, it has become their credo. During the hunt, a triple-amputee said about his time after Vietnam, "You can either go forward or go backward. I've chosen to go forward." These same sentiments were shared by the 1998 group.

Gary Bartlett, Jim Brunotte, Bill Johnston and Bud Marsh — who between them sacrificed a dozen limbs and other body parts in Vietnam — made the 1998 hunting trip to Montana. Johnston, a thrice-wounded Marine who lost both legs, captured the spirit of all the men who have overcome such severely disabling war wounds.

"People look at my condition and say, 'What a tragedy.' But I don't think so. It's a trade-off: Because of my disability I've been able to spend more time with my kids. Life is full of opportunities. You can deal with things as problems or as opportunities."

Chapter 11
Honoring the Troops in Life and Death

Miss Kansas, Kim Dugger, sings the national anthem to open the VFW Heart of America Rally held on June 1, 1991, at Richards-Gebaur Air Force Base outside Kansas City, Mo. More than 75,000 spectators gathered to honor troops who served during the Persian Gulf War.

Supporting troops in the field is a top VFW priority. Members have backed those serving from Korea and Vietnam to the Gulf and Bosnia. And they've memorialized Americans who sacrificed their lives on the battlefield.

Maintaining an active role in the community includes demonstrating concern for fellow citizens in uniform. Obviously, active duty personnel come from every town and city in the nation, and that's where VFW members enter the picture. Bolstering the morale of troops overseas in wartime and other periods of crisis is civic service at its best.

The link with home is as important to morale as hot chow and victory on the battlefield. Men on the line or stationed at a dreary foreign outpost depend on support from home to see them through a tour of duty. As we saw in Chapters 3 and 7, WWI Doughboys and WWII GIs were heaped with honors and universally praised by the citizens whose interests sent them overseas. And during both wars, VFW was in the forefront of the support movement.

Public backing for later wars was less than universal. In these cases, VFW efforts on behalf of the fighting men were even more important. The Korean War (1950-1953) was a prime example of dedicated VFW home front support.

VFW Washington Office Director Omar Ketchum summed up the situation early on: "In spite of the seeming apathy of the American people toward the men who are doing a magnificent job against superior numerical strength on that bleak and forsaken peninsula, the Veterans of Foreign Wars has not forgotten and is proud to present these benefits (for which the VFW has taken the lead) that are now available to those who have served on or after June 27, 1950." (Those benefits were outlined in Chapter 8.)

On the local level, VFW contributions were equally critical. American blood being spilled by the gallon in Korea was replaced at home and shipped across the ocean. Veterans who had fought on coral atolls, in Pacific jungles and on European battlefields knew just how precious whole blood was to badly wounded men. Members of Posts all over America literally rolled up their sleeves when VFW called for blood donations.

When Post 3042 in Laurel, Miss., answered the call, it set an area record. VFW mustered not only its own members, but enlisted housewives, oil field

With the Korean War in its third year and U.S. casualties steady, *VFW* magazine's February 1952 cover reminded members to donate blood to save American lives on the battlefields of that war-torn peninsula.

workers and businessmen. Any citizen who hailed a cab and named Post 3042 as the destination rode without charge.

The drive began, appropriately enough, on Pearl Harbor Day, 1950. The Red Cross bloodmobile arrived at the Post home and within two hours the initial supply of blood-collecting bottles and shipping crates was exhausted. More was rushed from Mobile, Ala. Volunteers from the Ladies Auxiliary and area hospitals stayed methodically busy throughout the day. Members of local labor unions and civic groups arrived to donate their pints of blood.

At 6 p.m., Dec. 7, at the end of a very long day, Hal Atkinson, chairman of the local VFW blood campaign, announced the record for the Mobile area — the 273 pints collected in one day at Pascagoula, La., had been broken. Atkinson and the others were not satisfied: They wanted to break the only other record remaining in the Southeast area of the Red Cross — 300 pints donated by the citizens of Charlotte, N.C.

Within two hours, the record fell. The 313th bottle was capped and placed in a shipping container. Prospective donors were still waiting in line when a Red Cross doctor said no more bottles were left. The volunteers would have to come back the following morning. It was a spirited achievement for a Post numbering 491 members. It gave other Posts something to shoot for during the rest of the war.

VFW faced a formidable challenge in the rehabilitation of disabled Korean War veterans. Quartermaster General Robert B. Handy, Jr., explained: "The job is even more complicated today. When we were at war with the Axis powers, Congress provided the Veterans Administration with a nearly unlimited budget. But during the last two years, the VA budget has been greatly curtailed. Branch offices have closed, field representatives discharged. As a consequence, VFW Post service officers are forced to absorb details of work

> "In spite of the seeming apathy of the American people toward the men who are doing a magnificent job against superior numerical strength on that bleak and forsaken peninsula, the Veterans of Foreign Wars has not forgotten them."
> **Omar Ketchum**
> **Director, VFW Washington Office**

VFW Post 3042 in Laurel, Miss., organizes a blood donor drive on Pearl Harbor Day, Dec. 7, 1950. Volunteers from the Ladies Auxiliary pitch in. By the end of the day, the Red Cross runs out of collection bottles. But an area record of 313 pints of whole blood collected in one day will be on the way to forward first aid stations and field hospitals.

steadily growing in volume."

To help fund growing programs, Handy issued a call for a doubling of sales of Buddy Poppies by doubling the number of VFW and Auxiliary members on the streets selling the bright red paper flowers.

In early summer 1951, VFW launched *Operation Vacation* — a special service program for disabled veterans and their wives. Every two weeks, medical authorities picked a wounded serviceman to receive a two-week vacation to Florida with all expenses paid.

The first so honored was Sgt. Phillip M. Sabato, an eight-year veteran of the Marine Corps who had been wounded and frostbitten during the fighting around Chinju Reservoir in North Korea. When he was able to travel, Sabato and his wife were sent from Washington National Airport by Maryland Republican Rep. James P.S. Devereux, who had commanded the Marines on Wake Island during its epic defense 10 years earlier.

The Sabatos were met at Miami airport by VFW representatives and chauffeured to their hotel to unwind on white beaches under a bright sun; terrain so unlike that of Chinju.

Walter E. Hogue, a Navy quartermaster first class, was another vet who discovered he was not among the forgotten when he returned to the States after a harrowing experience in Korean waters.

Hogue's minesweeper, the *Pledge*, swept the harbor prior to the Marine amphibious assault at Inchon on Sept. 15, 1950. The *Pledge* remained on station until it was blown up by a mine that killed seven sailors and wounded 43 others. Hogue, bleeding from a leg wound, was pulled from the water by a Navy frogman and recuperated in a stateside hospital. Thanks to *Operation Vacation,* Hogue and his wife, Kathleen, found convalescence considerably enhanced.

GIs in the war zone also performed their share of good deeds. Marines and Seabees of the 1st Marine Aircraft Wing formed the first VFW field unit in Korea — Ichibon VFW No. 1. They adopted an orphanage and asked for children's winter clothing from the States. National headquarters in Kansas City sent a check for $500, and *Operation Santa Claus* gathered momentum.

A letter from Maj. John E. Johnson of the Pusan Replacement Depot was published in *VFW* magazine asking — not for money — but clothing for the "ragged orphans in this war-torn city." He urged those at home to "clean out the attic — don't throw it away, mail it away." In Long Island City, N.Y., Post 5294 took him at his word and launched a community-wide campaign,

Commander-in-Chief Charles C. Ralls presents plane tickets to Miami, Florida, to Sergeant and Mrs. Phillip M. Sabato.

Luxury VACATIONS

For War Wounded Home from Korea Arranged by V.F.W.

VFW launches "Operation Vacation" in 1951 for disabled Korean War vets. Twice a month, a wounded vet and his wife are flown to Florida for an all-expenses-paid two-week holiday. Commander-in-Chief Charles C. Ralls presents plane tickets to Marine Sgt. and Mrs. Phillip M. Sabato.

Officers of VFW Field Unit Post No. 1 in Pohang, Korea, September 1952, announce their goal of 500 charter members during the coming year. All the members were attached to the 1st Marine Aircraft Wing.

In January of 1952, VFW launched a letter-writing campaign called *Be Sure to Write Today.* "The members of our own organization," said Commander-in-Chief Frank C. Hilton, "know from personal experience what Mail Call means. This is why we are sponsoring this letter-writing project."

The sheet music cover promoted the project's official theme song, written by composer John W. Miller.

sending more than 6,500 pounds of clothing to Pusan.

By the end of the war, American troops in Korea had donated more than $25 million out of their paychecks to help salvage the ruined land. Organized assistance arrived with the creation of the American-Korean Foundation. VFW became an active partner. As Foundation Chairman Gen. James A. Van Fleet, said: "The fighting must be followed by a victory over starvation, disease and despair. The help of every American in every American city, town and village is needed to win this victory."

VFW Commander-in-Chief Wayne E. Richards reminded members: "By working closely with other civic, veteran and fraternal groups, we have an opportunity to again demonstrate that the VFW community service program is one of positive action — and not merely lip service when our help is needed."

Early in May 1954, Junior Vice Commander-in-Chief Timothy J. Murphy flew with other veterans organization leaders to Korea under the sponsorship of the Foundation's "Veterans March for Korea" campaign.

Murphy met President Syngman Rhee and was a guest of the South Korea veterans association. "We learned," Murphy reported, "that no provisions were made to assist disabled South Korean veterans. Those who have lost arms and legs are unable to get artificial limbs. No vocational guidance is available for psychoneurotic treatment. No hospitals for men wounded in fighting against the Reds."

When he returned home, Murphy told fellow VFW members of the efforts GIs were making to alleviate the suffering of the Korean people. He urged VFW to do its utmost to support the Foundation "in the name of humanity"— and, more pragmatically — "to insure Korea against propaganda by underground Communists who are trying to exploit the misery that exists."

Long before it was over, the public lost interest in the Korean War. Most of its veterans quietly submerged themselves in society. Under these circumstances, it is no surprise that formal recognition of their sacrifices was virtually non-existent. All that changed, ironically, with the erection of a memorial to an even more controversial war. In the aftermath of the Vietnam War Memorial dedication during the early 1980s, a movement arose to build a Korean War memorial.

VFW was in the forefront of that effort. In August 1987, the organization presented a check for $200,000 to the American Battle Monuments Commission, the agency responsible for raising funds. VFW members ended up making the largest contribution of all veterans groups.

In the July 1995 issue of *VFW* magazine, Commander-in-Chief Allen F. Kent wrote: "Finally, after 42 years, Korean War vets are receiving the official and lasting recognition long their due. The VFW has proudly played a major part in making the memorial a reality. VFW members contributed more than $600,000, leading all veterans groups. We could do no less. Years of fund-raising and organizational promotion paid dividends."

The two-acre memorial is located in a small grove of trees called Ash Woods, near the Lincoln Memorial and directly across the Reflecting Pool from the Vietnam Veterans Memorial. An estimated 50,000 people turned out for the July 27 dedication. Before them appeared 19 life-like statues on patrol — 14 soldiers, three Marines, a Navy corpsman and an Air Force forward air controller. The stainless steel figures stand from 7 1/4 to 7 1/2 feet tall, frozen in time.

Nearby, a 164-foot reflecting wall of polished granite contains 2,500 images representing all branches and services that participated in the war. Engraved on the wall is the reminder that "Freedom is not Free." Etched on the apex: "Our nation honors her sons and daughters who answered the call to defend a country they never knew and a people they never met." The "Pool of Remembrance," 30 feet long, filled with continuously circulating water, is intended as a place of reflection on sacrifices made in the past.

Sadly, the description of Korea as the "forgotten" war is all too true when it comes to the government. Within three years of its dedication, the Korean War Memorial was in a disgraceful state of disrepair. Just two years short of

Past VFW Commander-in-Chief John Staum; Bob Currieo, past Washington Office executive director and Chief; and retired Marine Gen. Raymond G. Davis, then-chairman of the Korean War Veterans Memorial Advisory Board, pay tribute in 1995 to America's Korean War dead depicted on a 164-foot reflecting wall of polished granite containing 2,500 images.

the war's 50th anniversary, Congress had to appropriate $2 million to make it presentable.

Vietnam, more so than Korea, cried out for public displays of morale-boosting. Lengthier and more prone to overt hostility directed at its participants, the Vietnam War (1965-1973) was a true test of VFW's resolve to back the warriors no matter what the course or outcome of the war.

In 1965, Commander-in-Chief Andy Borg, a WWII Navy vet, visited Vietnam. He was outraged at the avalanche of media coverage of so-called "peace" demonstrations at home. Borg cabled an angry protest to the U.S. wire services. "Our fighting men," he said, "would like misguided protesters to shut up, and they told me so in no uncertain terms."

Borg returned home determined to provide tangible proof that Americans supported the men who daily faced death and wounds. He chose Veterans Day, 1965, to mount *Operation Boost*. Letters were sent to every VFW Post in the country asking for an all-out effort. The response was overwhelming. Hundreds of mayors issued proclamations calling on citizens to rally around the troops. More than 240 U.S. newspapers featured *Operation Boost* — some even contributed free ad space to promote the events. Radio and TV stations donated hundreds of hours for spot announcements.

On Veterans Day, a *VFW* magazine editor reported: "If patriotism had ever become old-fashioned, it roared back into style on Nov. 11. There were parades, speeches, special school and church programs, flags flying and cheers ringing loud and clear through the autumn air."

Borg was moved to comment: "When the annals of this wonderful organization are set down, historians will surely find that its members' support of U.S. fighting men in Vietnam was one of its most splendid moments. It would take a book to list all our projects. Together, they form a living memorial built by veterans of past wars to demonstrate to those fighting men that we were with them to a man."

In Huntsville, Ala., Post 2702 put together *Operation Sweet Tooth*, which

On July 27, 1995, the Korean War Veterans Memorial is dedicated in Washington, D.C. VFW members contributed more than $600,000, leading all veterans groups in making the memorial a reality. The 19 stainless steel figures, slightly larger than life, seem frozen in time.

dispatched crates of Christmas goodies unavailable in Vietnam. Marine Cpl. James E. Carter wrote from Da Nang: "The guys over here know that it is just a few idiots who are making trouble — they do not represent true Americans. They just want to enjoy the freedom you guys have won for us and not pay anything in return. I grew up as a free person in a free nation, thanks to you."

In 1966, national headquarters launched *Operation Assist*, a VFW-wide program. It was created to help families of men who found themselves in unfamiliar communities when suddenly husbands, fathers or sons were sent to Vietnam. Post members sought out families who needed help and provided it. Post 1881 of Cheyenne, Wyo., for example, started a scholarship fund for children of Wyoming servicemen killed in action.

Relatives of troops in Vietnam often felt like lepers because of anti-war demonstrations. In a counter move, Post 8253 in Hazleton, Pa., organized a "March for Freedom" that drew 20,000 people who closed ranks in a massive demonstration of support. The march boosted pride and morale among those at home who sweated out the safe return of their men overseas.

Americans in Vietnam were not thinking only of themselves. Maj. Gen. Lew Walt, commander of the Third Marine Amphibious Force, backed *Operation Handshake*, an effort that provided basic supplies that his Marines distributed to Vietnamese soldiers fighting alongside them.

One of the more unusual requests in the field came from a chaplain who wrote Post 342 in Rockford, Ill., asking for a bell to replace one stolen by Communists at a church and orphanage. A 600-pound bell was donated from an equally unusual source — a shrine erected by a father in gratitude for the safe return of five sons from WWII.

The Post secured the bell along with more than $300,000 worth of clothes, food, medical and school supplies for sick and needy Vietnamese. It required two Marine cargo jets to fly the bell and two tons of supplies to Vietnam.

In the wake of the Tet Offensive of 1968, VFW mobilized its members to come to the aid of the devastated South Vietnamese. Brutalized by the Communist forces, villagers cried out for help. Within six short months, $85,000 was raised for the Tet Aggression Relief Fund. Assistance was dispensed in the form of 10 deep water wells, antibiotics, personal items for 12,000 hospitalized Vietnamese veterans, medical equipment and necessary

Commander-in-Chief Andy Borg launches "Operation Boost" in 1965 to counter morale-eroding protests at home and abroad. On Veterans Day that year, there is a massive outpouring of support from citizens across the nation. Members of Post 379 in Yakima, Wash., display a support banner at the airport.

"When the annals of this wonderful organization are set down, historians will surely find that its members' support of U.S. fighting men in Vietnam was one of its most splendid moments."
Andy Borg
VFW Commander-in-Chief (1965-66)

1st Infantry Division officers brief Junior Vice Commander-in-Chief Joseph A. Scerra (without a cover) during a trip to Vietnam in 1966. Scerra said troop morale was "almost unbelievable." He added, "If we lose the war in Vietnam it will not be lost by our men. It will be lost in Washington."

The VFW Kings County Council of Brooklyn, N.Y., assembled 100,000 paperback books for servicemen in Vietnam in May 1970. Committee members (left to right): Meta Dreher, Carol Dreher, Mildred Hojnacki, Ted Tilton, Anna Graves, Robert Ramsey, Edward Ramsey, Irene Hauske, VFW County Council Commander John L. Fopeano, Chairman Alfred A. Manti, Jr., Henry Hojnacki and Edward Dreher.

essentials for handicapped vets at a rehabilitation center. James Weber reported: "As evidenced by the projects completed because of the generosity of the VFW and its Ladies Auxiliary, it is apparent that Americans are doing more than fighting a war in Vietnam."

During the war, *VFW* magazine served as a forum for servicemen to air their views. Letters came into the national office in Kansas City by the hundreds. None wanted sympathy for themselves — but they frequently expressed outrage, offered thanks for support and told stories of accomplishments few other media outlets bothered to report. Here are a few examples:

Chaplain G.P. Murray: "I spent eight months in a combat zone with a group of men who literally worked themselves to death on humanitarian projects. We built roads, dug water wells and did countless acts of civic improvement working in Catholic and Protestant orphanages. What's wrong with being on the side of freedom? What's wrong with helping a brother who is badly hurt and calling for help? What's wrong with speaking out against the godless ruthlessness of communism?"

Spec. 5 James E. Bohannon. U.S. Army: "Without my presence and a half-million others, free elections would never have taken place. That's why I'm here — to make those elections possible....so that school children here can learn about freedom, *their* heritage, just as I once learned."

Staff Sgt. R.P. Randall, U.S. Marine Corps: "The VFW should put even more pressure, for lack of a better word, on the legislative body of our government to stop playing games in Vietnam and either fight a no-holds-barred war or get out and stop wasting lives. Which is more important, world opinion or the lives of American fighting men?"

Spec. 4 David House, Spec. 4 George Wurtzinger, Spec. 4 John McDonald,

May 13, 1967, witnessed perhaps the largest troop support rally during the Vietnam War. Organized by *We Support Our Men in Vietnam*— the brainchild of VFW member Ray Gimmler— 250,000 marchers paraded down New York City's Fifth Avenue. A sea of American flags waved for 8 1/2 hours as placards proclaimed unqualified backing for GIs.

VFW aid was extended to allied war casualties. Funds were raised by VFW's Tet Aggression Relief Fund at the height of the Vietnam War in 1968-69. The project garnered $85,000.

Pfc. William Boufort and Spec. 4 M.J. Sullivan, Jr.: "We are proud to be Americans. The men here are disillusioned with the apathy shown by the American people. We have shed too much blood and lost too many lives to quit in our efforts here. We ask our fellow VFW members to write your congressmen; let your voices be heard. We do not consider flower power hippies or any other asinine faction to represent us."

Spec. 5 S.H. Schaefer III, 101st Airborne Division: "I am proud to be a member of the VFW — my father and grandfather are members of the same Post I am. Now that I am doing my small part for our country, I am grateful to be a member of what I feel is the finest organization in the States."

Cpl. Paul F. Southwood, 1st Marine Division, Chu Lai: "I volunteered for this second trip to Vietnam because I believed in what we are doing over here. I would be very proud to be a member of your fine organization and hope you will accept me."

If there was any doubt that most Americans backed their men fighting in Vietnam, it was dispelled by the largest supportive event staged on their behalf. Coordinated by VFW and every other veterans organization, 250,000 people marched

OUR TROOPS ARE DONATING—CAN WE DO LESS?

YOU CAN HELP OUR MEN HELP THE "TET" REFUGEES

GIVE TO THE V.F.W.

TET AGGRESSION RELIEF PROJECT

SEND YOUR DONATION NOW!
USE THE CONVENIENT COUPON BELOW

Make Check or Money Order Payable to:
V.F.W. "TET" PROJECT
V.F.W. NATIONAL HEADQUARTERS
BROADWAY AT 34th STREET
KANSAS CITY, MISSOURI 64111

Name _____
Address _____
City _____ State _____
Zip _____

THE "TET OFFENSIVE" last February in which Communist infiltrators brutally attacked 35 cities in South Vietnam has created another crisis in that war-torn land:

75,000 HOUSES DESTROYED
630,000 PEOPLE MADE HOMELESS
TO HELP these innocent victims, General Westmoreland is asking his troops to donate part of their pay to a refugee relief fund.

THE V.F.W. HAS PLEDGED ITS HELP
AT THE REQUEST of Commander-in-Chief Joseph Scerra, the National Council of Administration authorized a similar V.F.W. relief fund, to start a donation of $25,000 from National Headquarters. All members are urged to add their personal contributions.

THE MONEY will be administered in South Vietnam through General Westmoreland's headquarters to insure that every cent reaches the refugees.

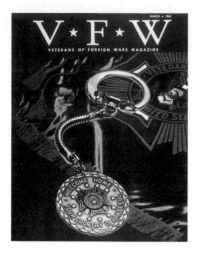

VFW members distributed thousands of key chain medallions to servicemen returning from Vietnam in 1968. The medallion is engraved with the words: "Welcome Home, Your Country is Grateful." Tears came to the eyes of one recipient, who said he didn't know anyone outside his own family cared.

Roger Staubach, Vietnam Navy vet and Dallas Cowboys quarterback from 1968-79, is a life member of Post 3359 in Garland, Texas. He has actively supported veterans causes, including construction of the Vietnam Veterans Memorial.

through the streets of New York City on May 13, 1967. Millions stood and cheered for more than eight hours as the marchers passed by.

The preamble for the *Support Our Men in Vietnam* parade committee read: "Peace is not the issue — all sane men are for peace. Our purpose is to morally support our servicemen in the field. The committee takes no position on the Administration's policy, nor does it dispute the right of dissent. It only opposes attacks on our nation and the impression given the world of a people who oppose their country. Above all, we are striving to assure our fighting men in Vietnam that they have the full respect, love, prayers and backing of the American people."

Raymond W. Gimmler, then a 43-year-old ex-Marine and still today a member of Post 3350 in East Rockaway, N.Y., was chairman of *We Support Our Men in Vietnam* and organized the parade. "A quarter million Americans — by AP and UPI count — marched 8 1/2 hours down Fifth Avenue with the idea of simply backing the fighting men," said Gimmler.

Under VFW leadership, the so-called "Silent Majority" was awakened with *Operation Speak Out*, a nationwide call to express inner feelings of patriotism. Participants represented a cross section of America. VFW was joined by 23 other organizations, encompassing other vets groups and fraternal orders.

During the week of Veterans Day, 1968, thousands of Americans gathered at the Washington Monument. In the House of Representatives, congressmen spoke for two hours backing U.S. policy and forces in Vietnam.

Commander-in-Chief Ray Gallagher was flooded with letters in 1969. President Richard Nixon wrote, "I salute the VFW and thank you." Kansas Sen. Bob Dole offered his support. Georgia Sen. Herman R. Talmadge said, "You have my full support in your efforts to counteract the vocal and militant minority that has been shaming our country."

Arizona Sen. Barry Goldwater, a WWII Army Air Forces veteran, told Gallagher he was gratified that "the VFW has taken the lead in encouraging the 199 million of our citizens who did not take part in the Moratorium to speak out." And Rep. Ed Foreman of New Mexico wrote, "I am confident that *Operation Speak Out* will demonstrate to Hanoi that we are not going to run up the white flag."

National headquarters had ordered, in 1968, thousands of key chain medallions engraved with the words, *Welcome Home, Your Country is Grateful,* for distribution to VFW members. Commander-in-Chief Richard Homan, a sergeant with the 610th Tank Destroyer Battalion in Europe during WWII, suggested that whenever a VFW member saw a serviceman just back from Vietnam, he should shake his hand and give him a medallion.

Homan was as good as his word when he clasped the hand of a captain just back from Southeast Asia. "When I gave him the medallion," Homan remembered, "tears came to his eyes. He said he didn't know anyone outside his own family cared."

During the 1971 National Convention in Dallas, Raymond J. McHugh, chief of the Copley News Service, summed up the complexities of Vietnam when he told members of a special caucus: "You are the victims of a nuclear age, a new era in which a nation dare not lose a war, but at the same time not win one, either."

By then, VFW's unflagging efforts on their behalf had attracted tens of thousands of Vietnam veterans to member rolls. On March 31, 1973 — immediately after the last GIs departed Vietnam — 60,000 Americans marched down Broadway in New York City in the 4 1/2 hour "Home With Honor" parade spearheaded by 1,000 Vietnam veterans as 150,000 citizens looked on. Later, the vets were honored at the Hotel Commodore. Once again, parade organizing was done by VFW member Ray Gimmler. "From 1965 on, 21 other large support demonstrations were held in the New York metropolitan area alone," said Gimmler.

Today, Vietnam vets comprise perhaps 25 percent of VFW's membership. They have played a prominent role in its continued growth. Beginning with the election of Billy Ray Cameron as commander-in-chief in 1984, nine Vietnam vets held the top position by 1998. Vietnam vets also are assuming the organization's mantle of leadership in the field: Many serve as Department and Post commanders. In addition, the head staffers in both Kansas City and Washington, D.C., are almost all veterans of the war in Southeast Asia.

"VFW played a definitive and extensive role. I needed money to get interest stimulated, and VFW was the only organization in Washington to come forward with money. Then VFW had fund-raising dinners, and everywhere I went VFW was right in the middle of it and actually contributed $300,000. VFW also stood by us and we added a statue and the flag. I am really lost for words to thank VFW for all the help it has given us. Individual members are the most wonderful people I have ever met in my life."
Jan Scruggs
President, Vietnam Veterans Memorial Fund

Memorialization of America's dead in Vietnam began fairly early on locally. Ten years after the war ended, the national Vietnam Veterans Memorial was dedicated to the 57,939 Americans who died in Indochina. An estimated 150,000 people crowded the Mall in Washington, D.C., to observe the five-day ceremonies that began on Nov. 10, 1982. Most were veterans and family members of the dead.

VFW's part in making the memorial possible was readily acknowledged by fund President Jan Scruggs: "VFW played a definitive and extensive role. I

needed money to get interest stimulated, and VFW was the only organization in Washington to come forward with money. Then VFW had fund-raising dinners, and everywhere I went VFW was right in the middle of it and actually contributed $300,000. VFW also stood by us, and we added a statue and the flag. I am really lost for words to thank VFW for all the help it has given us. Individual members are the most wonderful people I have ever met in my life."

When *National Salute II* rolled around in 1984, VFW was the only veterans group to contribute toward the statue dedication. Some $10,000 was given to pay for entertainment, which Frankie Valli and the Four Seasons

Wisconsin VFW members and others gather at the Vietnam Veterans Memorial in Washington, D.C. The group stands vigil for the POW/MIA cause during Veterans Week in November 1984.

turned over to the committee to defray operating expenses.

Commander-in-Chief Billy Ray Cameron, Marine Vietnam veteran, spoke at the statue dedication: "Like many of you, I have friends and comrades here memorialized — mute yet immortal. To me, this memorial has served its highest purpose: to reunite our beloved America with her bravest and best from the Vietnam era — the living as well as the dead and those still not returned from Southeast Asia.

"Speaking for the Veterans of Foreign Wars and our Ladies Auxiliary, we have always held to the ancient wisdom that says hate the war, yet honor the warrior. Jan Scruggs, you have performed a healing miracle."

Years later, an exact half-scale replica of the memorial was created by the

John A. Rodriguez of VFW Post 9186 in San Antonio, Texas, places a flag on the traveling replica of the Vietnam Veterans Memorial. The traveling Wall is half-scale, exact to the letter and inch.

The Wall, sanctioned by the Vietnam Veterans Memorial Fund, was dedicated on Nov. 8, 1996, and travels the nation.

Memorial Fund. It was dedicated in November 1996 and sent on tour across the country. "Maybe this is the way," Scruggs said, "to reach out and get high school kids interested in the Vietnam War and American history." The 1997 tour was nationally co-sponsored by VFW and Turner Broadcasting

System's TNT cable channel as part of its national veterans campaign known as "Operation TNT."

VFW was invited to be a co-sponsor by the Vietnam Veterans Memorial Fund (VVMF) as a means of furthering its commitment to community service. VFW's name and logo were prominently shown on the truck moving the wall.

David Montalvo, a Vietnam vet, visited the traveling wall in San Antonio, where more than 20,000 turned out during its three-day public display. Montalvo recalled, "It's very touching. I feel like it's a spiritual thing—people are getting in touch, somehow, with their lost loved ones."

Two other memorials were on the VFW agenda, too. The Vietnam Women's Memorial Project earned an early endorsement from VFW and ultimately received $76,000 in cash contributions. Broader in scope, the Women in Military Service for America Memorial garnered $118,000 from VFW donors. It was dedicated in October 1997.

Memorials are essential, but so is direct support to the troops. The United Service Organizations (USO) has assisted members of the armed forces by trying to bring a "touch of home" to them wherever they are stationed. Since that aim is fully compatible with VFW objectives, the organization granted financial support to USO to provide a reception center for traveling servicemen and women. Between 1982 and 1986, VFW National Headquarters sent USO $406,000 for a Washington, D.C., center. Additional donations were provided directly by Posts around the country and put into USO's building fund.

VFW continues to tangibly back USO's aims. Several overseas trips by the Dallas Cowboys' cheerleaders in the late 1990s during the holidays were VFW-funded. Keeping up morale in peacetime is one thing, boosting the morale of armed forces in the field in wartime is quite another. This is an area where VFW members excel.

During the Persian Gulf War (1990-91), VFW Post 5290 in Conyer, Ga., launches *Operation Second Front.* Boxes of items not readily available in Saudi Arabia are packed and shipped to servicemen there.

One soldier wrote back, "Thank you and God bless you."

Left to right: Department Secretary Jane Mitchell; District 19 Commander Bob Pickens; Post Commander Jim Whitten; Department Judge Advocate Glenn Mitchell; Post President Wilma Parrott; Department President Patsy Cates; Bob Phiel; Chairman Jack West; Sara Phiel and Georgia West.

U.S. forces found themselves immersed in a major military campaign as this decade opened. Approximately 600,000 GIs served in the brief Persian Gulf War of 1991. Starting with the 1990 troop build up in Saudi Arabia known as *Operation Desert Shield,* VFW lost no time in galvanizing home front support.

VFW members tied ribbons around trees and fence posts to show their support; others

initiated letter-writing campaigns. Post 5290 in Conyer, Ga., launched *Operation Second Front* and shipped cartons of canned treats and board games. A young soldier wrote back, "It does my heart good to know that there are people in the world like you. Thank you and God bless you!"

Post 6933 in Darien, Conn., decided to adopt a unit of its own — the Decontamination Platoon of the 197th Infantry Brigade. Out went magazines, cassette tapes and all manner of "junk food."

Children at the VFW National Home in Michigan kept up a letter-writing campaign that would last until *Operation Desert Storm* was over.

In Independence, Mo., Rose Hudson's mother remembered lighting a candle every night during WWII until the troops came home. Her daughter adopted the ritual. WWII vet Robert Fetch, a close neighbor and VFW member, recognized the significance of the remembrance candles. Each night, Fetch and Rose Hudson, as well as many others, set lighted candles on inner sills facing the street, the small flames glowing steadily to remind passersby of GIs overseas.

When the 1st Infantry Division — the "Big Red One" — shipped out for the Middle East it took along 10,000 boxes of care packages arranged by Post 8733 and its Ladies Auxiliary in Junction City, Kan. Post 3398 in Willow Grove, Pa., "adopted" the H & S Company of the 1st Marine Tank Battalion. Post Commander Andre Fleming remembered his days in Vietnam, recalling "the good feeling of receiving cards, letters and cookies from unknown but loving Americans."

VFW troop support from national headquarters during the Persian Gulf War fell into three phases: *Operation Hometown,* which eventually delivered 100,000 packages to U.S. forces in the Gulf; *Operation Homefront,* a nationwide toll-free family assistance hotline; and *Operation Homecoming* with its spectacular "Heart of America Rally" in Kansas City.

Operation Hometown started the show. In 1990, VFW representatives flew to Saudi Arabia to arrange distribution of the 100,000 packages to be sent from the States. Retail value of gift items surpassed $1 million early in the campaign. Various companies made generous donations.

Packages contained lip balm, sunglasses, greeting cards, music cassettes, baseball card books, shampoo, sewing kits, T-shirts, disposable razors, bandannas, hand lotion, hard candy, chewing gum, mouthwash, Frisbees, flycatcher insect traps,

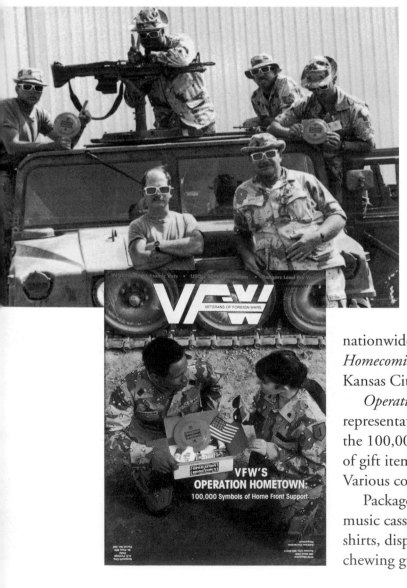

Staff Sgt. James Merriweather and Spec. Melissa Ross of the 1st Infantry Division in 1990 at Ft. Riley, Kan., open one of the gift boxes. The collective retail value of gift items surpassed $1 million. (Bottom photo)

GIs in the Saudi desert display frisbees and sun glasses, part of *Operation Hometown,* dispatched by VFW in 1990-91. Other useful items included books, stationery, video games, lip balm and insect traps.

VFW magazines, Ladies Auxiliary pencils, writing paper and envelopes and small American flags.

Benefits accrued at home as well. The first 50,000 boxes were packed by eager handicapped employees of the Rehabilitation Institute of Kansas City.

The second 50,000 were loaded by veterans under the Compensated Work Therapy Program at the VA Medical Center in Topeka, Kan.

Gen. H. Norman Schwarzkopf, head of the U.S. Central Command, received an *Operation Hometown* package. He wrote: "I received your *Operation Hometown* package. Thank you very much. ... That's just the kind of support that our young men and women need and deserve. ... Let me assure you that we will continue to prove we are worthy of your support. You are why we are here."

Operation Homecoming's "Heart of America Rally" took place June 1, 1991, at Richards-Gebaur Air Force Base outside Kansas City. More than 75,000 spectators gathered to honor troops and families of *Operation Desert Storm*. Some 2,500 *Desert Storm* veterans attended from six Midwest states. Children and adults alike crawled over modern weapons of war — tanks, Humvees, Bradley fighting vehicles, howitzers and aircraft spread across the tarmac. Families and veterans of earlier wars were treated to demonstrations of a Patriot missile battery and a variety of small weapons systems. Live music was occasionally drowned out by the sound of high-performance jets screaming overhead.

Commander-in-Chief James L. Kimery said that although the *Desert Storm* conclusion was an occasion to celebrate, the rally was "truly a celebration of the efforts of veterans and their families in all of America's wars."

Keynote speaker Maj. Gen. Thomas R. Olson, second-highest ranking Air Force general leading *Desert Storm* in Saudi Arabia, paid tribute to the rally organizers: "You are the stout hearts that maintain the strength we need to be the force we are."

Families were everywhere, waving miniature American flags donated by the Ladies Auxiliary. One of the honorees was Susan Pontius. She had to leave her husband and four children behind in Kansas City to serve as a nurse with the 410th Army Evacuation Hospital Unit. Seeing the flags fluttering in the hands of so many thousands prompted her to say, "I think this is just wonderful. It feels so neat to come home and feel that you are so welcome."

> "I received your *Operation Hometown* package. Thank you very much. ... That's just the kind of support that our young men and women need and deserve...Let me assure you that we will continue to prove we are worthy of your support. You are why we are here."
> Gen. H. Norman Schwarzkopf
> Commander, U.S. Central Command

Visitors to VFW's June 1991 "Heart of America" rally are treated to close-up views of some of the weapons used in the lightning desert war. Standing near a self-propelled 155mm howitzer, kids turn their attention skyward as military jets thunder overhead.

VFW Magazine: A Century of Covers

VFW magazine has transformed itself along with the changing times of the 20th century. VFW traces its roots to *American Veterans of Foreign Service*, which began publishing in November 1904 and was originally edited by founding member James Romanis. *Foreign Service* was launched in 1915 under William E. Ralston.

From 1927 until his death in January 1962, Barney Yanofsky — a professional journalist — served as editor. *Foreign Service* became *VFW* with the January 1951 issue. John Smith assumed Yanofsky's responsibilities until hiring James K. Anderson, who was editor from 1969-89. Richard K. Kolb, a Vietnam vet, is the current editor-in-chief.

A U.S. Marine fire team stops to plan its next move through some buildings where members later found a Somali weapons cache. The sweep occurred during *Operation Restore Hope* in January 1993.

VFW eagerly recruited veterans of Somalia after they were awarded the prestigious Armed Forces Expeditionary Medal.

Within little more than a year of the Gulf fight, GIs were back in harm's way. This time it was the East African country of Somalia. Dispatched in late 1992 to save the starving, U.S. soldiers and Marines ended up fighting for their own lives on occasion: 30 would lose their lives there before America pulled out in 1994. Numerous Posts "adopted" units serving in Somalia. Contributions to morale ranged from donating care packages to ensuring the names of those killed were added to war memorials.

Col. Lawrence E. Casper, CO of the 10th Mountain Division's Falcon Brigade, wrote from Mogadishu, Somalia's capital, in response to a Missouri Post's gifts. "Not only does your gift enhance the morale of our soldiers," he said, "but equally beneficial is the assurance that people back home do care about what we are doing. Your support helps motivate us as we execute our mission."

Lt. Col. Bill David, commander of the 10th's *Task Force 2-14*, wrote to *VFW* magazine: "We have been involved in all the fighting here in Mogadishu since Aug. 1, 1993, to include the rescue of 90 Rangers and the ensuing battle of Oct. 3-4. Contrary to what our liberal media would have the American public believe, the outcome of the fighting has been very much one sided — with the scales tipped in our favor. The professionalism, courage and valor of the American fighting man remains alive and well. It is truly a national treasure.

"I would appreciate a separate mailing of membership applications from your fine organization. I feel confident that we have a large number of soldiers who would feel honored to join the ranks of the VFW."

Veterans of *Operation Restore Hope* were awarded the Armed Forces Expeditionary Medal (AFEM) at VFW's urging. Staff teams from VFW National Headquarters and the Washington office fanned out to both ends of the country — from Camp Pendleton in California, home of the 1st Marine Expeditionary Force to Fort Drum in Watertown, N.Y., home of the 10th Mountain Division. VFW recruiters signed up 3,000 new members, waiving the usual dues and creating a reservoir of good will among America's active-duty combat Marines and soldiers.

Commander-in-Chief Jack Carney said: "It's VFW's way of showing our appreciation for a job well done. Recognition is due these outstanding men and women who served on the Horn of Africa. A free annual membership in our organization is the least we can do to express our gratitude."

Means of showing VFW's appreciation for service overseas were demonstrated again just two years later. In 1996, on another continent in the former Yugoslavia, U.S. troops were called to help settle ancient quarrels.

Bosnia is more than 6,000 miles from the nearest U.S. port of embarkation, but not out of range of VFW support missions. It occurred to Post Adjutant Gordon DeHart of Post 9574 in Aurora, Ill., to write directly to U.S. force headquarters in Tuzla and ask what was in short supply. DeHart was told books and magazines would fill the bill.

Post members solicited contributions, including a substantial gift from The Tri-Cities American Association of University Women's annual book sale. More than 1,000 books and numerous bundles of magazines were collected, packaged and sent on their way to U.S. troops. At Christmas 1996, the Post mailed 3,200 cards to the men and women overseas — each card bearing the lyrics of traditional carols as reminders of holidays past with friends and family.

From Post 7591 in Madison, Wis., members and its Auxiliary donated personal necessities and choice food items valued at $700. Post 1197 and its Auxiliary in Batavia, Ill., regularly dispatched gifts to servicemen and women. It also "adopted" particular units, including the 74th Engineer Company. Fifth-grade children showed their concern by writing letters included with Easter baskets.

These contributions did not go unnoticed. The Illinois Post and its Auxiliary, for instance, received a commemorative plaque and a certificate of appreciation from the 9th Engineer Battalion.

VFW magazine — maintaining a tradition harking back to WWI and more recently Bosnia — sent its own contributions. Cpl. David Strang, chaplain's assistant of the 4th Battalion, 12th Infantry, responded: "American support has always been the backbone of military success. If you wish to grant future assistance, paperback books, magazines, recent newspapers, religious literature, cookies, letters of encouragement and mostly, prayer, are the things that benefit the religious program and the soldiers most."

Contributions came from faraway places. Air Force Staff Sgt. Troy Wright, a life member of Post 1913 in Hopkinsville, Ky. — then based at Osan AFB in South Korea — came up with a novel idea. He asked for help from his hometown Post in securing "lots of instant oatmeal." Post Commander Roy M. Heirakuji got in touch with the Quaker Oats Company in Chicago and explained the VFW mission. Quaker Oats responded with four crates of the

Members of VFW Post 9574 in Aurora, Ill., load up boxes in 1996 destined for troops stationed in Bosnia. More than 1,000 books and numerous bundles of magazines are collected, packaged and sent on their way. Left to right: Post Commander Ray Hedrich, Quartermaster Franklin Hobart and Senior Vice Commander Dick Maudsley.

classic American cereal.

When *VFW* magazine's editor visited Bosnia in May 1996, he heard a common refrain. "The media doesn't care for the individual soldier — only stories that make big headlines," remarked GI Michael L. Smith. "That's why it is so important to see that VFW cares enough to visit troops over here."

VFW took the next step, securing tangible recognition for Bosnia vets for a job well done under hazardous conditions. VFW fought for nearly two years to have the prestigious Armed Forces Expeditionary Medal (AFEM) granted to them. With the help of New York Rep. Gerald Solomon in Congress, they were authorized the AFEM in late 1997.

VFW Post 11555 (Topeka, Kan.) Commander Sherry Blede hands out *Operation Uplink* phone cards to members of the 190th Air Refueling Wing deploying for Bosnia in 1997. Many troops say that *Operation Uplink* provides a vital link to home.

VFW now has a permanent way of lending a helping hand to Americans in uniform and away from home. A VFW innovation called *Operation Uplink,* implemented generally in August 1996, has proved a morale lifter to all the recipients of its pre-paid, long-distance calling cards. As the card holder cover says, "This is our way of helping hospitalized veterans and active-duty military personnel maintain ties with family and friends."

Cards have been distributed to vets in VA hospitals and troops on active duty in Bosnia, South Korea, Germany, Saudi Arabia, Kuwait and Panama. Telephone time is purchased with funds donated by Posts and Ladies Auxiliaries, corporate contributions and individuals.

VFW's *Operation Uplink* distributes thousands of free, long-distance phone calling cards to hospitalized veterans and active-duty personnel overseas.

The concept was introduced in August 1996. On July 4, 1998, the program was boosted with the distribution of 25,000 prepaid phone cards to military personnel at bases in the Washington, D.C., area.

VFW service officers and VA officials hand out the cards in VA hospitals. Commanding officers, Red Cross and USO volunteers give cards at military installations with help from respective VFW Departments. Europe's VFW Department service officer, Bruce Withers, found it gratifying how the cards touched soldier's lives. "Many troops said that *Operation Uplink* is the next best thing to being home," he commented.

On July 4, 1998, 25,000 cards were presented on five bases and at two VA/military medical facilities in the Washington, D.C., area. An additional 15,000 cards were donated by IDT Corp., a telecommunications company based in Hackensack, N.J. That brought to 70,000 the number of 10- and 20-minute cards handed out. At the start of 1999, the number of phone cards had surpassed 207,000, according to Ron Browning, head of VFW's Marketing Department. West Virginia Sen. John D. Rockefeller IV most appropriately labeled *Operation Uplink* a "lifeline."

VFW's future is intertwined with the young men and women who serve in the armed forces today. That's precisely why *Operation Uplink* was launched. It serves as a direct connection between VFW and the nation's

defenders. As Sgt. Russ Parsons, stationed on Okinawa, said, "This is a wonderful program, which helps build the morale of young warriors who are faraway from loved ones."

Ground breaking for the national World War II Memorial is scheduled on Veterans Day 2000. The National Mall site is at the east end of the Reflecting Pool between the Lincoln Memorial and the Washington Monument.

The main plaza will be seven feet below ground level. Designer Friedrich St. Florian envisions the memorial as a "solemn, contemplative place embedded in the earth."

VFW is undertaking a major fund-raising campaign in support of this long overdue tribute.

Veterans — present, future and past — are what VFW is all about. While serving the needs of Americans currently in uniform, the organization cannot neglect those who have given their all. VFW has now come full circle in its efforts to memorialize America's war dead. It took memorials to Vietnam and Korea to mobilize public opinion in favor of a monument of equal stature for World War II. Fund-raising is moving full steam ahead for the tangible tribute to be constructed on the Mall in Washington, D.C. A truly monumental undertaking, the $100 million World War II Memorial will capture center stage when completed. The American Battle Monuments Commission, which is coordinating the effort, hopes to break ground for the memorial by Nov. 11, 2000.

VFW's National Council of Administration approved setting aside $2.5 million to be used as matching funds for donations made by members and Posts. VFW will contribute $1 for each $2 raised. VFW donations will be made available at the time the memorial is actually built. This fulfills a vintage VFW objective: "To perpetuate the memory and history of our dead."

But VFW, of course, is primarily about the living. Remembering the sacrifices of Americans killed in battle is vital, but so is ensuring the welfare of today's veterans well into the 21st century. That mission shows no signs of slowing. As long as there is a war veteran in need, VFW will be there to assist.

For 100 years, the Veterans of Foreign Wars has lived up to its stated ideals of caring for the disabled, tending to families who lost loved ones in war, looking out for the nation's defense, promoting citizenship and contributing to the community. Our first century has proven VFW's inherent worth. That same sense of duty will no doubt be sustained in the 21st century.

VFW Post 7344 and other veterans groups in Blue Ash, Ohio, erected what is perhaps one of the most moving tributes to the nation's veterans, and especially those who died serving their country. Spanning the Revolutionary War to the Persian Gulf War, the memorial was dedicated in May 1991. It encompasses eleven life-sized sculptures representing all branches of the armed forces. Blue Ash is a small town near Cincinnati.

'To Perpetuate the Memory

Golden Triangle Veterans Memorial Park in Port Neches, Texas, a project of Post 4820, honors veterans of all 20th century wars who call the area home. Initiated in 1988, the park encompasses nearly 11 acres. Post members have devoted well over 50,000 man-hours to its development. Its value is estimated at $1 million. Displays include a F4-D jet fighter, M-6083 tank, Huey helicopter, anchor, 7-foot statue of a Marine, landing craft and a monument to the 36th Infantry Division.

Within Golden Triangle Park (lower left), separate plaques on a marble square list the names of veterans born in the area, who enlisted there, lived there later or died in and around Port Neches.

and

VFW Post 1949 in Enumclaw, Wash., pays tribute to hometown veterans killed in action. Korean War Navy vet Jack Warren's Purple Heart memorial was dedicated on May 25, 1997, at a cost of $58,000. It bears the names of 88 veterans who served in WWI through the Vietnam War. Left to right: Post members Milton Till, Frosty Hulsey, Les Walden, Howard Evans, Jr., Delman Till and Ted Rooks.

VFW Color Guard of Post 5975 commemorates Memorial Day 1995 in Marshall Cemetery at Marshall, Ill.

History of Our Dead'

Afterword

Education benefits will continue to be a key attraction for future active duty personnel. VFW intends to see that they receive them.

What were VFW's most lasting impacts in the 20th century? Views differ. So I queried just a few of the men whose opinions are based on long service to VFW. Some ideas are common, others may be controversial. But all agree the WWII-era GI Bill tops the list. VFW, though, takes pride in many others.

Cooper T. Holt, executive director of the Washington Office for some 30 years, ranks "our lasting ability to negotiate with Congress" as the key to the fact that "not one VA hospital was closed, the VA budget was not decreased." Holt is proud of VFW's role in forming the Senate Veterans Affairs Committee. He gives due credit to Texas Rep. Olin "Tiger" Teague and Mississippi Rep. G.V. Sonny Montgomery. "Veterans never had stauncher allies than these men," he said. As for the upcoming century, Holt warned in 1999 that VFW must not rest on its laurels. "The future," he said, " is not as bright as it once was as far as veterans legislation is concerned. The reason is simple — there are fewer vets in Congress than ever before.

"Unless we're vigilant, health maintenance organizations may invade VA hospitals. VA medical centers may not exist, as we now know them, within 10 years. We are lost unless we educate everybody from the top echelon down to the Post level and convince them of the urgency."

Larry Rivers — who was a commander-in-chief, Washington office executive director and adjutant general all between 1988-98 — looked back on VFW history and cited three of the orgainzation's greatest achievements.

"The GI Bill of World War II heads the list. We played a major role in pushing it through

Congress. Certainly, the Voice of Democracy program that provides a shining opportunity for students to think, and think deeply, along patriotic lines and give expression to their feelings. And making it among the top 25 in *Fortune's* poll of effective lobbyists was a signal triumph.

"Many often overlook VFW's many small, quiet—but meaningful—contributions over the years. One example: our successful efforts in 1998 to get permanent hardship duty pay for field teams searching for MIA remains."

In anticipating the 21st century, Rivers said: "The high level of staff expertise achieved over the years must be maintained to meet the demands of the coming century, which include changing demographics. Increasingly, among veterans there are more women and racial minorities, each with their own culture and problems."

Rivers believes "the days of the beer-hall atmosphere of VFW Posts are fading. Posts in the future will feature a new image: Recreation areas, child-care centers, specials for an increasing number of senior citizens. Posts will cater to youth and will establish closer ties with non-vets."

Rivers confidently concluded: "Some in the VFW today say we face a sea of problems. I say that we are surrounded by opportunities."

Veterans benefits originate and are ultimately preserved in the Capitol Building. VFW's National Legislative Service wages battles in the halls of Congress to promote and protect veterans rights. It has done so since 1919 and will continue in the 21st century.

Howard Vander Clute, also a past chief who served as adjutant general from 1981 to 1994, reflected on VFW's past and future. He cited Quartermaster General J.A. Cheatham as one of VFW's unsung heroes. "Cheatham," he said, "knew how to keep us afloat financially. He made sage investments, always. He was conservative in the way he handled funds, and expanded the Emblem & Supply Department as a source of increased cash flow. Above all, he had integrity and demanded high moral standards of those around him."

Vander Clute continued: "As far as the future is concerned, our main goal is to stabilize membership. WWII veterans still form our largest single membership pool. But we're losing 36,000 of them each month—that's 400,000 a year. Founder Jim Putnam long ago saw the dangers when he and the others formed the organization we have today. He watched the Civil War-era Grand Army of the Republic (GAR) fade away.

"If we need to go back to the early days and rename ourselves the Veterans of Foreign Service, that's OK with me."

Spanning the generations. W.E. "Dutch" Prough of Post 1536 in Sayre, Pa., shakes hands with Hal Eddy (a Grenada vet) of Post 2811 in Gainesville, Fla., at the national convention in New Orleans in 1991. Eddy's wife Tammy is at center.

VFW's future lies where it always has: with its core membership. VFW members slogged through the snows of North Russia in 1929 to retrieve the remains of comrades killed in a forgotten campaign. Posts and Auxiliaries supported troops overseas in every campaign waged during this century. Volunteers contributed money and time to victims of natural disasters. Activists wrote thousands of letters to sway their representatives in Congress when critical veterans legislation was under debate.

Posts keep alive the spirit of patriotism and when needs arise in a community, VFW members become an immediate, visible presence. Members demonstrate consistent concern for youth.

"Traditionally, VFW's areas of volunteer activism have reached into every sector of society. Our commitment to community service is second to none," said Commander-in-Chief Tom Pouliot. "Posts are the rock upon which this organization was built. And it is at the local level where our public face is best known. Post's good works are what creates a positive image. To steer VFW on a course of sustained growth and tap into the pool of 10 million eligibles, we must work more with the community at-large."

Members in the community are the essence of VFW. They range in age from their 20s to their 80s. Perhaps some of their words are the keys to the future. One of the youngest, Ian Welch, 23, of Post 6579 in New Lothrop, Mich., served in the Adriatic Sea off Bosnia as a crew member aboard the *USS Kearsage.* He joined simply because it was a family tradition. But he warns: "We need more younger members."

At the other end of the generational spectrum is Pacific WWII vet Dan Christenson of Post 8315 in Schertz, Texas. A member since 1945, he originally joined for camaraderie, benefits assistance and community service projects. "My spirit of patriotism," he said, "has not lessened over the years."

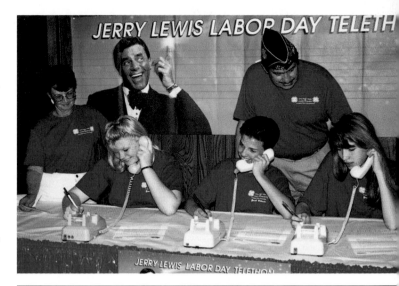

Members of Post 7945 in Thornton, Colo., help man the phones at a Jerry Lewis Labor Day Telethon, which raises funds for muscular dystrophy. Genevieve Pierce and Joe Archuleta supervise area high school students. Members at work in the community are the essence of VFW.

VFW is at the confluence of historical events. On the one hand, it is commemorating the 100th anniversary of its birth. On the other, the organization is at a crossroads regarding its long-term future. Both the new and old must be recognized equally. The marriage of an organization's heritage with its present mission ensures prestige today and guarantees success tomorrow. The year 1999 offered the opportunity to proudly proclaim the heritage bequeathed VFW by its predecessors.

At the same time, attention must be focused on what lies ahead. Today, only the veterans who served in the Persian Gulf War and the expeditionary campaigns of the 1980s and 1990s can ensure VFW's survival well into the next century. It is their youth and enthusiasm that will keep VFW in the public eye and keep the connection between the two alive.

Still, there is a common thread that cements the VFW foundation. Whether the pillars of that foundation originated in WWII, Korea, Vietnam, the Gulf, or all the campaigns in between, is not important. Our future hinges on the unity that derives from the universal experience of war and its aftermath. The particulars may have been different in each case, but the essence remains the same.

As members commemorate VFW's 100th anniversary, they simultaneously pay heed to the organization's destiny in the 21st century. That destiny will be shaped by how leaders and members alike accommodate the needs of the newest generations of overseas veterans and how they connect with the American public. On that basis, the future looks bright for the nation's premier war veterans organization.

Famed publisher Henry Luce characterized the 20th century as the "American century." Indeed, it was. But it also was VFW's century.

Spanish-American War

Philippine Insurrection

World War I

China Service

WWII–Asiatic-Pacific Campaign

WWII–European-African-Middle Eastern Campaign

WWII–American Campaign

WWII–American Defense

Army of Occupation–Europe

Army of Occupation–Far East

VFW Eligibility: 1898-1999

Listed below are the eligibility campaigns and their qualifying dates. They encompass a full century of overseas service.

SPANISH-AMERICAN WAR ERA AND BEYOND

Spanish Campaign Medal	Army	May 11-Aug. 16, 1898
	Navy	April 20-Dec. 10, 1898
Army of Cuba Occupation Medal	Army	July 18, 1898-May 20, 1902
Army of Puerto Rico Occupation Medal	Army	Aug. 14-Dec. 10, 1898
Philippine Campaign Medal	Army	Feb. 4, 1899-Dec. 31, 1913
	Navy	Feb. 4, 1899-Sept. 15, 1906
China Relief Expedition Medal	Army	June 20, 1900-May 27, 1901
China Relief Expedition Medal	Navy	April 5, 1900-May 27, 1901
Cuban Pacification Medal	Army	Oct. 6, 1906-April 1, 1909
Cuban Pacification Medal	Navy	Sept. 12, 1906-April 1, 1909
Nicaraguan Campaign Medal	Navy	July 29-Nov. 14, 1912

WORLD WAR I ERA

Mexican Service Medal	Army	April 12, 1911-June 16, 1919
	Navy	April 12, 1914-Feb. 7, 1917
Haitian Campaign Medal	Navy	July 9, 1915-Dec. 6, 1915
		April 1, 1919-June 15, 1920
Dominican Campaign Medal	Navy	May 4-Dec. 5, 1916
World War I Victory Medal	Army	April 6, 1917-April 1, 1920
(with Battle or Service clasp including	Navy	April 6, 1917-March 30, 1920
Siberia and European Russia)		
Army of Occupation of Germany Medal	Army	Nov. 12, 1918-July 11, 1923

EXPEDITIONARY ERA

Nicaraguan Campaign Medal	Navy	Aug. 27, 1926-Jan. 2, 1933
Yangtze Service Medal	Navy	Sept. 3, 1926-Oct. 21, 1927
		March 1, 1930-Dec. 31, 1932

WORLD WAR II

European-African Middle Eastern Campaign Medal	Dec. 7, 1941-Nov. 8, 1945
Asiatic-Pacific Campaign Medal	Dec. 7, 1941-March 2, 1946
American Campaign Medal	Dec. 7, 1941-March 2, 1946
(30 consecutive or 60 non-consecutive days outside the continental limits of the U. S.)	
American Defense Service Medal	Sept. 8, 1939-Dec. 7, 1941

CHINA SERVICE MEDAL

Navy/Marines (USS Panay, etc.)	July 7, 1937-Sept. 7, 1939
(Chinese Civil War, 1945-49) All Services	Sept. 2, 1945-April 1, 1957
(China/Formosa, 1950-57)	

ARMY OF OCCUPATION MEDAL

Italy	May 9, 1945-Sept. 15, 1947
Germany (except West Berlin)	May 9, 1945-May 5, 1955
West Berlin	May 9, 1945-Oct. 2, 1990
Austria	May 9, 1945-July 27, 1955
Korea	Sept. 3, 1945-June 29, 1949
Japan	Sept. 3, 1945-April 27, 1952

NAVY OCCUPATION SERVICE MEDAL

Italy	May 8, 1945-Sept. 15, 1947
Trieste	May 8, 1945-Oct. 25, 1954
Germany (except West Berlin)	May 8, 1945-May 5, 1955
Austria	May 9, 1945-Oct. 25, 1955
Asiatic/Pacific	Sept. 2, 1945-April 27, 1952

KOREAN SERVICE MEDAL
June 27, 1950-July 27, 1954
(War actually ended July 27, 1953.)

VIETNAM SERVICE MEDAL
July 4, 1965-March 28, 1973

SOUTHWEST ASIA SERVICE MEDAL .... Aug. 2, 1990-Nov. 30, 1995
(*Operation Desert Shield/Desert Storm*: Combat areas of operation only.)
Personnel assigned to support units serving in Israel, Egypt,
Turkey, Syria, and Jordan. .... Jan. 17-April 11, 1991

ARMED FORCES EXPEDITIONARY MEDAL
Lebanon .... July 1-Nov. 1, 1958
Vietnam .... July 1, 1958-July 3, 1965
Taiwan Straits .... Aug. 23, 1958-Jan. 1, 1959
Quemoy and Matsu Islands .... Aug. 23, 1958-June 1, 1963
Congo (Zaire) .... July 14, 1960-Sept. 1, 1962
Laos .... April 19, 1961-Oct. 7, 1962
Berlin .... Aug. 14, 1961-June 1, 1963
Cuba .... Oct. 24, 1962-June 1, 1963
Congo (Zaire) .... Nov. 23-27, 1964
Dominican Republic .... April 28, 1965-Sept. 21, 1966
Korea .... Oct. 1, 1966-June 30, 1974
Cambodia (*Bombing Campaign*) .... March 29, 1973-Aug. 15, 1973
Cambodia (*Operation Eagle Pull*) .... April 11-13, 1975
Vietnam (*Operation Frequent Wind*) .... April 29-30, 1975
Cambodia (Mayaguez Rescue) .... May 15, 1975
El Salvador .... Jan. 1, 1981-Feb. 1, 1992
Lebanon .... June 1, 1983-Dec. 1, 1987
Grenada .... Oct. 23-Nov. 21, 1983
Libya (*Operation El Dorado Canyon*) .... April 12-17, 1986
Persian Gulf (*Operation Earnest Will*) .... July 24, 1987-Aug. 2, 1990
Panama (*Operation Just Cause*) .... Dec. 20, 1989-Jan. 31, 1990
Somalia (*Operation Restore Hope*) .... Dec. 5, 1992-March 31, 1995
Haiti (*Operation Uphold Democracy*) .... Sept. 16, 1994-March 31, 1995
Operation Vigilant Sentinel (Persian Gulf) .... Dec. 1, 1995-Feb. 15, 1997
Operation Southern Watch (Iraq) .... Dec. 1, 1995-Open
Operation Northern Watch (Iraq) .... Jan. 1, 1997-Open
Persian Gulf Intercept Operations .... Dec. 1, 1995-Open
Bosnia (Operation Joint Endeavor / Joint Guard) ...... Nov. 20, 1995-June 20, 1998

NAVY AND MARINE CORPS EXPEDITIONARY MEDAL (post-WWII)*
Cuba ("Bay of Pigs" and before and after) .... Jan. 3, 1961-Oct. 23, 1962
Thailand .... May 16-Aug. 10, 1962
Gulf of Aden/Yemen .... Dec. 8, 1978-June 6, 1979
Indian Ocean Contingency Operation/ Iran Hostage Crisis .... Nov. 21, 1979-Oct. 21, 1981
Lebanon .... Aug. 20, 1982-May 31, 1983
Libya (*Operation Prairie Fire*, etc.) .... Jan. 20-June 27, 1986
Persian Gulf (*USS Stark*, etc.) .... Feb. 1-July 23, 1987
Panama (pre- and post-invasion)** .... April 1, 1988-Dec. 19, 1989
                                                    Feb. 1-June 13, 1990
Liberia (*Operation Sharp Edge*) .... Aug. 5, 1990-Feb. 21, 1991
Rwanda (*Operation Distant Runner*) .... April 7-18, 1994
* *Actually dates back to Feb. 12, 1874 and covers **52** landings before WWII.*   ** *Marines only.*

COMBAT ACTION RIBBON*
Navy/Marine Corps/Coast Guard .... March 1, 1961-Open

*Only two actions occurred when a campaign medal was not also authorized: USS Liberty (June 8-9, 1967) and
Operation Assured Response (Monrovia, Liberia, April 30-May 6, 1996).*

COMBAT INFANTRYMAN BADGE (Army) .... Dec. 6, 1941-Open

COMBAT MEDICAL BADGE (Army) .... Dec. 6, 1941-Open

KOREA DUTY**
Service on the Korean Peninsula, or in territorial waters
for 30 consecutive or 60 non-consecutive days. .... June 30, 1949-June 26, 1950
                                                    July 28, 1954-Sept. 30, 1966
                                                    July 1, 1974-Open

**Periods not covered by a campaign medal.

Navy Occupation

Korean Service

Vietnam Service

Southwest Asia
Service

Armed Forces
Expeditionary Medal

Navy Expeditionary
Medal

Marine Corps
Expeditionary Medal

Combat Medical
Badge

Combat Action Ribbon

Combat Infantryman Badge

Americanism Award

Armed Forces Award

Distinguished
Service Award

Dwight D.
Eisenhower Award

Emergency Services
Award

Gold Medal of Merit

Hall of Fame Award

J. Edgar Hoover Award

News Media Award

Space Award

James E. Van Zandt
Award

Convention Cities

1914 - Pittsburgh, Pennsylvania	1957 - Miami Beach, Florida
1915 - Detroit, Michigan	1958 - New York City, New York
1916 - Chicago, Illinois	1959 - Los Angeles, California
1917 - New York City, New York	1960 - Detroit, Michigan
1918 - Minneapolis, Minnesota	1961 - Miami Beach, Florida
1919 - Providence, Rhode Island	1962 - Minneapolis, Minnesota
1920 - Washington, D.C	1963 - Seattle, Washington
1921 - Detroit, Michigan	1964 - Cleveland, Ohio
1922 - Seattle, Washington	1965 - Chicago, Illinois
1923 - Norfolk, Virginia	1966 - New York City, New York
1924 - Atlantic City, New Jersey	1967 - New Orleans, Louisiana
1925 - Tulsa, Oklahoma	1968 - Detroit, Michigan
1926 - El Paso, Texas	1969 - Philadelphia, Pennsylvania
1927 - Providence, Rhode Island	1970 - Miami Beach, Florida
1928 - Indianapolis, Indiana	1971 - Dallas, Texas
1929 - St. Paul, Minnesota	1972 - Minneapolis, Minnesota
1930 - Baltimore, Maryland	1973 - New Orleans, Louisiana
1931 - Kansas City, Missouri	1974 - Chicago, Illinois
1932 - Sacramento, California	1975 - Los Angeles, California
1933 - Milwaukee, Wisconsin	1976 - New York City, New York
1934 - Louisville, Kentucky	1977 - Minneapolis, Minnesota
1935 - New Orleans, Louisiana	1978 - Dallas, Texas
1936 - Denver, Colorado	1979 - New Orleans, Louisiana
1937 - Buffalo, New York	1980 - Chicago, Illinois
1938 - Columbus, Ohio	1981 - Philadelphia, Pennsylvania
1939 - Boston, Massachusetts	1982 - Los Angeles, California
1940 - Los Angeles, California	1983 - New Orleans, Louisiana
1941 - Philadelphia, Pennsylvania	1984 - Chicago, Illinois
1942 - Cincinnati, Ohio	1985 - Dallas, Texas
1943 - New York City, New York	1986 - Minneapolis, Minnesota
1944 - Chicago, Illinois	1987 - New Orleans, Louisiana
1945 - Chicago, Illinois	1988 - Chicago, Illinois
1946 - Boston, Massachusetts	1989 - Las Vegas, Nevada
1947 - Cleveland, Ohio	1990 - Baltimore, Maryland
1948 - St. Louis, Missouri	1991 - New Orleans, Louisiana
1949 - Miami, Florida	1992 - Indianapolis, Indiana
1950 - Chicago, Illinois	1993 - Dallas, Texas
1951 - New York City, New York	1994 - Las Vegas, Nevada
1952 - Los Angeles, California	1995 - Phoenix, Arizona
1953 - Milwaukee, Wisconsin	1996 - Louisville, Kentucky
1954 - Philadelphia, Pennsylvania	1997 - Salt Lake City, Utah
1955 - Boston, Massachusetts	1998 - San Antonio, Texas
1956 - Dallas, Texas	1999 - Kansas City, Missouri

VFW Family Tree

The Veterans of Foreign Wars traces its origins to veterans of Cuba and the Philippines who formed separate groups in Ohio, Colorado and Pennsylvania. All had similar aims and were founded at, or shortly after, the turn of the century. Because of their common purposes, they all eventually united to form the premier veterans organization of America.

The tree below charts the VFW's organizational stages, showing all the parent groups and their paths to the creation of what we know today as the VFW. Leaders of both the predecessor groups and VFW appear in chronological order on the following pages with their terms in office.

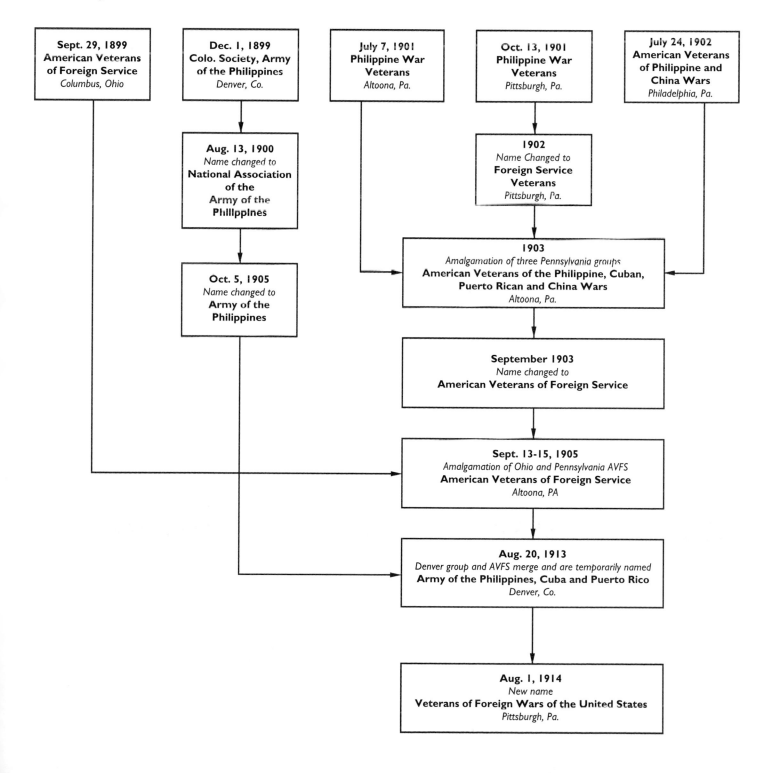

Sept. 29, 1899
American Veterans of Foreign Service
Columbus, Ohio

Dec. 1, 1899
Colo. Society, Army of the Philippines
Denver, Co.

July 7, 1901
Philippine War Veterans
Altoona, Pa.

Oct. 13, 1901
Philippine War Veterans
Pittsburgh, Pa.

July 24, 1902
American Veterans of Philippine and China Wars
Philadelphia, Pa.

Aug. 13, 1900
Name changed to
National Association of the Army of the Philippines

1902
Name Changed to
Foreign Service Veterans
Pittsburgh, Pa.

Oct. 5, 1905
Name changed to
Army of the Philippines

1903
Amalgamation of three Pennsylvania groups
American Veterans of the Philippine, Cuban, Puerto Rican and China Wars
Altoona, Pa.

September 1903
Name changed to
American Veterans of Foreign Service

Sept. 13-15, 1905
Amalgamation of Ohio and Pennsylvania AVFS
American Veterans of Foreign Service
Altoona, PA

Aug. 20, 1913
Denver group and AVFS merge and are temporarily named
Army of the Philippines, Cuba and Puerto Rico
Denver, Co.

Aug. 1, 1914
New name
Veterans of Foreign Wars of the United States
Pittsburgh, Pa.

AMERICAN VETERANS OF FOREIGN SERVICE, COLUMBUS, OHIO

James C. Putnam*
1899-1900

Maj. Will S. White*
1900-01-02

James Romanis*
1902-03-04-05

ARMY OF THE PHILIPPINES, CUBA AND PUERTO RICO, DENVER, CO.

Gen. Francis V. Greene*
1900-01

Gen. Irving Hale*
1901-02-03

Gen. Charles King*
1903-04

Gen. Wilder S. Metcalf*
1904-05

Col. Alfred
S. Frost*
1905-06

Gen. Arthur MacArthur*
1906-07

Capt H.A. Crow*
1907-08

Maj. P.J.H. Farrell*
1908-09

Col. Charles L. Jewett*
1909-10

A.H. Anderson*
1910-11

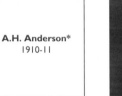

F. Warner Karling*
1911-12-13

PHILIPPINE WAR VETERANS
ALTOONA, PA.

H.O. Kelley*   G.O. Knoghton*
1901   1902

PHILIPPINE WAR VETERANS
PITTSBURGH, PA.

G.H. Smith*   James La Belle*   William A. Wein*
1901   1902   1903

AMERICAN VETERANS OF PHILIPPINES
AND CHINA WARS, PHILADELPHIA, PA.

Capt. Robert S. Hansbury*
1902

AMERICAN VETERANS OF FOREIGN SERVICE
PENNSYLVANIA

Capt. Robert S. Hansbury*
1903-04

H.O. Kelley*
1904-05

AMERICAN VETERANS OF FOREIGN SERVICE
OHIO AND PENNSYLVANIA

Charles H. Devereaux*
1906-07

David T. Nevin*
1907-08

J. Alfred Judge*
1908-09-10

George Metzger*
1905-06

Robert G. Woodside*
1910-11-12-13

VETERANS OF FOREIGN WARS

Rice W. Means*
1913-14, Colorado

Thomas Crago*
1914-15, Pennsylvania

Gus Hartung*
1915-16, Colorado

Albert Rabing*
1916-17, New York

William Ralston*
1917-18, Pennsylvania

F. Warner Karling*
1918-19-20, Missouri

*Deceased

Robert G. Woodside*
1920-21-22, Pennsylvania

Tillinghast Huston*
1922-23, New York

Lloyd M. Brett*
1923-24 Washington, D.C.

John H. Dunn*
1924-25, Massachusetts

Fred Stover*
1925-26, Pennsylvania

Theodore Stitt*
1926-27, New York

Frank T. Strayer*
1927-28, Indiana

Eugene P. Carver*
1928-29, Massachusetts

Hezekiah N. Duff*
1929-30, Michigan

Paul C. Wolman*
1930-31, Maryland

Darold D. DeCoe*
1931-32, California

Robert E. Coontz*
1932-33, Washington, D.C.

James E. Van Zandt*
1933-34-35-36, Pennsylvania

Bernard W. Kearney*
1936-37, New York

Scott P. Squyres*
1937-38, Oklahoma

Eugene I. Van Antwerp*
1938-39, Michigan

Otis N. Brown*
1939-40, North Carolina

Joseph C. Menedez*
1940-41, Louisiana

Max Singer*
1941-42, Massachusetts

Robert T. Merrill*
1942-43, Montana

Carl J. Schoeninger*
1943-44, Michigan

Jean A. Brunner*
1944-45, New York

Joseph M. Stack*
1945-46, Pennsylvania

Louis E. Starr*
1946-47, Oregon

Ray H. Brannaman*
1947-48, Colorado

Lyall T. Beggs*
1948-49, Wisconsin

Clyde A. Lewis
1949-50, New York

Charles C. Ralls*
1950-51, Washington

Frank C. Hilton
1951-52, Pennsylvania

James W. Cothran*
1952-53, South Carolina

Wayne E. Richards*
1953-54, Kansas

Merton B. Tice*
1954-55, South Dakota

Timothy J. Murphy*
1955-56, Massachusetts

Cooper T. Holt
1956-57, Tennessee

Richard L. Roudebush*
1957-58, Indiana

John W. Mahan
1958-59, Montana

Louis G. Feldmann*
1959-60, Pennsylvania

Ted. C. Connell
1960-61, Texas

Robert E. Hansen
1961-62, Minnesota

Byron B. Gentry*
1962-63, California

Joseph J. Lombardo*
1963-64, New York

John A. Jenkins*
1964-65, Alabama

227

Andy Borg*
1965-66, Wisconsin

Leslie M. Fry*
1966-67, Nevada

Joseph A. Scerra
1967-68, Massachusetts

Richard W. Homan
1968-69, West Virginia

Raymond A. Gallagher
1969-70, South Dakota

H.R. Rainwater*
1970-71, California

Joseph L. Vicites*
1971-72, Pennsylvania

Patrick E. Carr*
1972-73, Louisiana

Ray S. Soden
1973-74, Illinois

John J. Stang
1974-75, Kansas

Thomas C. Walker
1975-76, Connecticut

R.D. (Bulldog) Smith
1976-77, Georgia

John Wasylik
1977-78, Ohio

Eric Sandstrom
1978-79, Washington

Howard E. Vander Clute, Jr.
1979-80, New Jersey

T.C. Selman*
1980-81, Texas, (Died in Office)

Arthur J. Fellwock
1980-81-82, Indiana

James R. Currieo
1982-83, Arizona

Clifford G. Olson, Jr.
1983-84, Massachusetts

Billy Ray Cameron
1984-85, North Carolina

John S. Staum
1985-86, Minnesota

Norman G. Staab
1986-87, Kansas

Earl L. Stock, Jr.*
1987-88, New York

Larry W. Rivers
1988-89, Louisiana

Walter G. Hogan
1989-90, Wisconsin

James L. Kimery
1990-91, New Mexico

Robert E. Wallace
1991-92, New Jersey

John M. Carney
1992-93, Florida

George R. Cramer
1993-94, Illinois

Allen F. Kent
1994-95, Arizona

Paul A. Spera
1995-96, Massachusetts

James E. Nier
1996-97, Texas

John E. Moon
1997-98, Ohio

Thomas A. Pouliot
1998-99, Montana

John W. Smart
1999-2000, New Hampshire

John F. Gwizdak
2000-01, Georgia

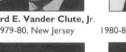

Chronology of VFW Milestones

ORGANIZATIONAL DEVELOPMENTS/PROGRAMS

VFW's accomplishments have spanned the gamut of activities, ranging from establishing national holidays to donating millions of dollars worth of college scholarships.

Note: In each case, this is the year the event occurred or the program, department or committee was created.

1899	American Veterans of Foreign Service (Columbus, Ohio) Army of the Philippines (Denver, Colo.)
1903	Three Pennsylvania groups form another AVFS
1904	First issue of *Foreign Service* (November)
1905	AVFS of Ohio and of Pennsylvania amalgamate
1912	*Foreign Service* made permanent
1913	Camps designated Posts
1914	Veterans of Foreign Wars born from merger of Ohio and Pennsylvania AVFS
	Ladies Auxiliary
	National Headquarters in Pittsburgh
1915	5,000 members
1916	First national essay contest
1917	Theodore Roosevelt becomes member
1918	National Headquarters in New York
1919	VFW's first lobbyist appointed
	National Service Bureau (NSB)
1920	Departments created (first in D.C.)
1921	60,000 members
	Women WWI vets qualify for membership
	Americanization Committee—first Americanization Day held April 27
	Legislation Division of NSB becomes separate entity
1922	Precise membership record-keeping
	Buddy Poppy program
	Hundreds of VFW Posts sponsor sports teams
1924	Members urged to become Boy Scout leaders
1925	VFW National Home in Michigan
	VFW's first Medal of Merit awarded to a Boy Scout for life-saving
	VFW's Awards and Citations Committee

	Americanization Essay Contest
1926	American Flag Movement is launched by VFW member Noel Gaines of Frankfort, Ky.
1927	VFW donates $10,000 to Mississippi Valley flood victims
	Aviator Charles Lindbergh becomes honorary VFW member
1928	VFW donates relief funds to American Red Cross
	Americanization Day (April 27) observed nationwide
	VFW proficiency medal for Citizens Military Training Camps (precursor to ROTC) candidates
1929	Two VFW members—Harold I. June and Charles Lofgren are on Byrd Expedition to Antarctica
1929-30	VFW recovery of U.S. remains from North Russia
1930	Anti-Communism rally in Union Square, N.Y.C.
	National Headquarters in Kansas City, Mo.
	First VFW scholarship award ($300) to a Boy Scout
1931	National Rehabilitation Service
	VFW succeeds in campaign to make *Star-Spangled Banner* the national anthem
1933	Department of Americanism permanent
1934	Employment & Civil Service Commission
	Sons of VFW
	VFW Committee on Junior Activities sponsors nationwide youth program
1935	VFW Citizenship Medal
1936	Boy Scout-VFW plan of cooperation
	Congressional Charter (P.L. 630)
1937	VFW HQ appropriates $10,000 for victims of Ohio River Valley floods
	VFW takes charge of Junior Softball from Amateur Softball Association (ASA)
	VFW inaugurates a permanent national youth program

1938	$25,000 donated to Red Cross for flood relief to victims
	Bicycle Safety Club program
1940	201,170 members
	Junior Rifle Clubs are formed with National Rifle Assn.
1941	VFW War Service Commission
	Boxing champ Gene Tunney becomes national director of Youth Activities
	Speak Up for Democracy radio program
1942	VFW Aviator Cadet program
1943	Extension Department
1944	Americanism Department (Youth Activities, Patriotic Instruction & Speakers Bureau) moves from D.C. to Kansas City
1945	Public Relations Department
1946	National Security and Foreign Affairs
	Membership reaches 1,544,444
	Athletics & Recreation Department
1947	Voice of Democracy with National Association of Broadcasters: Citizenship Award (first)
	National Marble Tournament held first in Boys Town, Nebraska
1947-48	First Community Service contest
1948	VFW contributes $56,000 to victims of Columbia River floods in Oregon
	Effective March 6, offices of the Commander-in-Chief and Adjutant General are relocated from Washington, D.C. to Kansas City
1949	VFW celebrates 50th Anniversary
1950	Life membership instituted
	Cooperative disaster relief plan with the Red Cross
1950-51	Nationwide community service wins Freedoms Foundation Award
1951	Adjutant General & Quartermaster General become two separate offices
	Foreign Service becomes *VFW* magazine (January)
	Permanent VFW Emergency Relief Fund established
	$35,000 in cash prizes are awarded to community projects
	Freedoms Foundation gives six awards to VFW
1952	Dunn family (Kansas flood victims) wins $75,000 farm in Washington courtesy of VFW
	National Teen-er Baseball: First annual tournament held in Hershey Park, Pa., following year

1953	VFW Junior Bowling sponsors 132 teams as part of the American Junior Bowling Congress
1955	Last Chief elected directly by delegates
	VFW joins National Conference of Service, Fraternal & Veterans Organizations on Juvenile Delinquency
1956	150,000 kids take part in national VFW marble competition
1957	Post 788 in Cedar Rapids, Iowa, sponsors Scout troop exclusively for mentally impaired boys. Total VFW Scout units enroll 50,000 boys.
1958	VFW becomes full partner in Voice of Democracy
	Encampments designated conventions
	May 1 becomes Loyalty Day (P.L. 529)
1959	Minnesota VFW/Ladies Auxiliary raises $325,000 toward dedication of the VFW Cancer Research Center at the University of Minnesota in Minneapolis. Largest single Department project ever undertaken.
1960	VFW Washington Memorial Building dedicated
1961	Insurance Department
	Teen-er Baseball leagues total 189 with 14,000 players in 22 states
	VFW-NRA Junior Postal Rifle Match winner receives first free deer hunt to Texas
	VFW assumes primary sponsorship of VOD — within four years 262,000 students participate
1962	Lite-A-Bike program: a $300,000 project with 3-M Company of St. Paul provides "Scotchlite" reflector tape. 50,000 VFW members from 4,500 Posts take part
1964	Community Activities Department
	VFW/Ladies Auxiliary contributes nearly $100,000 to earthquake victims in Anchorage, Alaska
	First VFW Congressional Award
1965	Programs is elevated to assistant adjutant general status
1966	Defensive Driving course with National Safety Council
1968	Tet Aggression Relief Project raises $85,000 for South Vietnamese civilians and disabled veterans
	Flag Act
1969	Life Insurance program
1973	Drug Awareness program
1974	VFW's 75th Anniversary
1977	Sons of VFW counts 800 units with 16,000 boys (ages 8-16)
1977-78	"Save Panama Canal" campaign

1978	Women again admitted to the VFW
	Department of Europe instituted
1979	VFW Political Action Committee
1981	VFW wins first-ever case for PTSD disability compensation
1982	Vietnam Veterans Memorial (VFW contributes $300,000)
	Hunter Safety program
1983	VFW helps sponsor Special Olympics
	VFW agrees to permit Red Cross to use VFW facilities as shelters and relief centers during natural disasters
1984	Membership passes 2 million mark
	First Vietnam veteran becomes Chief
	VFW contributes first installment of $70,000 to Vietnam Women's Memorial
1985	Home Protection program
1986	Keep America Beautiful involvement
	$406,000 is raised for United Service Organizations
1988	Post 2858 & Auxiliary in Tiffin, Ohio, raises $6,200 for Jerry Lewis' muscular dystrophy campaign
1990	VFW contributes first installment of $650,000 to Korean War Memorial
	VFW contributes $49,000 for California earthquake victims
1991	*Operation Hometown* (care packages for Gulf vets)
	Heart of America Rally for Gulf vets in K.C. draws 75,000
1992	Safety & Youth Activities expanded
	VFW disburses $197,000 to relieve victims of Hurricane Andrew and other disasters
1994	VA Golden Age Games sponsorship
	VFW Persian Gulf Registry
1995	Oklahoma City bombing victims receive $40,000 in VFW Post donations
1997	Citizenship Education and Community Service replace Americanism and Community Activities Departments
	75th anniversary of Buddy Poppy
	VFW gives $170,000 for victims of Red River floods in North Dakota and Minnesota
1998	VFW Posts raise $100,000 for March of Dimes
	VFW actively participates in Make A Difference Day and America's Promise—Alliance for Youth
	VOD gives $2.6 million in college scholarships

VETERANS BENEFITS & ISSUES

VFW has played an instrumental role in virtually every significant piece of veterans legislation passed in the 20th century.

Note: In each case, this is the year an act was passed or an institution established.

1917	War Risk Insurance Act Amendments
1918	Vocational Rehabilitation Act (P.L. 178)
1919	Census Act Rider on Veterans Preference Discharge Allowance
1920	Widows & Orphans Pension Act (Spanish-American War)
1921	Veterans Bureau Act
1923	Veterans Preference Point System
1924	House Veterans Affairs Committee
	World War Veterans Act
	World War Adjusted Compensation Act
1925	Senate Subcommittee on Veterans Affairs
1926	Spanish-American War benefits (P.L. 166)
	New Johnson Act increases WWI benefits
1930	Veterans Administration (VA)
	World War Service Disability Pension Act (P.L. 522)
1931	Bacharach Amendment (P.L. 743) allows borrowing on WWI bonus certificates
1933	Wagner-Peyser Act: Veterans Employment Service
1934	Pension for widows of WWI vets
1936	Bonus bonds to WWI vets made immediately redeemable. The bonds' collective worth: $2.4 billion.
1938	Armistice Day (Nov. 11) legal holiday (P.L. 510)
1940	Philippine Travel Pay Bill
	National Service Life Insurance
	Selective Service & Training Act
1943	Benefits to WWII vets (P.L. 10)
	Disabled Veterans Rehabilitation Act (P.L. 16)
1944	GI Bill of Rights (P.L. 346)
	Veterans Preference Act
	Mustering-Out Pay Act
	Extra pay for combat infantrymen
1946	Veteran Emergency Housing Act (P.L. 388)

1947	Bureau of Veterans Re-employment Rights (BVRR)	1984	Montgomery GI Bill

1947   Bureau of Veterans Re-employment Rights (BVRR)

1948   Cash subsistence for GI Bill increased

1950   Vocational Rehabilitation Act

1951   Servicemen's Indemnity & Insurance Acts

1952   Veterans Readjustment Assistance Act (Korean War GI Bill)

1954   Veterans Compensation Act

Nov. 11 as Veterans Day (P.L. 380)

1962   Veterans Benefits Act (Cold War GI Bill)

1966   Veterans Readjustment Benefits Act (P.L. 89-358) (Vietnam War GI Bill)

1970   Senate Veterans Affairs Committee

1972   Vietnam Era Veterans Readjustment Assistance Act (raised GI Bill stipend to $220 per month)

1973   Federal court agrees veterans preference applies to state jobs

1974   Vietnam Era Veterans Readjustment Assistance Act (vocational rehabilitation)

1976   Veterans Education & Employment Assistance Act

1977   Post-Vietnam Era Veterans Educational Assistance Act

1978   Veterans preference preserved

VA home loan increase

Veterans & Survivors Pension Improvement Act

Veterans Day returned to Nov. 11

1979   First joint meeting of House/Senate Veterans Affairs committees

Vietnam Veterans Outreach Program (P.L. 96-22) (creates Vet Centers for PTSD counseling)

Vietnam Era Veterans Week (May 28-June 3)

1980   VFW calls for Agent Orange study

VA home loan increase

Veterans Rehabilitation & Education Amendments

1981   Former POW Benefits Act

Veterans Health Care, Training & Small Business Loan Act

1982   Veterans Employment and Training Service (VETS)

Vietnam Veterans Memorial dedicated

1983   Emergency Veterans Job Training Act

1984   Montgomery GI Bill

Veterans Dioxin & Radiation Exposure Compensation Standards Act (P.L. 98-542): Agent Orange & Atomic Exposure

Vietnam Unknown placed in Tomb of Unknowns

1985   VA health care designated an "entitlement"

1987   New GI Bill Continuation Act (made permanent)

Korean War Memorial authorized

1988   Radiation Exposed Veterans Compensation Act

Department of Veterans Affairs Act

Veterans Judicial Review Act

Veterans Benefits & Improvement Act

1989   VA as Cabinet department

Court of Veterans Appeals

1990   Agent Orange service-connection

1991   Agent Orange Act (P.L. 102-4)

Persian Gulf War Veterans Assistance Act (P.L. 102-25)

Veterans Benefits Improvement Act (P.L. 102-86)

1992   Veterans Health Care Act

1993   Persian Gulf vet treatment law

1994   VETS succeeds BVRR

1995   Korean War Memorial dedicated

1996   Veterans Health Care Eligibility Reform Act

Veterans Benefits Improvements Act

1997   World War II Memorial fund-raising campaign launched

1998   Veterans Employment Opportunities Act

Veterans Programs Enhancement Act

1999   Soldiers', Sailors', Airmen's and Marines' Bill of Rights Act (S. 4) passed in the Senate

Staff: Year 1999

KANSAS CITY

Ainsworth, Jennifer
Allee, Margaret
Allen, Rebecca
Allgaier, Dan
Altis, Brenda
Alvarez, Julian
Atkins, Tommy
Atkinson, Carole
Bachand, Wayne
Bailey, Kindra
Bartels, Donald
Beauchamp, Tammy
Beck, Marian
Berkley, Geremie
Blankenship, Janie
Bleam, Connie
Bowden, Sharon
Brady, Amanda
Brandon, Peggy
Brook, Sandra
Brown, Becky
Brown, Kelly
Brown, Patricia
Browning, Ron
Cale, Bud
Cale, Phyllis
Campbell, Marjorie
Chinn, Brian
Christy, Dawn
Clifton, Nelda
Collier, Jennifer
Cookston, Cindy
Corum, Kim
Cox, Lucinda
Crawford, John
Crider, Robert
Crow, Robert
Crutcher, Ross
Crutcher, Steve
Curtis, Dolores
Cutright, Russell
Cutright, Sonja
Dady, Melissa
Dailey, Melodi
Danaher, Marilyn
Day, Melissa
Dickens, Deonne
Dickerson, Joanne
Dusenbery, Cindy
Dyhouse, Timothy
Edwards, Toya
Eidemiller, Sandra
Ellis, Earl
Eshnaur, Leonard
Ester, Brenda
Fast, Connie
Ferguson, Linda
Fitch, Kay
Foster, Ronald
Franke, Betty
Garrison, Darla
Gay, Randy

Gebo, Michael
Gilpin, Keri
Gjesfjeld, Johnna
Gniotczynski, Larry
Gniotczynski, Tammy
Gormalley, Michael
Greeley, Steven
Greene, Robert
Hailey, Jason
Hales, Mary
Hammett, Carol
Harmer, Kristine
Hensley, Terry
Hicks, Gary
Hoffman, Warren
Holland, Donald
Houseman, Aaron
Houseman, Tina
Housknecht, Gary
Johnson, Gina
Johnson, Samantha
Jones, Alan
Jones, Keeta
Jones, Kevin
Jones, Tammy
Kamen, Mary
Kane, Vanessa
Keller, Kristine
Kerns, Robert
King, Dora Jean
King, Phyllis
Kinney, Tiffanie
Kissell, Thomas
Kolb, Richard
Kunkle, Keren
Le Febvre, Lawrence
Lierz, James
Lindsey, Nancy
Ludwig, Dee
Lynn, Jean
Madison, James
Maher, Lawrence
Marcum, Sheryl
Mathis, Steven
Maucelli, Frances
McIntire-McCumbie, Pat
McDonald, Cynthia
McGinnis, Teresa
Merimee, Nancy
Miles, Ladonna
Miller, Ann
Miller, Gayle
Miller, Jennifer
Molthan, Albert
Moody, Brandi
Moran, Joseph
Morgan, Cheryl
Muff, Peter
Murray, Glenna
Mynatt, Barbara
Neilon, Alisa
Niblock, Janae
Nick, Judy

Northington, Jesse
Oak, Regina
O'Brien, John
Olsen, Magdalene
Pall, Laverne
Patterson, Jamie
Phillips, Lynda
Porter, Linda
Pratt, Mary
Pricer, Regina
Putthoff, Diane
Ramirez, Arthur
Rangel, Carmen
Rice, Jo Ann
Richardson, Judy
Ridgley, Joe
Roos, Michael
Rose, Rita
Rowoldt, James
Santillan, Monica
Scott, Gale
Senk, John
Shea, Daniel
Shewmaker, Rita
Sloan, Lori
Sloan, William
Smith, Elita Sue
Smith, Patricia
Smith, Sharon
Solis, Michelle
Sperry, Linda
Stewart, Melissa
Stillwell, Angela
Stone, Robert
Swindler, David
Sypko, Ted
Taylor, Lolita
Thomas, Tammy
Thorson, Gordon
Van Buskirk, Stephen
Vassholz, Marti
Vassholz, Mary Anne
Vetter, James
Watkins, Brandie
Wayman, Kelly
Weisbrod, Paula
Weissend, Billy
West, Lydia Jean
White, Rachelle
Whitlock, Brian
Widener, Robert
Wiesing, Nancy
Williams, Donna
Williams, Jean
Wilson, Susan

WASHINGTON

Aldana, Theresa
Amos, Carolyn
Andrew, Edward
Barnes, Ashley
Beavers, Patricia
Betz, Sylvia
Boone, Jesse
Bradshaw, William
Burns, Fredrick
Callaway, Valerie
Chaney, Gina
Cullinan, Dennis
Daniels, Sidney
Dargin, Sylvia
Davenport, Karen
Dozier, William
East, Mary
Edwards, Audrey
England, Judy
Estry, George
Felder, David
Gardner, Robert
Garnett, Nadia
George, Stanley
Grant, Erayna
Griffin, David
Grimm, Rodney
Harder, Bruce
Harrington, Alex
Hatfield, Wetzel
Haupt, Charles
Hawley, George
Hines, Rita
Hirst, Richard
Holland, Theresa
Jewell, James
Juarbe, Frederico
Lowe, Gloria
Magill, James
Mallard, Jennifer
Manhan, Robert
McFarland, Alice
McKinnon, Ronald
McNeill, John
Morris, Teresa
Olaseha, Doris
O'Toole, Robert
Pomeroy, Nancy
Rankin, Wayne
Richmond, Boyce
Sheets, George
Smith, Austin
Smith, William
Steadman, Kenneth
Stephens, Laverne
Torain, Alfonzo
Van Tassel, Karen
Vaughn, James
Wagstaff, Horace
Wallace, Jimmy
Wallace, Robert
Washington, Michael

America at War: The Lethal Toll

Expressly outlined in the VFW's constitution and congressional charter is the objective of keeping alive the sacrifices made by Americans on the field of battle throughout U.S. history.

In keeping with this tradition, the VFW believes it is appropriate to recognize and remember the war dead of every hostile U.S. military engagement.

Military Action	Hostile Deaths	Wounded	Non-Hostile Deaths
Revolutionary War (1775-1783)	6,824	8,445	18,500
Indian Wars (1789-1898)			
Soldiers[1]	2,125	2,156	N/A*
Indians[2]	4,000	N/A	N/A
Franco-American Naval War (1798-1800)	20	42	N/A
Barbary Wars (1801-05, 1815)	35	64	N/A
War of 1812 (1812-1815)	2,260	4,505	524+
Marquesas Islands (1814)	4	1	N/A
West Indies (1822-25)	3	5	N/A
Sumatra (1832)	2	11	N/A
Texas War of Independence (1835-36)[3]	704	138	N/A
Mexican War (1846-48)	1,733	4,152	11,550
China (1854-59)	15	32	N/A
Fiji (1855)	1	2	N/A
"Cortina War"/Texas Border (1859-60)	5	18	N/A
Civil War (1861-65)[4]　　**Total**	**204,070**	**382,881**	**413,952**
Union	110,070	281,881	249,952
Confederate	94,000	101,000	164,000
Japan (1863)	5	6	N/A
Formosa (1867)	1	0	N/A
Mexico (1870)	1	4	N/A
Korea (1871)	3	10	1
Spanish-American War (1898)	362	1,637	2,621
Philippines War (1899-1902)	1,053	2,840	3,220
Samoa (1899)	4	5	0
China/Boxer Rebellion (1900)	53	253	51
Moro Campaigns (1902-06, 1913)	130	300	N/A
Dominican Republic (1904)	1	0	0
Mexican Border (1911-1919)	20	N/A	N/A
Nicaragua (1912)	5	16	N/A
Vera Cruz (1914)	19	69	N/A
Haiti (1915-20)	10	26	136
Dominican Republic (1916-1922)	20	50	124
Mexico Punitive Expedition (1916)	18	30	9
World War I (1917-18)	53,513	204,002	63,195[5]
North Russia Expedition (1918-19)	146	307	100
Siberia Expedition (1918-20)	48	52	122
Nicaragua (1927-32)	47	66	89
Yangtze Service, China (1921-1941)	5	80	N/A

Military Action	Hostile Deaths	Wounded	Non-Hostile Deaths
North Atlantic Naval War (1941)	126	44	15
World War II (1941-45) **Total**	**293,121**[6]	**670,846**	**115,185**
European Theater	185,179	498,948	66,805
Pacific Theater	107,903	171,898	48,380
Trieste/Italy (1945-47)	6	14	N/A
Chinese Civil War (1945-47)	12	42	22
Cold War (1945-89)[7]	187	N/A	3,744
Philippines (1946)	1	N/A	N/A
Greek Civil War (1946-49)	1	1	2
Korean War (1950-53)	33,629	103,284	3,262[8]
Quemoy and Matsu (1954)	3	N/A	N/A
Lebanon (1958)	1	1	4
Bay of Pigs, Cuba (1961)	4	0	N/A
Laos (1961-62)	3	3	N/A
Vietnam War (1961-75)[9]	47,386	153,303[10]	10,818
Cuba (1962)	1	0	8
Panama Canal Riots (1964)	3	85	N/A
Dominican Republic (1965-66)	27	172	20
Guatemala (1965-68)	3	2	N/A
Korea DMZ (1966-69)[11]	89	131	814
USS Liberty off Israel (1967)	34	171	0
Terrorism (1968-1995) Service Personnel[12]	59	N/A	0
Mayaguez-Cambodia Incident (1975)	18	50	23
Iran (1980)	0	0	8
Lebanon (1982-84)[13]	266	169	2
Grenada (1983)[14]	10	100	9
El Salvador (1983-91)[15]	9	26	11
Southwest Africa (1984)	1	0	0
Honduras (1984, 1989)	1	28	N/A
Libya (1986)	2	0	0
USS Stark — Persian Gulf (1987)	37	21	0
Persian Gulf (1987-88)	2	10	14
Panama (1989-90)[16]	23	240	18
Persian Gulf War (1990-91) **Total**	**145**	**357**	**228**
Operation Desert Shield	0	0	108
Operation Desert Storm	145	357	120
Peru (1992)	1	5	N/A
Somalia (1992-94)	30	175	14
Haiti (1994)	1	3	2
Saudi Arabia (1996)	19	66	0
Kenya (1998)	3	0	0
Grand Total:	**652,529**	**1,541,554**	**648,417**

N/A = Figures not available.

Sources and Notes

1. Death total for soldiers includes *regulars* only, thousands more militiamen and volunteers also were killed.
2. Indian deaths are for after 1850 only. Don Russell, "How Many Indians Were Killed?" *The American West*, July 1973, p. 47.
3. *Texas Independence* by Andrew Jackson Houston (Houston: Anson Jones Press, 1938).
4. Non-hostile category includes 26,000 Confederate and 32,000 Union soldiers who died as prisoners of war. See *The Concise Illustrated History of the Civil War* by James I. Robertson, Jr. (National Historical Society, 1979), p. 61 and *Civil War Handbook* by William H. Price (L.B. Prince Co., 1961), p. 17.
5. Most of the non-hostile deaths in WWI were due to the flu epidemic that swept through Army camps in the U.S. in 1918.
6. WWII: The Army and Air Forces' total includes 39 deaths in unspecified locales.
7. 39 U.S. planes were shot down on Communist borders during the Cold War: 177 Americans were killed. Also, perhaps 10 Americans were killed in various ground incidents. As a direct consequence of the Cold War, 31 Americans were killed in air crashes during the Berlin Airlift (1948-49). In addition, however, thousands of GIs died accidentally in Germany: Between Oct. 1, 1979, and Sept. 30, 1991, alone, 1,415 died mostly in accidents; another 2,329 from 1965 through 1975.
8. The old, inaccurate figure of 20,617 was worldwide.
9. Included for Vietnam are the deaths of one soldier in 1956, one in 1957 and two in 1959.
10. Hospitalized wounded only. Also applies to the Korean War.
11. Included in the hostile deaths figure for Korea are 58 KIAs along the DMZ (7 were KIA between 1955-63), one sailor from the *Pueblo*, 31 crewmen of a recon plane shot down over the Sea of Japan and six soldiers killed in the DMZ between 1974-1977. 1 helicopter crewman was KIA Dec. 17, 1994. 814 non-hostile deaths since 1961.
12. Excluded from the terrorist total are those already counted in separate columns. The total includes, for instance, 16 military personnel killed on Pan Am Flight 103 on Dec. 21, 1988.
13. Includes 241 servicemen killed in the terrorist bombing on Oct. 23, 1983; four Marine guards in the embassy bombing; two who ran over land mines; one Navy pilot; and 18 Marines killed in action.
14. Casualties for Grenada are still confused. It appears that four Navy SEALs drowned; four Army Rangers were killed accidentally; and one soldier was killed accidentally in a strafing.
15. Of the 9 hostile deaths in El Salvador, only one soldier was actually killed in a firefight; 3 of the hostile deaths were from a helicopter downed in Honduras.
16. Of the 22 deaths due to hostile action in Panama, one occurred prior to *Operation Just Cause* and one after in a terrorist bombing. Of the 18 non-hostile deaths, 11 occurred Feb. 21, 1990, accidentally in a helicopter crash during an "air assault" against a village harboring Panamanian rebels. On June 10, 1992, another U.S. soldier was killed in an ambush.

Notes on Sources

The greater part of the research was conducted at VFW National Headquarters in Kansas City, Mo. Pertinent historical data came from the organizational archive and a large library dedicated to military and political history from the founding of the nation to the present day.

Interviews with VFW leaders, past and present, provided reflections on the organization's major achievements and its future.

Bound volumes of *Foreign Service* and *VFW* magazines dating back to 1904 provided the lion's share of historical information.

The volumes are rich in material dealing with the steady growth of the VFW. Particularly valuable are first-person accounts written by those who participated in the organization's achievements through nearly a century of war and peace.

VFW crusades for veterans rights and community action were — and are — promulgated in the pages of the official monthly journal. At policy level, the publication served as a sounding board and a campaign platform throughout the nation's often turbulent history. Cabinet-rank officials, generals, admirals and VFW commanders-in-chief signed pieces that contained information vital to veterans welfare and the security of the nation. "Political correctness" was never an issue.

At the grass-roots level, positive actions were taken by members of Posts and Auxiliaries to make communities a better place to live. And to provide healthy avenues for youngsters to explore. These activities were often chronicled in *VFW* magazine and its predecessor publications.

Selected Bibliography

Anderson, James K. *Veterans of Foreign Wars: 75 Years of Achievement.* Kansas City, Mo.: Booklet, 1975.

Annual Reports of the War Department, 1899-1901.

Bennett, Michael. *When Dreams Come True: The GI Bill and the Making of America.* Washington, D.C. : Brassey's, Inc., 1996.

Bottoms, Bill. *The VFW: An Illustrated History of the Veterans of Foreign Wars.* Rockville, Md.: Woodbine House, 1991.

Bozich, Stanley J. and Jon R. *"Detroit's Own" Polar Bears.* Frankenmuth, Mich.: Polar Bear Publishing Company, 1985.

Caute, David. *The Great Fear: The Anti-Communist Purge Under Truman and Eisenhower.* N.Y.: Simon & Schuster, 1978.

Committee on Foreign Affairs. *Report: MIA-POW Task Force.* Washington, D.C.: GPO, 1986.

Congdon, Don, ed. *The Thirties: A Time to Remember.* N.Y.: Simon & Schuster, 1962.

Crownover, Roger. *The United States Intervention in North Russia, 1918-1919.* Ann Arbor, Mich.: UMI, 1996.

Daniels, Jonathan. *The Time Between the Wars: Armistice to Pearl Harbor.* N.Y.: Doubleday, 1966.

Daniels, Roger. *The Bonus March.* Westport, Conn.: Greenwood Publishing Corp., 1971.

Ebersole, Marilyn and Kim Broers. *Celebrate 75 Years, 1914-1989: Ladies Auxiliary to the VFW.* Kansas City, Mo.: Lowell Press, 1989.

Eddington, Patrick G. *Gassed in the Gulf.* Washington, D.C.: Insignia Publishing Co., 1997.

Furnas, J. C. *The Americans: A Social History of the United States.* N.Y.: G.P. Putnam's Sons, 1969.

Gans, Herbert J. *The Levittowners: Ways of Life and Politics in a New Suburban Community.* N.Y., Pantheon Books, 1967.

Goldsmith, Katherine. *The Story of the Veterans of Foreign Wars of the United States; The First Fifty Years, 1899-1949.* An unpublished manuscript at national headquarters, Kansas City. Mo., n.d.

Goulden, Joseph C. *The Best Years:* N.Y.: Atheneum 1976.

Halberstam, David. *The Fifties.* N.Y.: Villard Books, 1993.

Halliday, E.M. *The Ignorant Armies.* N.Y.: Harper & Brothers, 1960.

Harper, Frank. "Fighting Far From Home: The First Colorado Regiment in the Spanish-American War." *Colorado Heritage,* Issue 1, 1988. Colorado Historical Society.

Harries, Merion & Susie. *Last Days of Innocence: America at War, 1917-1918.* N.Y.: Random House, 1997.

Hopson, Glover E. *The Veterans Administration.* N.Y.: Chelsea House, 1988.

Kennedy, David M. *Over Here: The First World War and American Society.* N.Y.: Oxford Univ. Press, 1980.

Lisio, Donald J. *The President and Protest: Hoover, Conspiracy and the Bonus Riot.* Columbia, Mo.: University of Missouri Press, 1974.

Manchester, William. *The Glory and the Dream: A Narrative History of America.* Boston, Mass.: Little Brown & Co., 1973.

McConnell, Malcolm & Theodore G. Schweitzer III. *Inside Hanoi's Secret Archives: Solving the MIA Mystery.* N.Y.: Simon & Schuster, 1995.

Messick, William L. *America's Fighting Presidents.* Summerland, Calif.: Harbor House (West), 1993.

Mitchell, Broadus. *Depression Decade: 1929-1941.* N.Y.: Rinehart, 1947.

Musicant, Ivan. *Empire By Default: The Spanish-American War and the Dawn of the American Century.* N.Y.: Henry Holt & Co., 1998.

Olson, Keith W. *The G.I. Bill, the Veterans and the Colleges.* Louisville, Ky.: Univ. Press of Kentucky, 1974.

Perrett, Geoffrey. *Days of Sadness, Years of Triumph: The American People, 1939-1945.* N.Y.: Coward, McCann & Geoghagan, 1973.

Reynolds, Quentin. *Known But To God: The Story of the "Unknowns" of America's War Memorials.* N.Y.: John Day Co., 1960.

Rochester, Stuart I. & Frederick Kiley. *Honor Bound: The History of American Prisoners of War in Southeast Asia, 1961-1973.* Washington, D.C.: Office of the Secretary of Defense, Historical Office, 1998.

Ross, David R.B. *Preparing for Ulysses: Politics and Veterans During WWII.* N.Y.: Columbia Univ., 1969.

Severo, Richard & Lewis Milford. *The Wages of War: When America's Soldiers Came Home—From Valley Forge to Vietnam.* N.Y.: Simon & Schuster, 1989.

Spiller, Harry, ed. *American POWs in Korea.* Jefferson, N.C.: McFarland & Co., Inc., 1998.

Stallings, Laurence. *The Doughboys: The Story of the AEF, 1917-1918.* N.Y.: Harper & Row, 1963.

Strait, Jerry L., and Sandra S. *Vietnam War Memorials.* Jefferson, N.C.: McFarland & Company, 1988.

VFW Magazine and *Foreign Service.* Bound Volumes, November 1904-1998.

Waters, W.W. *The B.E.F.: The Whole Story of the Bonus Army.* N.Y.: Arno Press, 1969.

Wecter, Dixon. *When Johnny Comes Marching Home.* N.Y.: Cambridge, Mass.: Houghton Mifflin, 1944.

Photo Credits

Unless noted here, all photos are from VFW photo files.

BACK COVER   Top, Del Ankers Photographers. Bottom, left to right, Edd White, Phil Licata, Post 4264 and VFW. Inside back flap, Rigmor Mason.

INTRODUCTION   p. 1, Tal Wilson. p. 6, George Wallace White, Post 1746. p. 8, Courtesy Sen. Chuck Hagel.

CHAPTER 1   p. 14, Post 1111, p. 17, left to right, top to bottom, VFW, VFW, VFW; Tom Dillard, Dallas Morning News; White House; Hal Williams & Bill Mott; White House. p. 21, bottom right, Del Ankers Photographers, Wash, D.C. p. 22, Scott Boatright. p. 24, top, Ladies Auxiliary; bottom, Military Order of the Cootie. p. 25, Trent Nelson. p. 26, bottom left, International News Photo; bottom right, O'Brien Photos.

CHAPTER 2   p. 29, National Archives. p. 30, top, DOD; bottom, Collier's Weekly. p. 32, Colorado Historical Society. p. 33, National Archives. p. 35, Colorado Historical Society. p. 36, U.S. Army Military History Institute. p. 40, U.S. Army. p. 41, U.S. Army.

CHAPTER 3   p. 44, Liberty Memorial Museum, Kansas City. p. 47, National Archives. p. 48, U.S. Army. p. 50, U.S. Army in Action Series. p. 51, Harris and Ewing. p. 53, Albert Fanning.

CHAPTER 4   p. 54, Liberty Memorial Museum, Kansas City. p. 56, UPI/Corbis-Bettmann. p. 58, John B. Seemiller. p. 59, top, Warner Bros.; bottom, Warner Bros. p. 60, National Archives. p. 61, top left, Robert Merrill. p. 62, International News Photos. p. 63, bottom, International News Photos. p. 64, bottom middle, National Home; bottom right, National Home. p. 66, top, Western Newspaper Union; bottom, U.S. Naval Institute. p. 67, Rider-Philpott Studio. p. 68, International Newsreel Photo. p. 69, Underwood and Underwood.

CHAPTER 5   p. 72, Press Photo Service. p. 73, National Archives. p. 75, International News Photos. p. 76, bottom, Detroit News. p. 77, bottom, Rod Rieser.

CHAPTER 6   p. 78, International News Photos. p. 80, top, Davenport Photographers. p. 81, Moynahan. p. 82, Acme. p. 83, top, E.F. Clark; bottom, Capitol Photo Service. p. 85, Acme. p. 88, UPI/Corbis-Bettmann. p. 89, Keystone View. p. 93-94, Keystone View. p. 95, Acme.

CHAPTER 7   p. 96, Acme. p. 102, Clark. p. 104, top,

National Archives; bottom, Denny Hayes, Dallas Times Herald. p. 108, Acme. p. 110, Special Collections, Univ. of Maryland Libraries. p. 111, top, Library of Congress; bottom, University of Wisconsin. p. 113, bottom, National Home.

CHAPTER 8   p. 114, Acme. p. 115, Bill Mauldin. p. 116, bottom, International News Photo. p. 118, Miami Herald. p. 119, National Archives. p. 120, Rider-Philpott Studio. p. 121, top, Bob Waters. p. 123, Randazzo and Morrison, Inc. p. 125, right, UPI/Corbis-Bettmann. p. 126, bottom, courtesy Freedoms Foundation. p. 128, UPI/Corbis-Bettmann. p. 130, U.S. Air Force. p. 131, Del Ankers Photographers. p. 132, Acme. p. 134, top, UPI/Corbis-Bettmann; bottom, White House. p. 136, Thomas Nielsen. p. 139, bottom, March of Dimes. p. 141, Joseph D. Poellot. p. 143, White House. p. 145, DOD. p. 146, Tim Westerberg. p. 148, Scott Boatright.

CHAPTER 9   p. 150, DOD. p. 151, Tulsa Tribune. p. 152, top, UPI/Corbis-Bettmann. p. 154, bottom, CILHI. p. 155, DOD. p. 156, U.S. Air Force. p. 157, courtesy Joe Lupyak. p. 159, St. Louis Globe-Democrat. p. 160, top, Post 6063; bottom, courtesy Douglas Peterson. p. 162, CILHI. p. 163, K.C. Clark.

CHAPTER 10   p. 166, Edd White. p. 168, Post 4987. p. 169, top, Audrey Carroll; bottom, Miller News Picture Service. p. 170-173, Ladies Auxiliary. p. 176, Post 7462. p. 177, Ron Harris, Daily Mountain Eagle. p. 179, left, University of Minnesota; middle-right, Tim Rummelhoff. p. 180, bottom, Post 1596 & 6791. p. 181, John Robison. p. 182, bottom, March of Dimes. p. 184, Empire Photographers. p. 185, bottom, Ed Barnola, Post 5253. p. 186, Shigeo Yokote. p. 187, top, Dept. of Minnesota; bottom, Post 10273. p. 189, bottom, Post 9785. p. 191, bottom, CBS Photo Archive.

CHAPTER 11   p. 199, Scott Boatright. p. 203, Eddie Hausner/NYT Pictures. p. 204, bottom, Dallas Cowboys. p. 206, top, Ankers Photographers; bottom, Kin Man Hui. p. 207, Post 5290. p. 208, bottom, Phil Licata. p. 209, Scot Morrissey. p. 210-211, Phil Licata. p. 212, DOD. p. 213, Post 9574. p. 214, top, Dept. of Kansas. p. 215, American Battle Monuments Commission. p. 216, top, Tony Walsh; bottom, Post 4820. p. 217, top right, Post 1949; top left, Post 4820; bottom, Robert Murphy, Post 5975.

AFTERWORD   p. 218, Sgt. Lance Bacon/U.S. Marine Corps. p. 219, Architect of the Capitol. p. 220, Phil Licata. p. 221, Post 7945.

APPENDICES   p. 224, all photos, Phil Licata.

Index